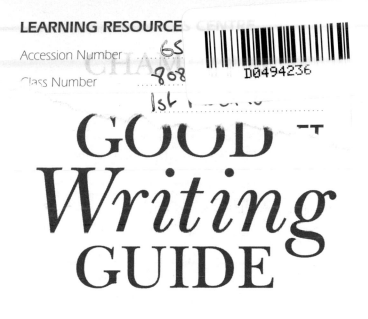

GOOD
Writing
GUIDE

by

Ian Brookes and Duncan Marshall

CHAMBERS

An imprint of Chambers Harrap Publishers Ltd
7 Hopetoun Crescent
Edinburgh, EH7 4AY

First published by Chambers Harrap Publishers Ltd 2004

A CIP catalogue record for this book is available from the British
Library.

ISBN 0550 10087 3

Publishing Manager: Patrick White

Editorial Consultant: Martin Manser

Editorial Assistance: Christina Gleeson and Liam Rodger

Prepress: Vienna Leigh

Designed and typeset by Chambers Harrap Publishers Ltd, Edinburgh

Printed and bound by in Great Britain by Mackays of Chatham Ltd

Contents

How to Use This Book

It is not necessary to read the whole book from start to finish to get the most out of it. This book is designed to be useful both as a self-help guide and as a reference book. Some users may wish to study it in detail, whereas others may wish to keep it at hand to provide advice on specific questions as these arise in the course of writing.

You are recommended to look briefly through Part One to get an idea of its contents. Some of the things covered in this part of the book will probably be familiar to you already. Others may not be, and you can start to make a note of these things and add them to your armoury of language skills. You do not need to memorize every rule and definition, but it is important that you start to form a clear idea of which areas of language are likely to cause problems, and how you can expand your range of skills. That way, when you come across one of these areas, you can go back to the relevant part of the book to seek advice.

You are recommended to look at Part Two in more detail. This sets out the processes that you need to go through when you write. As you become more and more experienced as writer, these processes should become more and more natural until eventually you go through them without consciously thinking about them or needing to refer to the book.

You are recommended to use Part Three as and when you need to produce a certain type of writing. This part of the book gives you examples of the writing you should be aiming to produce and provides tips on how to go about creating a wide range of documents.

When you want to use the book to find out about a specific subject, use either the table of contents at the front of the book or the index in the back of the book to find out where the subject is discussed. This should lead you to the place in the text where you can find what you are looking for.

However you choose to use this book, you should find plenty of information and practical advice in it. It should help you to approach the task of writing with increased confidence and to become a more fluent and successful writer.

Introduction

The purpose of this book is to help you to write well. Writing *well* involves not only writing *correctly* – following the rules of spelling, grammar and punctuation – but also writing in a clear and persuasive manner. The advice included in this book should help you to produce *good writing* – clearly written and persuasively worded documents. Moreover, it should also encourage you to become *a good writer* – the sort of person who is able as a matter of course to create documents that hold your readers' interest and communicate ideas and information effectively.

What happens when we write?

Before we think about what it takes to become a good writer, we should first take a bit of time to think in more general terms about what actually happens when you put pen to paper or, as is increasingly common, you start tapping away at a computer keyboard.

Unless you are keeping a diary, writing a shopping list or making notes, writing is not just a way of recording information; it is a way of communicating with other people. Like all communication, it involves both the sending and the receiving of information – in other words, it is a two-way process.

This might sound obvious, but the two-way nature of communication is often overlooked when people write. Most of us learn to read and write at an early age and then practise constantly throughout our lives, so we tend to forget that reading and writing are in fact highly artificial kinds of communication. Writing involves:

- ➤ sitting alone and retreating unsociably inside ourselves, especially when surrounded by other people

- ➤ generating information manually, using our hands to produce a series of marks on paper or dots on a screen

- ➤ sending information in code form to someone who is in fact somewhere else, often a person we know nothing about and might never meet

- ➤ waiting, perhaps for several weeks, while our message travels

through time and space, and then maybe waiting even longer
for a response – without knowing for certain that the original
message has been understood or even received in the first place

For all the reasons given, it feels very much like a one-way process
when we write. By contrast, when we speak we communicate directly
and instantly with people, and they communicate directly and instantly
with us, either on the telephone or face to face. Even if people meet
and do not have a conversation as such, the visual cues produced by
their body language can show clearly and immediately how they feel.
This means that the combination of spoken language and body
language is generally highly effective in putting across what we want to
say and how we feel, so there is little potential for failure in
communication. For example, someone who is giving a presentation or
lecture can respond to the reaction of an audience (its enthusiasm,
hostility or confusion as expressed by words, sounds or gestures) and
change his or her way of speaking more or less in mid-sentence to take
account of the audience's needs. If we are in the audience and are
unsure about something the speaker says, we have opportunities to
question or challenge the speaker in order to obtain more information
or put a different point of view. Or we could yawn constantly, or we
could stare at the ceiling. In each case our response should be clear to
the speaker and should encourage the speaker to make some changes.

Of course, we have all experienced occasions when speakers have failed
to take this ever-present opportunity to modify what they say or the way
they say it. Some speakers still seem to ramble on endlessly about not
very much in spite of the evident boredom of their audience; others seem
to be blissfully unaware that nobody in the room understands the obscure
jargon they are using. These breakdowns in communication occur when
speakers are unaware of the requirements of their audience.

If awareness of the audience is important when communicating face to
face in a situation such as a presentation or lecture, it is even more
important when communicating in writing, which involves an audience
that is unknown and unseen. Whether this audience consists of one
reader (for a letter) or several million readers (for a newspaper article),
the writer still has to keep the audience in mind.

What makes a good writer?

Just as good speakers are aware of the effect that their words are having and can modify what they say accordingly, so too good writers are aware of their readers. Different situations may call for different approaches to writing: a formal report for a business client has completely different requirements to a text message to a friend. Good writers think about who their readers are. They are able to recognize the sort of communication that is required, understand what their readers' expectations of that communication will be and adapt their approach accordingly.

Because the readers of a document are often unseen and unknown, it can sometimes be difficult to satisfy their requirements completely. However, an awareness of the existence and expectations of readers will usually go a long way towards pleasing most of the people most of the time, even if you cannot please all of the people all of the time.

Being aware of the reader is a key to good writing, but there are also other factors to take into account. In order to produce effective writing, the writer has to be able to deploy a range of language skills: a wide vocabulary enables the writer to select exactly the right word for the occasion; an understanding of the basic rules of spelling and grammar helps the writer to set out the message clearly and with no opportunity for misunderstanding; an awareness of the traps that writers can fall into helps to avoid using words that might irritate, confuse or enrage the reader. All of this constitutes the writer's 'tool kit'. The first part of this book is devoted to setting out all of the aspects of language that a good writer needs to think about, and provides a handy resource for you to refer to.

A good writer also needs to understand about the process of writing. The best results are rarely achieved simply by picking up a pen and keeping going to the end of the page. It will pay dividends to think about some of the techniques that can help to create good writing: how to set about writing a document in a methodical way, how to arrange what you have to say in the most effective manner, and what tricks you can use to make sure that your readers remain engaged and entertained from start to finish. The second part of this book deals with these issues and provides you with a basic method that can be applied to any writing task.

Finally, we have seen that a good writer has to adapt to the particular requirements of the situation. This means that a good writer will be familiar with the conventions surrounding a range of different types of writing. The final part of this book looks at the different writing tasks that you may have to face in the real world, and what the requirements of each type of writing are.

The five Cs

There are, therefore, a number of different elements that go into becoming a good writer. However, as a useful summary of the criteria for good writing, you can memorize **the five Cs**. These are a simple and easily remembered list of the hallmarks of good writing. Put simply, good writing should be:

- correct
- consistent
- clear
- complete
- concise

Correct writing involves making sure that you write according to the rules of standard English.

Consistent writing involves making decisions about how you are going to present information and sticking to these decisions throughout the document.

Clear writing involves making sure that your writing can be understood by the people who will read it. This involves using words that will be understood, and presenting information in a straightforward structure so that your readers know what is going on.

Complete writing involves presenting all of the relevant information, including explanations of anything that might be unclear.

Concise writing involves getting to the point quickly and not wasting your readers' time with irrelevant information.

Paying attention to the five Cs will keep you in good shape whatever it is that you are writing. We shall have cause to remind ourselves about them at various occasions in this book.

Part One

The Writer's Tool Kit

A good writer needs to know a few things about how language works. This knowledge might be thought of as **the writer's tool kit**: the writer keeps it stored away (either in the head or in a place where it can be easily looked up), and uses it to find ways of expressing ideas in a way that is appropriate to the situation. The aim of this opening part of the *Good Writing Guide* is to describe all of the aspects of English you need to know about in order to have confidence when you write.

We start by looking at language in general, beginning with **words**, the basic units writers work with. We look at the way that different words belong in different situations, and at ways of increasing your stock of words so that you always have a suitable word at your disposal. Looking at the different kinds of words brings us on to the **different forms of English** and when it is appropriate to use each form. We look in particular at how to write in **plain English**, a form of English that is recommended for straightforward written communication.

The second part of this section deals with more specific subjects and describes the basic rules that you will need to follow when you are writing. We set out some important rules concerning **spelling**, **grammar** and **punctuation**, and also look at **dealing with special types of information** such as speech, abbreviations and numbers. This part of the book sets out a lot of rules and conventions for writing. You do not need to master every one of these before you move on, but you will find it useful to be familiar with the sort of subjects that are covered there. That way you know where to go for help when these difficulties crop up when you write.

The third part of the writer's 'tool kit' concerns the **resources** that a writer can call upon for help. We look at how using dictionaries, thesauruses and other reference books can help you when you write, and we also look at how you can make use of the vast amount of information available on **the Internet**.

Finally, we look at what might be called the 'occupational hazards' a writer needs to be aware of. These are the traps that can cause a breakdown in communication between the reader and the writer. We look at some **commonly confused and misused words** you should be aware of, and at the barriers to communication that can be created by **ambiguity**. We also look at some areas of language that should be treated with caution, such as **jargon**, **clichés** and **buzz words**, and at the importance of using **sensitive language**.

This part of the book therefore covers a very wide area, and should provide you with the background information necessary to approach the task of writing with confidence.

Words

Two kinds of words

Words are the basic units writers work with. When we talk about
people who are good writers, we sometimes say that they are 'good
with words' or that they 'have a way with words'. So one of the most
important elements in a writer's 'tool kit' is a decent stock of words to
draw on.

Broadly speaking, there are two kinds of words: those you can choose
and those you cannot choose.

Words you cannot choose

The words you cannot choose are words such as *the, of, and, to, a, in,
that, it, I* and *was*. These are the nuts and bolts of language, the
'grammatical' words everyone is so familiar with that nobody even
notices them. They make up most of the language we use. (In fact, it
has been estimated that the ten words mentioned account for about a
quarter of everything we write and say.) They occur all the time in
everyday use, and people rarely have problems with them, but it is not
possible to say very much just using these words.

Words you can choose

However, there are other words that name and describe things and
actions, and provide the 'content' in language. These words occur less
frequently in everyday situations. It is possible to speak English
perfectly well without using many of them at all, and you might need
to look some of them up in a dictionary to check the meaning. It is a
command of these sorts of words that gives you a good vocabulary.
Although you don't need to use these words when you write, the
bigger your stock of words is, the more things you can achieve.

The two types of words might be compared to the mortar and stones
used for building a wall. The stones might vary in size and shape, and
some builders might use a lot of small stones where others might
choose a few larger ones, but whatever their size and shape they need

to be fitted together with skill, and it is the mortar of 'grammatical' words that binds them together.

Many of the words that you can choose have a particular **register**. They are used in some types of writing but are not suitable for other types. When you are thinking about using a word, it is important that you have a clear picture of the register of the word. Is the word going to make your writing sound stuffy? Or light-hearted? Or old-fashioned?

Formal and informal words

Certain words are generally used in formal writing, such as legal documents or academic essays, whereas others are restricted to more informal writing such as personal letters or e-mails.

In the table below, the words in the left-hand column would be appropriate in more formal writing, whereas those in the right-hand column would be more appropriate for informal writing:

FORMAL WORD	NEUTRAL WORD	INFORMAL WORD
appropriate	steal	pinch
circumspect	cautious	cagey
discomposed	annoyed	miffed
effrontery	cheek	brass neck
fracas	fight	dust-up
opulent	luxurious	swanky
propensity	liking	soft spot
risible	ridiculous	daft

Literary and poetic words

Certain words are generally avoided in normal speech but are characteristically used in poetry or self-consciously literary writing. These words are often thought of as reflecting a specially intense, heightened state of mind. The words in the right-hand column fall into this category:

NEUTRAL WORD	LITERARY WORD
grow	burgeon
poet	bard
sad	dolorous
shining	effulgent
sparkle	coruscate
speed	celerity
sweet	dulcet

Other types of word

Besides formal words, informal words and literary words, there are numerous other registers:

- ➤ Old-fashioned and archaic words have fallen out of everyday use and will make your writing sound dated. For example, *raiment* is an archaic word for *clothing*, and *oft* is an archaic form of *often*.

- ➤ Euphemistic words are used as polite alternatives to words that the writer wants to avoid. For example, *facility* may be used as a euphemism for *lavatory*, and *passing* may be used as a euphemism for *death*.

- ➤ Derogatory words are used with the aim of expressing disapproval. For example, *blockhead* and *bimbo* are derogatory words.

- ➤ Facetious words are used when the writer is being light-hearted or playful. For example, *hostelry* is a facetious word for *pub*, and *imbibe* is a facetious word for *drink*.

Writers who develop a wide vocabulary are better equipped to choose a word that has the appropriate register for any particular occasion.

Some tips for expanding your vocabulary

Before we become confident enough to use a word ourselves, we need to see or hear it used in a number of different places so that we get a feel for how it works. For this reason, it is unlikely that you will suddenly be able to bring about a huge increase in your stock of words. However, there are things that you can do to build up your vocabulary over a period of time:

> There are many words that you are familiar with but do not use when you sit down to write. Such words are said to form your **passive vocabulary**. One way to become a more effective writer is to transfer words from your passive vocabulary to your **active vocabulary**, the words that you do use when you speak or write. The more frequently you encounter words, and the more you think about what they mean and how they are used, the sooner words will move from your passive vocabulary into your active vocabulary.

> The more you read, the more you are likely to come across unfamiliar words and see how they are used. However, this is less likely to happen if you read books that use a very simple vocabulary, or – at the other end of the scale – books that use so many difficult words that you lose patience with them.

> Think about words that you find particularly effective and see if you can use these in your own writing.

> Listen to people – either people you know or people on television or radio – who have an impressive vocabulary. We tend to imitate what we hear more readily than what we read.

> When you see or hear an unfamiliar word, don't ignore it, but make an effort to find out what it means.

> Get into the habit of using a dictionary and a thesaurus. A dictionary will help you to pin down the precise meaning of a word and may give you examples of how the word is actually used. A thesaurus will offer you a range of alternative words that you can use instead of a common word.

> Crosswords and word games can be entertaining ways of introducing you to new words.

Some useful words for your vocabulary

To start you off in your quest to improve your writing skills, here are a few words that would be a useful part of any writer's active vocabulary. You may be aware of their meanings already, but you might not be in the habit of using them when you write.

Look at how they are used in the examples, and think of occasions when you might use them in your own writing:

alacrity quick and cheerful enthusiasm: *He responded to the request with alacrity.*

audacious bold and daring: *an audacious plan to revitalize the business*

corollary a natural or obvious consequence: *As a corollary of this initiative, departments were permitted to provide courses of shorter duration.*

deleterious harmful or destructive: *a deleterious effect on the environment*

incipient in an early stage: *an incipient feeling of rage*

ineluctable not able to be avoided, resisted or escaped from: *the ineluctable course of history*

insidious developing gradually and imperceptibly; treacherous: *the insidious effects of pollution*

minutiae small and often unimportant details: *bogged down in the minutiae of politics*

potent strong, powerful: *a potent symbol of change; a potent combination of speed and strength*

precarious unsafe; insecure; dangerous: *clinging on to a precarious position; a precarious grip on power*

precipitous dangerously steep: *a precipitous drop; a precipitous fall in the share price*

reciprocal involving both giving and receiving: *a reciprocal arrangement with a company in Brazil*

tendentious having a particular bias or underlying purpose: *a tendentious argument*

You can find more lists of words that might be useful additions to your vocabulary on pages 331 and 378.

Different Forms of English

In the previous chapter we saw that certain words tend to be used only in specific types of English. This leads to the question of how many different types of English there are, and what characteristics each have.

Although we tend to think of English as a single language, it exists in many different spoken and written forms, and it is quite natural for people to change from one form to another in response to the situation they find themselves in. The language used at a job interview will probably differ greatly from the language used at a party; you will use a different style of English when writing an e-mail to a friend than you would when writing a letter to a business associate. In fact, one feature of effective speakers and writers is their ability to adjust the way they communicate whenever necessary, allowing them to be easily understood and accepted by different people in different circumstances. In this chapter, we look at some of the different ways people use English, and consider why an awareness of this variation is useful.

Standard English

Most people grow up with the idea that there is a particular way of speaking and writing English that is the correct way. This 'official' standardized version of the language is known as **Standard English**, and most of what you read and write will have been produced in accordance with the rules of Standard English. It is used more or less everywhere – in books, in newspapers, in magazines, on television, on the radio, at work, for writing letters and in everyday speech. As you might imagine, this book is written using Standard English.

Although the idea of Standard English suggests a fixed, unchanging version of the language, what is acceptable and what is unacceptable has in fact changed over the years. The language used by Chaucer and Shakespeare is very different from the language we use today, and what is considered acceptable practice now may well have been frowned upon in the past. The process of language change is continuous and is still going on today.

The idea of a Standard English provides us with a useful goal to aim for when we write. We feel that if we can write in Standard English, everybody will able to understand what we say and recognize our writing as correct. However, in reality it is quite difficult to pin down exactly what Standard English is. Many people have different ideas about what is correct. This comes about because English is used in different parts of the world, in different social situations, and to talk about different topics. In each case, the form of English that is used may be slightly different.

Regional variations

English has now become the most widely spoken language on earth. When a language is only spoken in one community, it might be possible for a single, standardized form to exist. However, when a language is spoken in many different regions and many different countries, each area tends to develop its own variety, with its own pronunciation, spellings and words.

These varieties of English are known as **dialects**. A regional **dialect** is not the same thing as a regional **accent**. An accent is a particular way of pronouncing English. A dialect does not involve pronunciation but involves the use of different words or ways of organizing words. So, if a woman speaks with a Jamaican accent she could be speaking Standard British English, but if she uses a Jamaican dialect, she will be using a regional variety of the language spoken only by people in or from a particular part of Jamaica.

Dialect words fall into four main categories:

> Some dialect words are equivalents of words in British English. (American English uses *sidewalk*, *faucet* and *diaper* as equivalents of the British English *pavement*, *tap* and *nappy*.)

> Some dialect words are special meanings of existing words. (South African English uses *robot* to mean a *traffic light* and *canteen* to mean a *pub*.)

> Some dialect words are terms that have been coined for local

wildlife, plants, foods or natural features. (Australian English contains words such as *butcherbird* and *cheesewood* to name local fauna and flora.)

➤ Some dialect words are borrowed from local languages that speakers come into regular contact with. (Indian English borrows words from languages such as Hindi and Punjabi, some of which – for example, *guru, bungalow, chutney* and *pyjamas* – have now become part of Standard English.)

There are, therefore, different versions of English that are regarded as standard in Britain, the United States, Canada, the Caribbean, Australia, New Zealand, South Africa, India, South-East Asia and everywhere else where English is spoken.

Within each of these regions there also exist considerable variations. Just as people in different parts of the British Isles express themselves differently in speech (and, to a lesser extent, in writing), so speakers of English in different parts of the Caribbean and different parts of Australia use English differently. This means that it is not even possible to speak of a fixed Caribbean English or Australian English.

In the past, there has been a tendency to discount regional uses of English as being incorrect or inferior, used only by those who have not been properly educated. However, the diversity of English is now more widely recognized and celebrated. Writers such as Linton Kwesi Johnson, Roddy Doyle and Irvine Welsh have used regional dialects with great success.

The way you use dialect in writing depends on the effect you want to have on your readers. Regional words and phrases can help to create a sense of place in creative writing. However, there are occasions when clear communication with the speaker of a different dialect is called for. On such occasions, dialect forms may be a barrier to communication, and it is more appropriate to use Standard English.

Degrees of formality

As well as expressing themselves differently in different parts of the world or parts of the country, people also communicate differently in different social situations.

Formal situations – where it is considered appropriate to keep a distance between the writer and the reader – are characterized by a particular style of English that combines Standard English with its own vocabulary and sentence structure:

Patrons are kindly requested to refrain from smoking.

In Standard English, the same message might be communicated rather differently:

Please do not smoke.

At the other end of the scale, informal situations – where there is less likelihood of causing offence – allow for another style of language:

You smoke, we choke!

There are also various degrees of formality and informality. How formal or informal you choose to be is a decision that you have to make based on the type of language that is used around you, and what kind of impression you want to create. Some people are better than others at sensing the nature of the situation and adjusting their language use to suit the circumstances.

Formal English

Formal language is designed to place a distance between the writer and the reader. The reader is regarded as a person of authority, and is treated with respect by the writer. This makes it appropriate for documents such as business letters, essays and reports.

The main features of formal language are:

> The full forms of words are used. Words such as *television* and *memorandum* would be preferred to *TV* and *memo*.

> Contractions are not used. *I am* and *we are* would be preferred to *I'm* and *we're*.

> Longer words are used.

> Old-fashioned forms of words may be preserved. It is acceptable to use words such as *abide* and *deem* instead of *stay* and *think*.

> It uses some words that are not used in Standard English, especially words that are derived from Latin and Greek. For

example, *desist*, which comes from Latin, has a more formal tone than *stop*.

➤ It uses longer sentences, with more subordinate clauses (see pages 230–4).

➤ It tends to use the passive voice more often (see page 228).

➤ There is a greater insistence on traditional rules of grammar, such as not splitting infinitives and not ending sentences with prepositions (see pages 88–92).

➤ Phrasal verbs (see page 62) are less commonly used. *Extract* and *insert* may preferred to *take out* and *put in*.

Informal English

Informal language breaks down the barriers between the writer and the reader. The reader is regarded as an equal, and the writer may even make jokes at the reader's expense. This makes it appropriate for casual writing such as informal letters and notes to close colleagues.

The main features of informal language are:

➤ Shortened forms of words are used. Forms such as *TV* and *memo* would be preferred to *television* and *memorandum*.

➤ Contractions are used frequently. *I'm* and *we're* may be preferred to *I am* and *we are*.

➤ Short words are generally preferred to long words.

➤ It uses simplified descriptions in place of technical words. An optometrist may be referred to informally as an *eye doctor*, and a particle accelerator may be informally called an *atom smasher*.

➤ It uses many words that are not accepted in Standard English, especially humorous or facetious turns of phrase.

➤ It uses simple sentences, with few subordinate clauses.

➤ It tends to use the active voice rather than the passive.

➤ There is a greater tolerance of unconventional grammar, and many traditional rules can be disregarded.

➤ Phrasal verbs are more commonly used. *Take out* and *put in* may be used instead of *extract* and *insert*.

Forms of English in electronic communication

An extreme example of informal language can be found in the style used to compose electronic communications. Because e-mail and text messages are generally casual and highly compressed forms of communication and can be written, sent and received within a matter of minutes, the usual rules of written spelling and grammar are often ignored when these messages are composed.

Both forms allow writers to take liberties with the use of capital letters. It is not unusual to for e-mail messages to avoid the use of capital letters altogether, while text messages may consist of nothing but capitals. Because speed is an important consideration, both e-mail and text messages use abbreviations for commonly used phrases, such *imo* for *in my opinion* and *lol* for *laugh out loud* or *lots of love.*

It would seem very odd to receive a text message in which every word was spelt out in full. However, a person marking a student's essay might be surprised and unimpressed to receive an essay written in 'text'.

As with all forms of English, the writer needs to judge what type of language is appropriate. Being sensitive to this, and also being able to adapt to different circumstances, marks out effective language users.

> The varieties of English used in e-mail and text messages are discussed in more detail on pages 302–6.

Technical language

Experts and specialists in a subject will often use words for which the ordinary speaker of English has no use. This means that most subjects have developed a specialist vocabulary of technical terms.

The use of technical vocabulary allows specialists to analyse and discuss in detail a huge range of things that other people have no awareness of. Another advantage of this type of language is that it is concise, using a single term rather than an explanation or a description.

Technical language is very common in science, medicine and law. More familiar technical terms are encountered in everyday activities such as sport, music and cookery.

Technical language may come from various sources:

➤ Some technical terms are special meanings of existing words. (Computing uses special meanings of *spider*, *mouse* and *crawler*; cricket uses special meanings of *duck*, *gully* and *hook*.)

➤ Some technical terms have been coined on the basis of existing words. (Many scientific terms are based on Latin or Greek words: *arachnophobia*, meaning 'fear of spiders', is based on the Greek words for *spider* and *fear*.)

➤ Some technical terms have been borrowed from other languages. (Biology and law use words from Latin; music uses words from Italian; cookery and fencing use words from French.)

The disadvantage of technical language is that it is not easily understood by non-specialists. Indeed, it can be used quite self-consciously by specialists to make themselves seem more important or clever than everyone else, and to keep non-specialists from understanding their subject.

➡ See pages 190–1 for advice on how to get around the problems presented by technical language when you want to communicate with non-specialists.

House style

The fact that there are so many different forms of English can present problems when you come to write. Different users of English tend to develop their own ideas about what is normal or acceptable as far as using informal and technical language and regional variations.

Moreover, even if people have broadly similar ideas about the register and tone of their language, they may have different ideas about technical details such as the use of punctuation marks and spelling.

Many companies and organizations have therefore established a **house style**. This means that they have particular rules about the language that should be used or the ways text is organized and laid out. Because English is a very flexible language, there are often a number of ways of doing things, none of which is necessarily incorrect.

House rules exist to make sure that everyone does things the same way, avoiding the possibility of misunderstandings and making things easier to organize. They also allow an organization to present a consistent identity to the public and to its employees. This is particularly important when many different people within an organization are producing written material, and all of the writers have their own natural style and their own ideas about what makes up Standard English.

Areas that are covered by house style might include:

- how to deal with words that can be spelt in more than one way
- whether to use American or British spelling forms
- when to use capital letters
- when and how to use abbreviations
- how to deal with foreign words and phrases
- how to use punctuation
- whether to write numbers as figures or words
- how to present dates
- when to use italics

> Recommended approaches to these points of style are set out on pages 112–25.

Plain English

What is plain English?

Plain English is a particular type of Standard English that is recommended for effective communication.

The main features of plain English are:

> Vocabulary is kept as simple as possible, so that as many people as possible can understand what you write. Unnecessarily difficult, old-fashioned and technical words are avoided.

> Meaningless words and phrases are eliminated so that every word serves a purpose.

> Excessive formality is discouraged.

> The emphasis is on communicating clearly rather than creating striking effects.

> Sentences are short and simple. An average sentence length of around 15 words is recommended, and the maximum sentence length is around 30 words.

> Paragraphs are kept short.

> The document should be easily understood by anyone with basic literacy skills.

> The document should be easily understood by people who are not experts in the subject being discussed. The use of jargon and buzz words (see pages 190–1) is discouraged.

> Information is broken down into easily manageable portions.

Simple sentences

As a general rule, shorter and more straightforward sentences are easier to understand than longer, more complex sentences.

You can keep sentences short by trying to describe or explain only one thing in each sentence.

You can keep sentences simple by writing in what is called the **active voice**. (This concept is explained more fully on pages 227–8.) This means always writing from the point of view of the person doing the action rather than the person on the receiving end of it: if you are describing a robbery, it is simpler to say that *two women robbed a shop* than *a shop was robbed by two women.*

However, you need to strike a balance between writing short, simple sentences and limiting your ability to say what you mean.

Short sentences are often used in children's reading books:

Peter is in the tree. He is playing. He is having fun.

They can also be appropriate for instructions, where a process is broken down into separate stages:

Fill the container. Allow to stand for two minutes. Stir well.

Although constant stopping and starting might be suitable for instructions or for the needs of young children, in many other situations it can appear unnatural and restrictive.

For example, using only very short sentences does not allow you to indicate the relationship between two events. When you want to indicate that something happened *after* something else, or *because of* something else, or *in spite of* something else, you need to join the two events together in a single sentence. This can create slightly longer sentences, but should not prevent the sentence from being clearly understood:

I missed the bus because I arrived late.

She won the race even though she was not feeling well.

However, the more ideas you combine in a sentence, the greater chance there is of creating confusion:

As a result of the consultation, many different approaches have been tried, and we are confident that we have found the best one.

A person reading this sentence might conclude that the result of the consultation was twofold: (1) that many approaches were tried, (2) that the writers are confident they have found the best one; they might equally conclude that the writers' confidence has nothing to do with the consultation. When this sort of thing becomes unclear, it is time to start thinking about dividing the sentence into smaller units of meaning:

As a result of the consultation, many different approaches have been tried. We are confident that we have found the best one.

> ➡ You can find out more about sentences and how to construct them on pages 223–35.

Removing unnecessary words and phrases

Sentences can also become too long because they contain words and phrases that are not necessary. If splitting up a long sentence into several shorter sentences is not possible, see if you can shorten the sentence by eliminating any unnecessary words and phrases:

> ➤ Try to avoid using several words where one would do (see pages 257–8).

> ➤ Try to avoid words and phrases that do not add anything to the meaning (see pages 258–9).

> ➤ Try to avoid spending time telling your readers things they already know.

The extract below gives an extreme example of an unnecessarily long sentence. It comes from an application form intended for use by the general public, and consists of a single sentence containing 92 words:

> *If it is not possible by the date that the application form should be returned to this office to submit the necessary evidence to verify any information included on the form regarding the amount of income received by you and/or your parents or spouse during the relevant period, it is suggested that the completed application form should, nevertheless, be returned by the appropriate date and that the evidence of income e.g. certificate of employer, Income Tax form P60, Income Tax Assessment Form, etc, should be submitted as soon as it is available.*

The idea at the heart of this sentence can, in fact, be represented in about fifty words, as indicated by the bold letters:

> ***If it is not possible by the date that the application form should be returned*** *to this office* ***to submit the necessary evidence*** *to verify any information included on the form regarding the amount of income received by you and/or your parents or spouse during the relevant period,* ***it is suggested that the completed application form should, nevertheless, be returned by the appropriate date and that the evidence of income*** *e.g. certificate of employer, Income Tax*

> form P60, Income Tax Assessment Form, etc, **should be submitted as soon as it is available**.

However things can be made even simpler. Presumably, the form itself makes clear what kind of evidence needs to be supplied and who the evidence applies to. So, if the language is simplified the sentence can be reduced to 24 words:

> If you cannot send supporting evidence with your form, send the form now and send the supporting evidence as soon as it is available.

Simple vocabulary

Another feature of plain English is the idea of using simple words wherever possible. There are many words that writers get into the habit of using because they think they sound impressive. However, these words can often get in the way of the meaning, and there is often an alternative word that is more widely understood.

If you want your writing to be understood by the widest possible range of readers, you should consider finding simple alternatives for the difficult words listed below:

DIFFICULT WORD	SIMPLE ALTERNATIVE
accede to	agree to
alleviate	ease, lessen, reduce
apprise	inform
ascertain	find out, discover, establish
aspiration	wish, hope, desire
attain	reach, achieve
avail oneself of	use
bestow	give
cease	stop
desirous of	wanting, wishing for
desist	stop
eschew	avoid
endeavour	try
evince	show, display

DIFFICULT WORD	SIMPLE ALTERNATIVE
henceforth	from now on
heretofore	formerly
imbibe	drink
initiate	begin, start
latitude	freedom
manifest	show, display
multiplicity	lot
necessitate	need, require, demand, involve, entail, call for
opine	suppose
parameter	limit
proceed	go
purchase	buy
proclivity	liking, preference
replete	full
reside	live, stay
residence	home
salubrious	healthy
veracity	truth
wherefore	why

When should I use plain English?

The principles of plain English can be successfully applied to most writing tasks. However, they are particularly important when you want as many people as possible to read and understand what you write, and when it is important that there is no doubt about your meaning. This means that you should use this style when your intention is:

- ➤ to inform
- ➤ to advise
- ➤ to instruct
- ➤ to educate

You can allow yourself a little more freedom when you know that the people who are going to read your document are knowledgeable about the subject. You might use more technical vocabulary if you were writing a scientific report than if you were writing for the general public. However, that does not mean that you should lose sight of the importance of writing in clear, straightforward sentences.

There are a few types of writing where keeping the reader's interest and attention is as important as making your meaning clear. In order to do this you might introduce more complex sentence structures and vocabulary. A more elaborate style might be appropriate when your intention is:

> to persuade
> to entertain

Spelling

The task of communicating successfully in writing is made much easier if you follow the standard procedures for setting out words. The following chapters of this book are designed to help you by setting out the basic rules of spelling, grammar and punctuation.

The importance of correct spelling

The idea that spelling is important is sometimes thought of as an old-fashioned one. However, there are good reasons for using correct spelling as often as you can. These reasons also apply to correct grammar and punctuation, which will be covered in the following chapters.

Firstly, correct and conventional spelling makes life easy for your readers, whereas incorrect or unconventional spelling can get in the way of your meaning.

Secondly, using correct spelling indicates that you take pride in your work. Correct and consistent spelling may be taken as a sign of a tidy mind at work, and this encourages readers to take you and your writing seriously. Conversely, incorrect or inconsistent spelling suggests sloppiness or laziness – qualities that you do not want to project. This means that correct spelling is especially important in documents on which you are judged as a person. An employer who notices a spelling mistake in a letter of application or a CV may need no further excuse to throw your application onto the reject pile.

There are several ways that you can ensure your writing is free from spelling mistakes:

> ➤ Take note of any incorrect spellings marked by the spellchecker on your computer. However, keep in mind the limitations of spellcheckers (see pages 220–1).

> ➤ Check spellings in a dictionary if you are not sure (see pages 126–30).

> ➤ Learn the basic rules of spelling listed below.

> ➤ Familiarize yourself with those words that are difficult to spell

and make an effort to learn the correct way to spell them.
There is a list of difficult words on pages 46–8 and there are
some tips for learning spellings on pages 44–6.

Some basic spelling rules

Here are some simple rules, most of them to do with forming words
from others. This is not a complete list, and there are some exceptions
to these rules (not all of which are shown). However, knowing these
basic rules is a good starting point for being able to spell well.

The explanations of these rules involve certain technical terms, which
may require explanation:

A **syllable** is a part of a word that consists of a single sound. The
word *telling* has two syllables, while *important* has three.

A **vowel** is any of the letters *a, e, i, o* or *u* (and sometimes *y*) that
represent a sound made with the mouth open. A syllable usually
contains one vowel or a group of vowels making one sound.

Vowels may be called **long vowels** or **short vowels** depending on
how quickly they are pronounced. Short vowels tend to be represented
by a single letter, as in *cap*. Long vowels tend to be represented by a
group of letters, as in *sleep*. A letter *e* at the end of a syllable can turn
a short vowel into a long vowel, as in *cape*.

A **consonant** is any letter that is not a vowel. Consonants represent
sounds made with the mouth closed.

When a word contains more than one syllable, one of the syllables is
pronounced more strongly than the others. This syllable is said to be
stressed. In the word *telling* the stress falls on the first syllable,
while in *important* it falls on the second syllable.

Rules for adding *–ing, –ed, –er* and *–s*

The **base form** or **infinitive** of most verbs does not change when
–ing, –ed or *–er* is added to the end of the verb to create additional
forms:

stay – staying – stayed

walk – walking – walked – walker

If the base form of the verb has only one syllable and ends in a single vowel followed by a single consonant, then the last letter has to be doubled before *–ing*, *–ed* or *–er* is added:

run – running – runner

pot – potting – potted

stir – stirrer – stirred

If the base form of the verb has two or more syllables and ends in a single vowel followed by a single consonant, whether or not you double the final letter depends on the pronunciation. If you pronounce the word with a stress on the final syllable, then you have to double the final letter before you add *–ing*, *–ed* or *–er*:

regret – regretting – regretted

prefer – preferring – preferred

distil – distilling – distilled – distiller

But if the stress is not on the final syllable, the final letter is not doubled:

enter – entering – entered

gossip – gossiping – gossiped

If the last syllable has a short vowel and ends in *–l* you have to double the letter *l*, regardless of where the stress comes:

equal – equalling – equalled

repel – repelling– repelled

If a verb ends in *–c*, then a *k* is added before *–ing*, *–ed* or *–er*:

panic – panicking – panicked

picnic – picnicking – picnicked – picnicker

If a word ends with a 'silent *e*', the final *–e* is dropped before adding *–ing*, *–ed* or *–er*:

hope – hoping – hoped

love – loving – loved – lover

mine – mining – mined – miner

But notice that verbs ending in *–oe, –ee* and *–ye* do not drop the final *-e* before adding *-ing*:

> *agree – agreeing – agreed*
>
> *hoe – hoeing – hoed*
>
> *dye – dyeing – dyed*

If a verb ends in *–ie*, the *–ie* is changed to *–y* before the ending *–ing* is added:

> *die – dying*
>
> *lie – lying*

This does not happen when the ending *–ed* is added. This time, the *–e* is dropped before *–ed* is added:

> *die – died*
>
> *lie – lied*

With verbs that end in a consonant followed by *–y*, the opposite happens. The *–y* ending is kept when *–ing* is added to avoid having an awkward double *i* which would look unusual and be tricky to say. But *–y* is changed to *–i* when *–ed* or *–er* is added:

> *cry – crying – cried – crier*
>
> *try – trying – tried – trier*
>
> *marry – marrying – married*

The present tense of these verbs is formed by changing the *–y* to *–ies*:

> *cry – cries*
>
> *try – tries*
>
> *marry – marries*

But if a verb has a vowel before the *–y*, keep the *–y* ending when you add *–s* and *–ed*:

> *stay – stays – stayed*
>
> *play – plays – played*

But watch out for exceptions:

> *lay – lays – laying – laid*

pay – pays – paying – paid

say – says – saying – said

The present tense of verbs ending in *–ch, –sh, –s, –x* and *–z* is formed by adding *–es*:

touch – touches

wash – washes

hiss – hisses

fix – fixes

waltz – waltzes

Rules for making plurals

Often plurals can be formed simply by adding *–s*:

horse – horses

banana – bananas

Plurals of nouns ending in *–ch, –sh, –s, –x* and *–z* are formed by adding *–es*:

church – churches

flash – flashes

loss – losses

box – boxes

waltz – waltzes

But if the noun ends in *–ch* and it is pronounced *k*, then you only add *–s* to form the plural:

stomach – stomachs

monarch – monarchs

Plurals of nouns ending in *–f* and *–fe* are sometimes formed by changing the *–f* or *–fe* to *–ve* before adding *–s*:

scarf – scarves

hoof – hooves

knife – knives

But this not always the case:

roof – roofs

belief – beliefs

chief – chiefs

proof – proofs

safe – safes

Plurals of nouns ending in a consonant followed by *–y* are formed by changing the *–y* to *–ie* and adding *–s*:

berry – berries

hanky – hankies

fly – flies

The plural of nouns that have a vowel before the *–y* are simply formed with *–s*:

boy – boys

day – days

Plurals of nouns ending in *–o* are often formed by just adding *–s*:

piano – pianos

radio – radios

zoo – zoos

But some add *–es* instead:

potato – potatoes

tomato – tomatoes

hero – heroes

echo – echoes

And some can add either *–s* or *–es*:

banjo – banjos or *banjoes*

domino – dominos or *dominoes*

manifesto – manifestos or *manifestoes*

Some nouns change their vowels to form the plural:

foot – feet

goose – geese

tooth – teeth

man – men

A few nouns form the plural by adding –*en*:

child – children

ox – oxen

Words that have come into English from other languages often have plurals that do not follow these rules. This happens when the plural form is taken from the original language, which forms plurals in a different way from English.

Some naturalized Latin words ending in –*us* form plurals ending in –*i*:

cactus – cacti

stimulus – stimuli

Some naturalized Latin words ending in –*x* form plurals ending in *ces*:

appendix – appendices

matrix – matrices

Some naturalized Latin words ending in –*a* form plurals ending in –*ae*:

formula – formulae

vertebra – vertebrae

Some naturalized Greek words ending in –*on* form plurals ending in –*a*:

criterion – criteria

phenomenon – phenomena

Some naturalized Greek words ending in –*is* form plurals ending in –*es*:

crisis – crises

analysis – analyses

Sometimes naturalized words have two plural forms: one based on the original language, and one based on the regular English spelling rules:

appendix appendixes or *appendices*

> *stadium* – *stadiums* or *stadia*
>
> *antenna* – *antennas* or *antennae*

Naturalized French words ending in *–eau* have two plural forms: one (based on French spelling rules) ending in *–x* and one (based on English spelling rules) ending in *–s*:

> *gateau* – *gateaus* or *gateaux*
>
> *plateau* – *plateaus* or *plateaux*

Rules for adding *–ish* and *–y*

Adjectives can often be formed simply by adding *–ish* or *–y* to a noun:

> *tiger* – *tigerish*
>
> *dream* – *dreamy*

However, if the noun has only one syllable and ends in a single vowel followed by a single consonant, then the last letter has to be doubled before *–ish* or *–y* is added:

> *fad* – *faddish*
>
> *grit* – *gritty*

If a word ends in a 'silent *e*', the final *–e* is usually dropped before adding *–ish* or *–y*:

> *white* – *whitish*
>
> *grease* – *greasy*

However, there are a number of exceptions to this rule:

> *price* – *pricey*
>
> *same* – *samey*
>
> *mate* – *matey*

Rules for adding *–er* and *–est*

Comparatives and superlatives can often be spelt simply by adding *–er* or *–est* to an adjective:

> *hard* – *harder* – *hardest*
>
> *loud* – *louder* – *loudest*

However, if the adjective has only one syllable and ends in a single vowel followed by a single consonant, then the last letter has to be doubled before –er or –est is added:

red – redder – reddest

big – bigger – biggest

If an adjective ends in –e, the final –e is dropped before adding –er or –est:

white – whiter – whitest

simple – simpler – simplest

free – freer – freest

If an adjective has two or more syllables and ends in –y, you have to change the –y to –i before adding –er or –est:

angry – angrier – angriest

funny – funnier – funniest

But watch out for these one-syllable adjectives ending in –y:

dry – drier – driest

sly – slyer – slyest

shy – shier or *shyer – shiest* or *shyest*

> **!!!** Remember that some adjectives have irregular comparative and superlative forms (see page 67).

Rules for adding –ly

The ending –ly is often added to the end of adjectives to make adverbs:

foolish – foolishly

strange – strangely

surprising – surprisingly

If an adjective ends in a consonant followed by –le, the final –e is dropped before adding –ly:

simple – simply

double – doubly

The adjectives *true, due, whole* and *eerie* also drop the final *–e* before *–ly* is added:

> *true – truly*
>
> *due – duly*
>
> *whole – wholly*
>
> *eerie – eerily*

If an adjective ends in *–y*, the *–y* ending is changed to *–i* when *–ly* is added:

> *happy – happily*
>
> *weary – wearily*

But again there are some exceptions:

> *dry – drily* or *dryly*
>
> *shy – shily* or *shyly*

If an adjective ends in *–ic*, the ending *–ally* (rather than just *–ly*) is added:

> *basic – basically*
>
> *economic – economically*

But an exception to this rule is:

> *public – publicly*

Rules for adding *–able* and *–ible*

The ending *–able* is often added to the end of a verb to make adjectives:

> *remark – remarkable*
>
> *respect – respectable*

If a word ends in a 'silent *e*', the final *–e* is dropped before adding *–able*:

> *advise – advisable*
>
> *debate – debatable*

However, if the word ends in *–ce* or *–ge*, the *–e* is kept when adding *–able*:

> *notice – noticeable*
>
> *change – changeable*

There are a few other short words that end in a 'silent *e*', when the *–e* may be kept when adding *–able*:

like – likeable or *likable*

size – sizeable or *sizable*

love – loveable or *lovable*

If the word has only one syllable and ends in a single vowel followed by a single consonant, then the last letter has to be doubled before *–able* is added:

hit – hittable

If the word has two or more syllables and ends in a single vowel followed by a single consonant, whether or not you double the final letter depends on the pronunciation. If you pronounce the word with a stress on the final syllable, then you have to double the final letter before you add *–able*:

regret – regrettable

forget – forgettable

An exception to this rule happens with words ending in *–fer*. The final letter is not doubled:

prefer – preferable

transfer – transferable

With verbs that end in a consonant followed by *–y*, the *–y* ending is changed to *–i* when *–able* is added:

justify – justifiable

The ending *–able* is more common than *–ible*, and is used to make new words with this ending, but it is worth remembering some of the common adjectives that end in *–ible*:

audible	*flexible*	*negligible*
comprehensible	*gullible*	*permissible*
credible	*illegible*	*reversible*
edible	*incredible*	*sensible*
eligible	*legible*	*visible*

Words with the ending *–ible* are often derived from a verb that has changed in some other way:

defend – defensible

permit – permissible

neglect – negligible

Many *–ible* words do not seem to be related to a verb at all:

credible	*ostensible*
fallible	*possible*

Rules for adding *–ful, al–* and *–til*

Remember that when the word *full* becomes the suffix *–ful* it drops the final *l*:

hope – hopeful

faith – faithful

colour – colourful

The same rule applies to the words *all* and *till* which drop the final *l* when used as a prefix or suffix:

all – already – altogether

till – until

If the word to which *–ful* is added ends in *–y*, the *–y* ending is changed to *–i*:

beauty – beautiful

pity – pitiful

fancy – fanciful

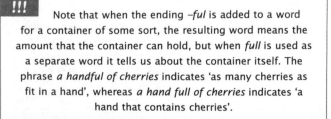

!!! Note that when the ending *–ful* is added to a word for a container of some sort, the resulting word means the amount that the container can hold, but when *full* is used as a separate word it tells us about the container itself. The phrase *a handful of cherries* indicates 'as many cherries as fit in a hand', whereas *a hand full of cherries* indicates 'a hand that contains cherries'.

Rules for adding *–ize* or *–ise*

It is acceptable in British English to use either *–ize* or *–ise* for most verbs that end in this sound:

> *characterize* or *characterise*
>
> *realize* or *realise*
>
> *apologize* or *apologise*

It is worth learning some of the common words that can only be spelt with *–ise* at the end:

advertise	*despise*	*rise*
advise	*devise*	*supervise*
arise	*exercise*	*surprise*
comprise	*improvise*	*televise*
compromise	*revise*	

There are also a few that are always spelt with *–ize*:

capsize	*prize*	*size*

And remember that a few words are spelt *–yse*:

analyse	*catalyse*	*paralyse*
breathalyse	*electrolyse*	*psychoanalyse*

The '*i* before *e* except after *c*' rule

You will have probably heard the rule '*i* **before** *e* **except after** *c*'. This works when the word has an '*ee*' sound, as in *deep*.

After any letter except *c*, *i* comes before *e*:

beli**e**ve	si**e**ge
chi**e**f	ni**e**ce

But after *c*, *e* comes before *i*:

ce**i**ling	perc**ei**ve
rece**i**pt	rec**ei**ve

However, there are some very common exceptions to this rule that are worth learning:

weird	protein	species
seize	either	
caffeine	neither	

If the word has an '*ay*' sound, as in *hay*, then it is usually written *ei*:

weigh	vein
eight	veil

There are also some words where the *i* and *e* produce a sound that is neither '*ee*' nor '*ay*'. If these letters come in the first syllable of a word, they are usually spelt *ei*:

height	their	heir

If these letters come towards the end of a word, they are almost always spelt *ie*:

ancient	glacier	society

Rules for adding endings to *-our*

When you add the endings *-ant*, *-ary*, *-ation*, *-iferous*, *-fic*, *-ize* or *-ise*, or *-ous* to words that end in *-our*, you take the *u* out of the *-our*:

glamour – glamorize

humour – humorous

honour – honorary

You leave the *u* in if you are adding the endings *–able, –er, –ism, –ist* or *–ite*:

> *honour – honourable*
>
> *favour – favourite*

Rules for the endings *–ous* and *–us*

The ending *–ous* is mainly used in adjectives:

famous	*enormous*
anonymous	*poisonous*

The ending *–us* is mainly used in nouns:

cactus	*octopus*
circus	*thesaurus*

> **!!!** Some words that originally came into English from Latin, such as *emeritus*, are exceptions to this rule, because many Latin adjectives end in *–us*.

Rules for words that can end in *–se* or *–ce*

Some words, such as *license* and *licence*, are often confused in spelling. The correct spelling depends on whether the word is being used as noun or as a verb. Remember that in British English the ending *–se* is used in verbs, and the ending *–ce* is used in nouns:

USE –SE FOR VERBS	USE –CE FOR NOUNS
to **practise** juggling	went to football **practice**
I was **advised** to keep quiet.	a piece of good **advice**
to **devise** a test	a nuclear **device**
to **license** a drug	a driving **licence**

> !!! It may help if you remember that *ice* is a noun.

Rules for words ending *–ceed*, *–cede* and *–sede*

There are three words that end in *–ceed*:

proceed	*succeed*	*exceed*

And only one word that ends in *–sede*:

supersede

All the others with the same final sound end with the letter pattern *–cede*:

precede	*accede*	*secede*
concede	*cede*	
recede	*intercede*	

American spelling

There are a number of minor differences between **British English** and **American English** spelling. Here are some of the most important ones.

When the endings *–ing*, *–ed* and *–er* are added to verbs ending in *l* and *p* in British English, the *l* and *p* are doubled:

travel – travelling

kidnap – kidnapped

In American English, they are not doubled:

travel – traveling

kidnap – kidnaped

> !!! It is worth noting that the British spellings are exceptions to the rule described on page 25. The American spellings agree with this rule.

When British spelling allows verbs to end either in *–ize* or *–ise*, American spelling always uses *–ize*:

characterize	realize	apologize

American spelling also uses *–yze* where British spelling uses *–yse*:

analyze	breathalyze

Most words that end in *–our* in British English end in *–or* in American English:

color	humor	rumor

> **!!!** *Saviour* and *glamour* are exceptions to this and are spelt the same way in both British and American English.

Many words that end in *–re* in British English end in *–er* in American English:

center	theater	fiber

> **!!!** Most words that end in *–cre* or *–gre* are exceptions to this: *acre*, *massacre* and *ogre* are spelt the same way in both British and American English.

American writers tend to replace the *oe* and *ae* with a single *e* in words that come from Latin and Greek:

fetus	anesthetic	anemia
diarrhea	cesium	

However, note that *fetus* is also the approved British spelling in scientific writing.

Most words spelt *–ogue* in British English are spelt *–og* in American English:

dialog	*catalog*
prolog	*analog*

Some words that end in a stressed vowel followed by *l* in British English have the *l* doubled in American English:

enroll	*fulfill*	*enthrall*

Nouns that end in *−nce* in British English are spelt *−nse* in American English:

defense	*license*	*pretense*

Here is a short list of other common words spelt differently in American English:

BRITISH SPELLING	AMERICAN SPELLING
doughnut	*donut*
jewellery	*jewelry*
skilful	*skillful*
axe	*ax*
plough	*plow*
cheque	*check*
programme	*program*
sceptic	*skeptic*
tyre	*tire*
sulphur	*sulfur*
gauge	*gage*

One word or two?

Sometimes there is confusion about whether a word is written as a single word or as two words. Moreover, sometimes a single word can sound similar to a phrase of two or more words, but mean something different. Use the following guidelines:

Write *all right* as two words. You never need to write *alright*:

I'll be **all right** when I get my breath back.

Write *a lot* as two words:

She has **a lot** of friends in London.

Already is an adverb expressing things to do with time:

Are you leaving **already**?

All ready is a phrase made up of words with two separate meanings:

If you are **all ready**, we can go.

Altogether means 'completely' or 'in total':

Altogether we've collected £50.

I'm not **altogether** happy with your essay.

All together means 'all in a group':

I'll put these books **all together** on the shelf.

> **!!!** If you are not sure which to use, try this test: *all together* can be separated by other words (*I'll put all these books together on the shelf*), but *altogether* cannot be separated.

Anyone means 'any person at all':

Anyone could tell you that.

Any one means 'any single one'. It can refer to people or things:

Choose **any one** of these cards.

> **!!!** If you are not sure which to use, try this test: *anyone* can be replaced by the word *anybody* (*Anybody could tell you that*), but *any one* cannot.

Cannot is generally written as one word:

He **cannot** sing.

Can not is only used when *not* is linked to the following words and needs to be emphasized:

41

*He **can not** only sing but he can dance as well.*

If *ever* is being used to give extra emphasis to words such as *why*, *how* or *where*, it is written as a separate word:

*What **ever** shall we do?*

*How **ever** did you manage that?*

If *ever* means 'any (thing, place, way etc) at all' it is joined to the word it is modifying to form a single word:

*Do **whatever** you please.*

*Go **wherever** he tells you.*

> **!!!** A single word, such as *whenever*, is usually part of a statement; separated words such as *when ever* are usually part of a question.

Every one means 'each individual one' and can refer to people or things:

*I looked at all the cups, and **every one** had a chip in it.*

Everyone means 'every person, all people':

***Everyone** thinks I'm crazy.*

*In this street, **everyone** has a car.*

> **!!!** If you are not sure which to use, try this test: *everyone* can be replaced by the word *everybody* (*Everybody thinks I'm crazy*), but *every one* cannot.

For ever is more often written as two words, but *forever* is also correct. Some people think that *forever* should mean 'continually' (*I'm forever getting this wrong*), and *for ever* should mean 'for all time' (*I'll love you for ever*), but it is not necessary to use the words in this way.

Always write *in fact* as two words:

*He was, **in fact**, more than capable of doing the job.*

Always write *in spite of* as three words:

> She succeeded **in spite of** the odds.

Always write *instead of* as two words, since *instead* is one word:

> Today I will have coffee **instead of** tea.

There is a distinction between *into* and *in to*. The word *into* is a preposition. It tells you there is movement from outside something to a position inside, or movement against something, or a change of state or condition:

> He walked **into** the room.

> He bumped **into** the door.

> The wizard turned them **into** frogs.

The phrase *in to* consists of the adverb *in* plus the preposition *to* acting as separate words:

> He came **in to** tell us the news.

In this sentence *in* is linked with *came* and *to* is linked with *tell*.

Maybe means 'perhaps':

> **Maybe** he will come this afternoon.

May be is a phrase made up of the verb *may* and the verb *be*:

> He **may be** coming this afternoon.

No-one means 'no person':

> There's **no-one** there.

No one means no single individual, either a person or a thing:

> **No one** person could possibly eat all that.

> **!!!** If you are not sure which to use, try this test: *no-one* can be replaced by the word *nobody* (There's nobody there), but *no one* cannot.

Onto is a single preposition:

> The book fell **onto** the table.

On to is the adverb *on* plus the preposition *to* acting as separate words:

> He went **on to** talk about his schooldays.

In this sentence *on* is linked with *went* and *to* is linked with *talk*.

Overall is a word meaning 'including everything':

> Isabel was left in **overall** control.

> Their work is quite good, **overall**.

Over all is a phrase made up of words with two separate meanings:

> She ruled **over all** the lands west of the river.

Sometime means 'at some point in time':

> I'll do it **sometime**.

Some time means 'a little time':

> I'll need **some time** to do this.

Thank you is usually written as two words:

> **Thank you** for the book.

It is sometimes written *thank-you* if you are not addressing someone directly:

> I'd like to say **thank-you** for the book.

Four tips for learning tricky spellings

There are a number of strategies you can use to help memorize the spelling of a word. Different words are suited to different strategies, so decide which one will be most helpful for each word.

TIP 1: BREAK DOWN THE WORD

Try breaking the word down into its component parts and saying them out loud or to yourself.

Some words are easiest to learn by sounding out individual letters:

> d–i–a–r–y

Some words are easiest to learn by sounding out individual syllables:

re–spon–si–bil–i–ty

Some words can be broken down into known 'roots' – components from which the word is created. These roots are spelt the same in every word in which they occur:

tele–phone

care–ful–ly

TIP 2: WORDS WITHIN WORDS

Many tricky words contain common words inside them. For example, the word *favourite* contains *our* and *rite*. Finding and remembering these 'words within words' can help you to learn a difficult spelling.

The 'words within words' strategy can be particularly useful for remembering the spelling of unstressed or silent vowels, for example *get* in *veg**et**able* or *par* in *se**par**ate*.

TIP 3: MNEMONICS

A mnemonic is a phrase that helps you to remember something. For example, people learning to read music learn the notes on the lines of the treble clef (E, G, B, D and F) by the phrase *Every Good Boy Deserves Favour*.

Mnemonics can also help you to remember difficult spellings. The best are simple and catchy, and create a vivid picture in your head:

*r**hythm** **h**elps **y**ou **t**o **h**ear **m**usic*

Mnemonics can help you remember the difficult part of a word:

*the **lieutenant** will **lie** ut**terly** still*

The most helpful mnemonics are often the ones that you make up yourself, creating phrases that have a special meaning for you.

TIP 4: LOOK – COVER – WRITE – CHECK

Look – cover – write – check is a four-stage strategy for learning difficult spellings. First you **look** at the word, then you **cover** it over and **write** it down from memory, then you uncover it to **check** that you have spelt it correctly.

When you first look at the word, or if you get the spelling wrong, try to concentrate on the parts that you have problems with, or that are not spelt as they sound.

Commonly misspelt words

The following list contains words that are commonly misspelt. You might find it helpful to go through and pick out words that you find difficult. You can then use the tips on pages 44–6 to help you to memorize these difficult words:

abbreviation	biscuit	disappear
abscess	blancmange	disappoint
absence	broccoli	doubt
accelerator	business	draughty
accessible	calendar	ecstasy
accidentally	catarrh	eczema
accommodation	ceiling	embarrass
achieve	cemetery	embodiment
acquiesce	changeable	encyclopedia
address	chaos	environment
advertisement	character	exaggerate
aerial	committee	exceed
aeroplane	competition	excellent
aghast	connoisseur	excerpt
almond	conscientious	exercise
annihilate	consensus	exhaust
argument	correspondence	experience
asphyxiate	courteous	fascinate
assassinate	definitely	fluorescent
asthma	deliberate	foreign
autumn	description	friend
bachelor	desperate	fulfil
beautiful	diarrhoea	gauge
believe	dilemma	genuine
berserk	diphtheria	ghastly

ghost	liaise	phlegm
gorgeous	lieutenant	physics
gorilla	liquefy	playwright
government	liquorice	pneumonia
grammar	maintenance	precede
guarantee	manageable	prejudice
guard	manoeuvre	privilege
guilty	marriage	proceed
gymkhana	martyr	professor
haemorrhage	mayonnaise	pronunciation
harass	medicine	psychiatry
height	millennium	publicly
humorous	miniature	pyjamas
hygiene	minuscule	questionnaire
hypocrisy	miscellaneous	queue
idiosyncrasy	mischievous	receipt
illiterate	misspell	receive
immediately	mortgage	recommend
independent	moustache	reconnaissance
indispensable	naive	refrigerator
innocuous	necessary	remember
inoculate	neighbour	reminiscence
instalment	niece	repetition
interrogate	noticeable	reservoir
irrelevant	nuisance	restaurant
irresistible	obscene	rhinoceros
jealous	occasion	rhyme
jeopardy	occurrence	rhythm
jewellery	opportunity	righteous
jodhpurs	parallel	sacrilegious
khaki	parliament	satellite
knowledgeable	permanent	sausage
laughter	perseverance	scissors
leisure	pharaoh	secretary
leopard	phenomenon	seize

separate	subterranean	valuable
sergeant	subtle	vegetable
sheikh	succeed	vehicle
shriek	success	verruca
siege	succinct	villain
sieve	supersede	Wednesday
silhouette	surprise	weight
sincerely	susceptible	weird
skilful	technique	wholly
solemn	temperature	woollen
soliloquy	tranquillity	wrath
sovereign	truly	yacht
spaghetti	turquoise	yield
sphinx	unfortunately	yoghurt
squabble	unwieldy	zealous
suave	vacuum	zoological

Grammar

What is grammar?

The word 'grammar' refers to the set of rules describing the different ways words are arranged into sentences.

If there were no rules about this, a writer could throw words into a sentence in any order:

Man tiger kill.

Tiger kill man.

Kill man tiger.

Readers coming upon such sentences would not have any guidance to help them to work out who was doing the killing, when the killing was happening, or what the relationship between *man* and *tiger* might be.

Grammar provides the writer with an order to put the words into so that they take on a definite meaning. It also provides the reader with rules for working out the meaning. The order in which the words appear is extremely significant: there is a big difference between *The man killed the tiger* and *The tiger killed the man.*

Everyone who has learned to speak, read and write must have gained a certain knowledge of these rules in order to be able to arrange words into patterns that other people can understand. This is usually achieved quite easily and unconsciously.

However, written language makes special demands on grammar. Firstly, we do not have the opportunity to supplement our writing with gestures or intonation in order to help get our point across. Nor do we have the opportunity of seeing our readers' reaction and using it to make adjustments to what we write in mid-sentence. Secondly, we may not know who is going to read what we write. Because of this there is a greater chance that what we write will not be understood by the people who read it. Grammar helps us out by providing a standard set of rules that we can expect all of our readers to know. An understanding of the standard rules for arranging words into sentences will help us to get our point across clearly, and also to create a good impression on our readers.

This book will help you by explaining some of the rules of grammar and then (on pages 84–92) discussing a few points that you need to be aware of if you want to be an assured and confident writer.

But before we look at the rules that apply to arranging words into sentences, it will help to get a clear understanding of the different functions that words can have in a sentence.

Parts of speech

Just as the engine of a motor vehicle needs to have various components, with each component performing a different function for the engine to work effectively as a unit, so too a sentence needs to have different types of words performing various functions. Some types of word (nouns) tell us *what things we are talking about*, others (verbs) express *what is going on*, while others (adverbs) describe *how things are being done*, and so on. The different types of word are called the **parts of speech** (or sometimes **word classes**). Together they combine to build up sentences that can convey descriptions of events or explain ideas and arguments.

There are seven main functions that a word can have in a sentence, each corresponding to a part of speech:

- nouns
- verbs
- adjectives
- adverbs
- pronouns
- prepositions
- conjunctions

We shall look at each of these types of word in turn. In addition to these, we shall also look at two further parts of speech:

- interjections
- determiners

What you need to know about nouns

A simple definition of a noun is that it is a 'naming word'. The words for all of the things you can see if you look around the room or out of the window are nouns. For example *dog, fish, table, phone* and *Peter* are all nouns.

Words such as *tranquillity, courage* and *chaos*, that give names to concepts, ideas or impressions, are also nouns. In fact, most words in the dictionary are classified as nouns.

A noun has some significant features that can help you to identify it and understand how it works:

> ➤ It often has two forms, the **singular** (referring to one thing) and **plural** (referring to more than one thing). For example *dog* and *child* are singular forms, whereas *dogs* and *children* are plural forms.

> ➤ It may be preceded by a word such as *a, the, my* or *some* (known as a **determiner**).

> ➤ It may be followed by an **apostrophe** then –*s*, or sometimes just an apostrophe, when showing that something belongs to someone (*my sister's phone, Peter's courage*).

> ➡️ The rules for the correct position of the apostrophe are given on pages 109–11.

Because there are so many nouns and they can refer to so many different things, it is sometimes helpful to think in terms of different categories of noun. Nouns can be categorized in a variety of ways:

> ➤ proper nouns and common nouns
> ➤ concrete nouns and abstract nouns
> ➤ countable nouns and uncountable nouns

Proper nouns and common nouns

A **proper noun** is a name of a particular person, place or thing. Because proper nouns are always unique individuals, they are spelt with capital letters. Proper nouns include *David, Saturn, October,*

Germany, Tokyo, Stonehenge, Rembrandt, Ramadan, Heinz and *Tuesday*.

A name can consist of more than one proper noun, and the name of a person or place might also include a title of some kind:

> *William Caxton*
>
> *President Kennedy*
>
> *Downing Street*
>
> *the Gobi Desert*

Sometimes a proper noun is used in a general way to refer not to the owner of that name, but to anyone or anything with a quality that is popularly associated with it:

> *a budding Einstein*
>
> *a modern-day Stonehenge*

Any noun that is not a proper noun is a **common noun**. Whereas proper nouns name individual people and things, common nouns name types of thing of which there may be any number of particular instances. Common nouns are not written with a capital letter:

PROPER NOUN	COMMON NOUN
Saturn	*planet*
Queen Victoria	*monarch*
October	*month*
Germany	*country*

Concrete nouns and abstract nouns

Common nouns can themselves be further divided into two categories: **concrete nouns** and **abstract nouns**.

A **concrete noun** is one that refers to a thing with a physical existence – something you can see and touch. Concrete nouns include *car, baby, tree, water, floor, giraffe, pen, sodium* and *garden*.

An **abstract noun** is one that refers to an idea, state or quality. These things do not have a physical existence – you can't see or touch them.

Abstract nouns include *strength, poverty, redness, modernism, radioactivity* and *directness*.

Countable nouns and uncountable nouns

Another useful distinction that is sometimes made is that between **countable nouns** and **uncountable nouns**. As the name suggests, a **countable noun** refers to something that can be counted. In other words, a countable noun has a singular form and a plural form:

dog – dogs

fish – fishes

knife – knives

idea – ideas

woman – women

Uncountable nouns refer to things that cannot be counted. Some uncountable nouns are concrete nouns describing matter or materials. These include *air, sodium, sand, wood, greenery, butter* and *wine*.

Other uncountable nouns are abstract nouns describing qualities, emotions, feelings and ideas. These include *beauty, anger, heaviness, truth* and *surrealism*.

Many uncountable nouns also have countable senses that refer not to the material or quality itself, but to a specific amount or instance of it:

UNCOUNTABLE SENSE	COUNTABLE SENSE
I like **coffee**.	*Two black* **coffees**, *please.*
These fanatics have no fear of **death**.	*The explosion caused many* **deaths**.
There was a burst of frantic **activity**.	*one of her favourite* **activities**
the sound of breaking **glass**	*a* **glass** *of wine*

Collective nouns

A **collective noun** refers to a collection of people or objects. There are three types of collective noun.

One type of collective noun is **always singular** and is used with the words *item of* or *article of*. Nouns such as *clothing, furniture, cutlery, equipment* and *luggage* fall into this category:

> The cutlery **is** polished every week.

Another type of collective noun is **always plural** but has no final *-s*. Nouns such as *cattle, police* and *people* fall into this category:

> The police **were** looking into the matter.

However, the most significant collective nouns are the **group nouns**. These refer to groups made up of individuals, and include words such as *army, audience, band, club, committee, company, crowd, family, firm, government, group, party, public, staff* and *team*.

Are group nouns singular or are they plural? See the discussion on page 91.

What you need to know about verbs

A simple definition of a verb is that it is a 'doing word'. A verb usually denotes an action, such as *jump, sleep, cry* or *eat*, but some verbs denote a state, such as *remain* or *be*.

Just as nouns may exist in more than one form depending on whether they are singular or plural, verbs may exist in more than one form. If we consider a verb such as *jump*, the form of the verb may change depending on:

> ➤ **person**: the form may vary according to who is doing the jumping. If it is *I* (the so-called **first person**) or *you* (the **second person**) the form of the verb is *jump*; if it is someone else (the **third person**) the form is *jumps*.

> ➤ **number**: the form may vary according to how many are jumping. For example, one person *jumps* (**singular**), but two people *jump* (**plural**).

> ➤ **tense**: the form may vary according to when the jumping is taking place. For example, yesterday *I jumped* (**past tense**), but today *I am jumping* (**present tense**) and tomorrow *I will jump* (**future tense**).

Some of the different forms of the verb *jump* are represented in the table below:

	PRESENT TENSE	PAST TENSE
FIRST PERSON SINGULAR	*I jump*	*I jumped*
SECOND PERSON SINGULAR	*you jump*	*you jumped*
THIRD PERSON SINGULAR	*he/she jumps*	*she/she jumped*
FIRST PERSON PLURAL	*we jump*	*we jumped*
SECOND PERSON PLURAL	*you jump*	*you jumped*
THIRD PERSON PLURAL	*they jump*	*they jumped*

The verb *jump* is a **regular verb**: its different forms are created according to predictable patterns. Some common verbs are **irregular**: their different forms are not predictable:

	PRESENT TENSE	PAST TENSE
FIRST PERSON SINGULAR	*I am*	*I was*
SECOND PERSON SINGULAR	*you are*	*you were*
THIRD PERSON SINGULAR	*he/she is*	*he/she was*
FIRST PERSON PLURAL	*we are*	*we were*
SECOND PERSON PLURAL	*you are*	*you were*
THIRD PERSON PLURAL	*they are*	*they were*

Verb forms

Each verb may exist in up to five different forms:

BASE FORM (INFINITIVE)	THIRD PERSON SINGULAR OF THE PRESENT TENSE	PRESENT PARTICIPLE	PAST TENSE	PAST PARTICIPLE
jump	*jumps*	*jumping*	*jumped*	*jumped*
sew	*sews*	*sewing*	*sewed*	*sewn*

You will notice that for regular verbs, such as *jump*, the last two of these forms are actually the same. Most verbs behave in the same way as *jump*, creating the different forms by adding *-s*, *-ing* and *-ed*. For irregular verbs, the way that the third form is produced can vary slightly, and the way that the last two are produced can vary quite a lot.

The **base form** is the one all the others are formed from, and the one that is used to show the present tense after *I*, *you*, *we* and *they*. It is also the form of the verb that you will see if you look it up in a dictionary.

The **third person singular** of the **present** tense is regularly formed by adding *-s* to the base form:

>*it cuts*
>
>*he finds*
>
>*she learns*

The **present participle** is formed by adding *-ing* to the base form. This part of the verb is often used in combination with another verb such as *is* or *was*:

>*it is cutting*
>
>*she is finding*
>
>*he was learning*

The simple **past tense** is regularly formed by adding *-ed* to the base form:

>*I jumped*
>
>*you watched*
>
>*she learned*

Some verbs do not add *-ed*, but form the past tense irregularly:

>*find – found*
>
>*break – broke*
>
>*forget – forgot*
>
>*shrink – shrank*

The **past participle** of regular verbs (and also many irregular verbs) is often identical in form to the past tense. However, some irregular verbs use different forms for the past tense and past participle:

>*break – broken*
>
>*forget – forgotten*
>
>*shrink – shrunk*

The past participle of the verb is often used in combination with another verb such as *has* or *was*:

it was broken

we had forgotten

it has shrunk

> **!!!** Don't confuse the past tense of the verb with the past participle. See the discussion on pages 84–5.

Main verbs and auxiliary verbs

When we describe an action, we sometimes use one of these verb forms on its own, but sometimes we use one of the verb forms in combination with another verb.

You can use the first two of the five verb forms described above on their own to convey the present tense (*I jump, he jumps*), and the fourth of these forms on its own to convey the past tense (*I jumped*). However, these one-word or 'simple' tenses are not sufficient to convey all the possible shades of meaning about when an action took place or is taking place.

We can greatly extend the number of ways we use verbs by using the base form, the present participle form or the past participle form in combination with certain other verbs, especially the verbs whose base forms are *be, have* and *do*. This allows us to create 'compound' tenses that can convey the past (*I was jumping, she has jumped*), the present (*you are jumping, he does jump*) or the future (*you will jump*).

This means that verbs can be divided into two major groups: **main verbs** and **auxiliary verbs**.

A **main verb** is what we normally think of as the 'doing' bit of the verb and it contains what we probably regard as the meaning of the verb:

jumps

learned

shrank

An **auxiliary verb** is so called because it performs an auxiliary or helping role in combination with a main verb. The highlighted words in the following examples are auxiliary verbs:

> **have** *jumped*
>
> **am** *cutting*
>
> **does** *find*
>
> **was** *learning*

Sometimes we find two auxiliary verbs used in combination with a main verb:

> **has been** *broken*
>
> **is being** *done*

The three principal auxiliary verbs (*be*, *have* and *do*) can also act as main verbs in their own right. These verbs are irregular and exist in more forms than other verbs. For example, *am*, *are*, *is*, *was* and *were* are all forms of the verb *be*.

Besides these three verbs, there are a number of other auxiliary verbs that only exist in one form. These include *can*, *could*, *might*, *will*, *would*, *shall*, *should*, *ought to* and *must*.

Using combinations of the main verb and various auxiliary verbs, you can construct more complex versions of any verb:

> We **will have to return** *later*.
>
> She **ought to have arrived** *before now*.
>
> They **should have been working** *this afternoon*.

> The auxiliary verbs *will* and *shall* are sometimes used as if they were interchangeable, but some people insist on observing a distinction between them. See the discussion on pages 90–1.

Active and passive forms of verbs

In addition to having different forms to indicate the person and the tense, verbs also have different forms according to whether the sentence is written in the **active voice** or the **passive voice**. (For more information about active and passive sentences, see pages 227–8.)

In sentences when the verb describes *what action the subject is doing* or *what state the subject is in*, the active form of the verb (often thought of as the 'normal' form) is used:

> *Elephants **destroyed** the field of maize.*

> *The hotel **serves** breakfast until nine o'clock.*

However, when sentences are written in the passive voice (so that instead of describing *what action the subject is doing*, the verb describes *what is being done to the subject*), the form of the verb consists of the past participle preceded by an auxiliary verb that is a form of *be*:

> *The field of maize **was destroyed** by elephants.*

> *Breakfast **is served** until nine o'clock.*

The infinitive form of the verb

When the base form is preceded by *to*, it produces what is traditionally referred to as the **infinitive**:

> *to jump*

> *to sew*

The infinitive is used after certain verbs, such as *try, need, like, hope, mean* and *tend*:

> *I shall try **to be** more careful next time.*

> *You need **to go** early to avoid the crowds.*

> *I would really like **to meet** him.*

The infinitive is often used when explaining a reason or purpose:

> *Bring her a cushion **to sit** on.*

> *I went out **to get** some fresh air.*

The infinitive form of the verb can also be used like a noun to express the general activity of doing something:

> ***To play** really well takes hours of practice.*

> ➡ What is a 'split infinitive', and is it a sign of bad writing? See the discussion on pages 88–9.

Transitive verbs and intransitive verbs

An important way of classifying verbs involves the distinction between **transitive verbs** and **intransitive verbs**.

Consider the following sentences:

> *Maggie **examined** her coat.*
>
> *I **phoned** Alan.*
>
> *Dave **sneezed**.*
>
> *The video **is rewinding**.*

The person or thing that is carrying out the action (*Maggie, I, Dave, the video*) is known as the **subject** of the verb and the person or thing on the receiving end of the action (*her coat, Alan*) is known as the **object**. A transitive verb requires an object, but an intransitive verb does not require one.

So the verbs in the following sentences are transitive:

> *Maggie **examined** her coat.*
>
> *I **phoned** Alan.*

Whereas the verbs in the following sentences are intransitive:

> *Dave **sneezed**.*
>
> *The video **is rewinding**.*

Some verbs can be either transitive or intransitive. For example *cook* can be used transitively, as in:

> *We cooked a meal.* (*We* is the subject; *a meal* is the object.)

It can also be used intransitively, as in:

> *She can't cook.* (*She* is the subject; there is no object.)

Finite verbs and non-finite verbs

A verb is a **finite verb** when it is used in combination with a subject and gives information about the subject. A finite verb always has a

tense, which indicates when the action was done (whether in the past, present or future):

> She **watched** the game.

> We **shall watch** the game.

Non-finite verbs are forms of the verb that do not indicate when the subject of a sentence performed an action. The **infinitive** form and the **participle** forms of the verb are non-finite verbs:

> **to watch** the game

> **watching** the game

The distinction between finite verbs and non-finite verbs becomes important when we think about sentences (see pages 223–35). For a sentence to be complete, it must contain a finite verb.

Using verbs as nouns

Sometimes you might come across a word that seems to be the *-ing* form of a verb, but which behaves like a noun, much in the way that the infinitive form does:

> **Swimming** is a terrific form of exercise.

> There were a lot of **comings** and **goings**.

> I need to do a bit of **decorating**.

This type of word is known as a **verbal noun** or, technically, a **gerund**.

Using verbs as adjectives

The *-ing* form (or **present participle**) of a verb can also be used as an adjective, describing a noun in terms of what the person or thing is doing:

> a **crying** baby

> a **depressing** experience

The **past participles** of verbs can also be used as adjectives, describing nouns in terms of what has been done to the person or thing:

frozen peas

an *abandoned* car

Phrasal verbs

A **phrasal verb** is an expression that consists of a verb followed by a **particle**, which can be either a **preposition** (such as *for*) or an **adverb** (such as *down* or *up*). Taken together, the verb and the particle have a meaning that could not be understood from the usual meanings of the words:

I need some time to **wind down**.

Look up the word in the dictionary.

He's **heading for** trouble.

A phrasal verb in which the particle is a preposition needs a word to act as an **object** in order to complete the meaning, whereas one in which the particle is an adverb is complete by itself: you always *head for somewhere*, but when you relax, you simply *wind down*.

Sometimes a phrasal verb has two particles, an adverb then a preposition:

I don't have to **put up with** all this nonsense.

You can't just **walk away from** your problems.

She's **going out with** Darren.

Phrasal verbs are usually formed from very common verbs. The same verb can be used with different prepositions or adverbs to create several different phrasal verbs:

I'm looking **for** Mark Dawes. (preposition)

Look **out**! (adverb)

She's always looked **up to** him. (adverb + preposition)

What you need to know about adjectives

A simple definition of an adjective is that it is a 'describing word'. The role of an adjective is to describe or give information about a noun. For example, in the sentences below, the highlighted words are adjectives:

*The **ginger** cat was drinking milk from a **chipped** saucer.*

*The cat was extremely **fat**.*

*They saw an **old** house with a **rambling** garden.*

Adjectives can be categorized in various ways:

> according to position

> according to meaning

> according to grammatical role

Categorizing adjectives according to position

Adjectives may be categorized as **attributive**, **predicative** or **postpositive**, depending on their position in a sentence. The names of the various categories of adjective might not seem very welcoming, but the divisions themselves are all straightforward, and it is useful to be aware of them.

If an adjective comes immediately before the noun, it is categorized as **attributive**:

*a **green** scarf*

*an **old** man*

*an **enormous** house*

Some adjectives can only be used attributively:

*my **elder** brother* (you can't say *My brother is elder.*)

*the **sole** survivor* (you can't say *The survivor was sole.*)

*the **main** road* (you can't say *The road is main.*)

If an adjective comes after the noun and requires a **linking verb** such as *be, become, get, seem* or *feel*, it is categorized as **predicative**:

*His scarf is **green**.*

*He's getting **old**.*

*Their house seems **enormous**.*

Some adjectives can only be used predicatively:

*My grandfather is still **alive**.* (you can't say *my alive grandfather*)

*The train is **due**.* (you can't say *the due train*)

*Dinner is **ready**.* (you can't say *the ready dinner*)

Most adjectives can be used in either position without any change in meaning. Some, as we have seen, can only be used in one position or the other. However, there are certain adjectives that change their meaning depending on whether they are being used attributively or predicatively:

ATTRIBUTIVE USE	PREDICATIVE USE
my late husband	*My husband was late.*
the faint glow from the fire	*I feel faint.*

The final class of adjectives, which come after the noun and do not require a linking verb, are known as **postpositive** adjectives:

*prizes **galore***

*the president **elect***

*the devil **incarnate***

Many of these postpositive adjectives occur in fixed noun–adjective combinations:

*attorney **general***

*mother **superior***

*court **martial***

Categorizing adjectives according to meaning

Another way of categorizing adjectives is as **qualitative adjectives**, **classifying adjectives** or **colour adjectives**, depending on the sort of information they provide about the noun they describe.

Probably the most familiar adjectives are the **qualitative adjectives**, which describe what a person or thing is like in terms of particular qualities, such as:

➤ size or extent (*a **tall** glass, the journey was very **long***)

➤ shape (*a **square** table, the windows are **round***)

➤ character (*a **funny** story, a **kind** man*)

➤ age (*a **young** woman, an **ancient** tradition*)

Qualitative adjectives also express the writer's personal opinion or feeling:

*a **horrible** day*

*We had a **lovely** time.*

> Many qualitative adjectives are **gradable**, meaning that they can exist in several forms to indicate different levels of extent or intensity. See pages 66–8.

Classifying adjectives describe a person or thing in terms of its belonging to a certain class or category, such as:

➤ frequency or period (*a **daily** paper, the **latest** fashions*)

➤ shape (*an **oval** table, **hexagonal** tiles*)

➤ nationality or origin (***Russian** vodka, a **Japanese** word*)

➤ material (*a **plastic** cup, a **wooden** door*)

➤ type (*an **urban** landscape, a **nuclear** reactor*)

It is possible to use several classifying adjectives together to describe a noun. When several adjectives are used in this way, they usually follow the order shown above, so that shape comes before nationality, material comes before type, and so on:

*the **latest full-length English woollen winter** coats*

As the name suggests, **colour adjectives** specify colour. They can be used together with qualitative adjectives such as *bright, dark, light, deep* and *pale*. When used along with other adjectives, qualitative adjectives come first, then colours, then classifying adjectives:

*my **old black leather** jacket*

Colour adjectives are different from other adjectives because they can also be used as **uncountable nouns** (*a horrid shade of pink*) and **countable nouns** (*the lilacs and purples that we chose for the bedroom*).

In addition, certain colours are actually derived from nouns (*ginger, cream, terracotta*) or are formed from a combination of noun and adjective (*sky blue, emerald green*).

Categorizing adjectives according to grammatical role

Two further sets of adjectives can be categorized according to their grammatical role within a sentence.

Emphasizing adjectives are, as the name suggests, used to emphasize the degree to which a particular quality exists. They are only used attributively, and without any other kind of adjective being present:

> *The meeting was an **absolute** disaster.*

> *I felt like a **complete** idiot.*

> *It rained for the **entire** weekend.*

Other emphasizing adjectives include *sheer, total* and *utter*, along with the various swearwords that can occupy this role.

Specifying adjectives are often used to introduce more specific information about number or identity. They come after a determiner and before a noun, and are themselves acting as secondary determiners:

> *We waited a **further** three weeks.*

> *The **following** people have been selected.*

> *the **same** old story*

> *the **usual** suspects*

Other specifying adjectives include *additional, certain, existing, extra, final, first, last, main, next, only, other, particular, past, previous, remaining* and *specific*.

Different forms of the adjective

Many adjectives, especially qualitative adjectives, are **gradable**, meaning that they have different forms depending on how intense the quality is that you are describing, or how much you want to emphasize a particular personal response:

*I want a **bigger** glass.* (not just *a **big** glass*)

*That is the **ugliest** dog I've ever seen.* (not just *an **ugly** dog*)

Gradable adjectives can exist in three different forms: the **positive** (or **absolute**) form, the **comparative** form and the **superlative** form. These different forms are shown below using the adjectives *big* and *beautiful* as examples:

POSITIVE	COMPARATIVE	SUPERLATIVE
big	bigger	biggest
beautiful	more beautiful	most beautiful

Shorter words (words of one syllable and some words of two syllables) form the comparative and superlative in the same way as *big*, by adding -*er* and -*est*:

long – longer – longest

tough – tougher – toughest

happy – happier – happiest

> ➡ The rules relating to how spellings change when these endings are added to a word are explained on pages 30–1.

You cannot add -*er* and -*est* to longer words, so the comparative and superlative forms of these are created by using *more* and *most* in front of the positive form:

awkward – more awkward – most awkward

sentimental – more sentimental – most sentimental

The adjectives *good* and *bad* are exceptions to the normal pattern, and have irregular comparative and superlative forms:

POSITIVE	COMPARATIVE	SUPERLATIVE
good	better	best
bad	worse	worst

Although **classifying adjectives** are not generally gradable, some of the more common and less precise shapes such as *round* and *thin* are gradable. In addition, some adjectives that are normally considered as classifying adjectives possess an extra, gradable sense if a category has become associated with a particular quality:

*a **more wooden** performance*

*the **most Victorian** attitudes*

Although the less common **colour adjectives** are not generally gradable, some very common ones are gradable:

*the **whitest** teeth I've ever seen*

*the grass is always **greener***

> **!!!** Don't use the superlative form of the adjective when you are making a comparison between two things. See the discussion on pages 86–7.

Using nouns as adjectives

Most nouns can be used in the same way as adjectives, in that they can be placed in front of another noun to give more information about what sort of thing the noun is. When a noun is used to 'modify' another noun in this way it is called a **modifier**. It is very common to see nouns used in this way:

*a **fish** tank*

*a **car** tyre*

***dog** food*

*a **music** magazine*

Many of these modifier–noun combinations have become so well established that they are treated as single words in their own right:

***shoe**lace*

***door**knob*

***tooth**brush*

Note that verbal nouns or gerunds are also often used as modifiers:

***swimming** trunks*

***steering** wheel*

***building** materials*

What you need to know about adverbs

Adverbs are used to add something extra to the meaning expressed by various parts of speech, and even the meaning of whole sentences. They often occur towards the end of the sentence and give a sense of completing it or rounding it off.

The most useful way to think about adverbs is that their role in the sentence is to answer certain questions the writer might want to answer for the reader, such as:

> how? (*She played **well**; They reacted **sluggishly**.*)

> where? where to? where from? (*She's **here**; I'm getting **nowhere**.*)

> how far? (*It stretches **endlessly**; He ran **miles**.*)

> how long? (*I waited **forever**; I paused **momentarily**.*)

> when? (*Are you free **tomorrow**?; I saw him **recently**.*)

> how often? (*They are paid **monthly**; We **seldom** discussed it.*)

> to what extent? (*I don't like it **much**; She's **highly** intelligent.*)

Some of the most familiar adverbs are formed by adding the ending -*ly* onto an adjective:

quick – quickly

sad – sadly

hasty – hastily

However, not all words ending in -*ly* are adverbs. Some are adjectives, including *costly, friendly, lively, lonely, silly* and *ugly*.

Phrases that act as adverbs

Although there are many single-word adverbs, it is also common for a group of words within a sentence to perform the function of an adverb. Such groups of words are known as **adverb phrases** or **adverbials**:

*handle **with care***

*the one **on the left***

*We walked **all the way**.*

*I waited **for ages**.*

*I'll see you **after the party**.*

*We **hardly ever** go there.*

*I agree **with all my heart**.*

Words that can behave as adjectives and adverbs

Some adjectives can also be used as adverbs in certain situations, depending on their position in the sentence:

ADJECTIVAL USE	ADVERBIAL USE
a **daily** newspaper	The newspaper is delivered **daily**.
an **hourly** bus service	He is paid **hourly**.
a **fast** car	He drives **fast**.
a **long** journey	I won't stay **long**.

Sentence adverbs

Sentence adverbs comment on or 'qualify' a whole sentence rather than referring to a particular word or group of words within a sentence. Unlike most other adverbs and adverbials, they do not come at the end of the sentence.

The most common sentence adverbs are single words ending in *-ly*, which are often used at the beginning of a sentence as a way of establishing the attitude of the writer:

Unfortunately, *we won't be able to come.*

Amazingly, *no-one was injured.*

Personally, *I think it's terrible.*

Other sentence adverbs of this kind include *clearly, fortunately, frankly, hopefully, obviously* and *thankfully*.

Sentence adverbs can also link two ideas or pieces of information in some way, for example by contrasting or qualifying what has already been said:

'You don't look very well.' '**On the contrary**, I've never felt better!'

We don't want to go. **However**, we have no choice.

Other sentence adverbs and adverbials of this kind include *even so, nevertheless* and *on the other hand.*

Because they are not part of the rest of the sentence, sentence adverbs are usually separated from the rest of the sentence by a comma (at the beginning of a sentence), or by two commas (in the middle of a sentence):

Fortunately, I was able to escape in time.

The export division, **on the other hand**, is in a healthy position.

> ➡ Sentence adverbs are extremely useful for linking together sentences and paragraphs to create a fluent style in your writing. See the discussion of linking devices on pages 252–3.

Technical adverbs

Certain adverbs that end in *-ly* can be used to express a point of view that refers to a particular subject area or field of knowledge. These **technical adverbs** are widely used as a way of compressing phrases such as *from an economic perspective* or *technically speaking*:

Economically, it was a disaster.

Technically, a gorilla is an ape rather than a monkey.

Their position in the sentence can vary, as can their use with commas. When they come at the start of a sentence, they are treated as sentence adverbs, and it is generally best for them to be followed by a comma. However, they can also be found in other positions in a sentence:

Is this discovery **historically** significant?

How are they coping **financially**?

Different forms of the adverb

Like adjectives, many adverbs are **gradable** and have **positive**,

71

comparative and **superlative** forms. There are two kinds of regular gradable adverb.

Words that are adjectives and act as adverbs only because of their position in the sentence use the same forms as adjectives throughout:

*He drives **fast** and works **hard**.* (positive)

*He drove **faster** and worked **harder** than ever.* (comparative)

*He drives **fastest** and works **hardest** when he's angry.* (superlative)

For adverbs that end in *-ly*, the comparative and superlative forms are created by using *more* and *most* in front of the positive form:

closely – more closely – most closely

nervously – more nervously – most nervously

The adverbs *well* and *badly* are exceptions to the normal pattern, and have irregular comparative and superlative forms:

POSITIVE	COMPARATIVE	SUPERLATIVE
well	better	best
badly	worse	worst

What you need to know about pronouns

Pronouns are short words that can act as substitutes for nouns. Words such as *you, them* and *it* are pronouns.

Pronouns save writers from having to spell out names again and again:

*Jim is a good worker, but I don't really trust **him**.*

*Sally told me that **she** had forgotten the key.*

Pronouns can act as substitutes not just for a noun, but also for a **noun phrase** – a cluster of words that acts as a noun. This can save a lot of time:

*I fell in love with **the big red sandstone Victorian house with the huge garden that I had seen the previous week**, and decided to buy **it**.*

The use of pronouns is so common that people often overlook them, but they perform a vital function, and without them language soon begins to sound awkward and repetitive. For example, without the use of pronouns, that last sentence would have to be written as:

> The use of **pronouns** is so common that people often overlook **pronouns**, but **pronouns** perform a vital function, and without **pronouns** language soon begins to sound awkward and repetitive.

Unlike nouns, adjectives and adverbs, you cannot devise a new pronoun to describe something new; they are a fixed set of words. There are several different kinds of pronoun, each of which has a specific use:

- personal pronouns
- the impersonal pronoun
- possessive pronouns
- reflexive pronouns
- interrogative pronouns
- relative pronouns
- demonstrative pronouns
- indefinite pronouns
- reciprocal pronouns

Personal pronouns

Personal pronouns stand in place of a person or thing. Different words are used to indicate the **person** and **number** (see page 54 above), and whether the pronoun is acting as the **subject** or the **object** of the verb (see page 60 above):

	SUBJECT	OBJECT
FIRST PERSON SINGULAR	*I*	*me*
SECOND PERSON SINGULAR	*you*	*you*
THIRD PERSON SINGULAR	*he – she – it*	*him – her – it*
FIRST PERSON PLURAL	*we*	*us*
SECOND PERSON PLURAL	*you*	*you*
THIRD PERSON PLURAL	*they*	*them*

In modern Standard English, the second person subject and object are the same in both the singular and the plural form: *you* in fact does the job of the four words (*I, me, we, us*) used by the first person in these positions. In earlier English there were different forms for the second person singular (*thou* for the subject, *thee* for the object) and the second person plural (*ye*). Some non-standard and dialect versions of English make a similar distinction between the second person singular (*you*) and a second person plural (*yous*).

Note that different words are used for the third person singular pronoun depending on the **gender**: *he* is used to represent things that are masculine, *she* for things that are feminine and *it* for things that are neither masculine nor feminine.

The impersonal pronoun

In certain sentences that do not have a clearly identifiable subject for the pronoun to refer to, the word *it* is used. This is called the **impersonal pronoun**:

> *It is nine o'clock.*

> *Has it stopped raining?*

> *It would be pointless to argue with him.*

Possessive pronouns

Possessive pronouns refer to things that belong to a specified person:

> *The black pen is **mine**. (mine = my pen)*

> ***Hers** is the red coat. (hers = her coat)*

> ***Ours** are in this box. (ours = our things)*

FIRST PERSON SINGULAR	*mine*
SECOND PERSON SINGULAR	*yours*
THIRD PERSON SINGULAR	*his – hers*
FIRST PERSON PLURAL	*ours*
SECOND PERSON PLURAL	*yours*
THIRD PERSON PLURAL	*theirs*

Reflexive pronouns

Reflexive pronouns are used when the person or thing referred to is the same as the subject of the verb:

*Frank has a high opinion of **himself**.*

*I had to pinch **myself**.*

They can also be used to add emphasis:

*You didn't do too badly **yourself**.*

*Even Tony **himself** was surprised.*

FIRST PERSON SINGULAR	*myself*
SECOND PERSON SINGULAR	*yourself*
THIRD PERSON SINGULAR	*himself – herself – itself*
FIRST PERSON PLURAL	*ourselves*
SECOND PERSON PLURAL	*yourselves*
THIRD PERSON PLURAL	*themselves*

Interrogative pronouns

Pronouns can be used when asking questions. These are known as the **interrogative pronouns**, because you would use them when questioning or interrogating someone:

Who *was on the phone?*

*To **whom** should I address my correspondence?*

Whose *are these?*

Which *is the least expensive?*

What *is your address?*

Relative pronouns

Relative pronouns are used to refer back to a person or thing mentioned earlier in the sentence:

*the man **who** lives across the street*

*the person to **whom** I spoke*

*the people **whose** car was stolen*

All of the words that can be used as interrogative pronouns can also function as relative pronouns, except that *that* is used instead of *what*:

*the wine **that** was cheapest* (not *the wine what was cheapest*)

Relative pronouns may either be **defining relatives** or **non-defining relatives**. Defining relatives specify which particular person or thing is meant:

*The book **that** I ordered has finally arrived.*

*I think the man **who** lives across the street is a spy.*

In these examples, the information introduced by the relative pronoun specifies which particular book and which particular man is meant.

Non-defining relatives merely provide additional information:

*I got the Spanish red wine, **which** was cheapest.*

*I had a word with my friend Alex, **who** lives nearby.*

In these examples, the information introduced by the relative pronoun is not essential to indicate which particular wine and which particular friend is meant.

You should be able to tell the difference between a defining relative and a non-defining relative because there should be a comma before a non-defining relative but not before a defining relative.

Moreover, some writers insist on a distinction between *that* and *which*, using *that* as a defining relative pronoun and *which* as a non-defining relative pronoun:

*I returned to the house **that** I had visited the previous year.*

*They live in a beautiful house, **which** is close to the sea.*

However, *that* and *which* are increasingly used interchangeably, especially as defining relatives.

For more information about *who* and *whom*, see pages 89–90.

Demonstrative pronouns

Pronouns can be used as the equivalent of pointing to something.
Words that do this are known as **demonstrative pronouns**. If the
thing is relatively close, you use *this* (or *these* in the plural); if the
thing is relatively far away, you use *that* (or *those* in the plural).
Because they are often used to refer to things that a person can see,
they tend to be used in speaking more than in writing. However, they
might also be used in writing to refer to something that has been
mentioned in the previous sentence:

> *Do not worry about the notes.* **Those** *have all been destroyed.*

> *I enclose a map. Please bring* **this** *with you.*

> These words can also be used as determiners.
> See page 83.

Indefinite pronouns

The **indefinite pronouns** refer to people or things without
specifying who they are or which ones they are.

One group of these begins with *some–, no–* or *every–*, and ends with
–body, –one or *–thing*:

> *I hope you meet* **someone** *nice.*

> **Everything** *went wrong.*

These pronouns always take a singular verb:

> **Nobody** *knows his name.*

Another group of indefinite pronouns is used to refer to general
amounts and quantities. This group includes: *some, any, none, all,
both, each, most, several, enough, few, many* and *half*:

> **Many** *will try;* **most** *will fail.*

> *The students were tested and* **all** *passed.*

> *There is only* **half** *left.*

Like the demonstrative pronouns, these pronouns, along with *either*
and *neither*, can also operate as determiners when the thing or person
they are referring to is the subject or object of the sentence.

Reciprocal pronouns

The only other pronouns are the **reciprocal pronouns**, *each other* and *one another*, which are always plural:

> *The mothers in the group can support **each other**.*

> *You and Marie know **one another**, don't you?*

What you need to know about prepositions

Like pronouns, **prepositions** are a fixed set of words. Most of them are short words, such as *in*, *at* or *on*. In addition, some phrases, such as *in front of* or *instead of* act as prepositions.

Some prepositions indicate the **place** where something is or the nature of its movement from one place to another. Prepositions of place include *in, at, on, over, under, against, near, next to, among, towards, on top of, into, out of, down, up, through, between, from* and *via*:

> *the house **near** the park*

> *She sat **next to** me.*

> *I saw you **at** the cinema.*

> *I keep my bike **in** the cellar.*

Some prepositions indicate **time**. Prepositions of time include *before, after, during, throughout, until, at* and *in*:

> *I'll see you **at** nine o'clock.*

> *I waited **until** Donna arrived.*

> *It happened **in** July.*

Some prepositions indicate the **relationship** between events and items. Prepositions of relationship include *in spite of, by means of, but for, according to, as well as, including, excluding, about, together with, in spite of* and *with*:

> *Everything was done **according to** the rules.*

> *We had a great time **in spite of** the weather.*

> *There are twelve of us **including** the kids.*

> *a man **with** white hair*

A preposition always has a noun or pronoun that is 'on the receiving end' of it. This word is the **object** of the preposition. If this word is a pronoun, the pronoun is in the object form (see page 73):

*She smiled at **me**.*

*I gave the pen to **him**.*

The object of the preposition usually follows immediately after it. However, in some sentences, the preposition can be separated from its object. This can happen, for example, in questions and exclamations beginning with *what, where, who, which* and *how*, and in sentences where the preposition is part of a phrasal verb:

***Which airline** are you flying **with**?*

***What a state** she's **in**!*

*He needs **a tissue** to blow his nose **on**.*

> ➡ Is it acceptable to end a sentence with a preposition?
> See the discussion on pages 91–2.

Words that can behave as prepositions and adverbs

Some prepositions can also be used as adverbs in certain situations, depending on their position in the sentence:

PREPOSITIONAL USE	ADVERBIAL USE
running **down** the steps	He sat **down**.
to put it **in** the box	Please come **in**.
walking **through** the park	A stream ran gently **through**.
They huddled **under** an umbrella.	The business went **under**.

What you need to know about conjunctions

A simple definition of a conjunction is that it is a 'joining word'. The role of a conjunction is to link words or groups of words together. Like pronouns and prepositions, they are a relatively small fixed set of words.

There are two kinds of conjunction:

> co-ordinating conjunctions
> subordinating conjunctions

Co-ordinating conjunctions

There are only a few **co-ordinating conjunctions**; the main ones are *and*, *but* and *or*.

The conjunction *and* signals an addition:

*bread **and** butter*

*two men **and** three women*

The conjunction *but* signals a contrast:

*tired **but** happy*

*He is very able **but** rather lazy.*

The conjunction *or* signals an alternative:

*tea **or** coffee*

*You can pay by cheque **or** credit card.*

When words or groups of words are joined in lists, a conjunction is generally only used before the last item, and other items are linked by a comma:

*She speaks French, German **and** Russian.*

It is, however, possible to use conjunctions in other parts of a list:

*You can have eggs **or** rolls **or** kippers **or** cereal.*

Co-ordinating conjunctions are often used in pairs. These pairs of conjunctions include *both ... and ...*, *either ... or ...* and *neither ... nor...*:

*She has degrees in **both** law **and** medicine.*

*I have visited **neither** Florence **nor** Milan.*

Co-ordinating conjunctions are useful when you want to make a series of short, simple sentences into a longer sentence:

*In summer they play golf **and** in winter they go skiing.*

Because their role is to join things together, co-ordinating conjunctions do not generally stand at the start of a sentence. However, it is permissible to begin a sentence with a conjunction to indicate a link with the previous sentence:

We are making the slogan 'Quality is Everything' a way of life. And that is not all.

Subordinating conjunctions

Subordinating conjunctions are used to introduce a piece of information that elaborates on or explains the information in the main part of the sentence (see pages 231–4 for a fuller explanation of these 'subordinate clauses').

Common subordinating conjunctions include *whether, because, if, until, that, in case, as if, unless* and *even though*:

*I wonder **whether** we'll get to meet her.*

*Take an umbrella **in case** it rains.*

*You should help her **because** she's your sister.*

What you need to know about interjections

Interjections are a special type of word. They are different from other parts of speech because they do not combine with other words in sentences. They stand on their own, and usually express a strong emotion. Words such as *hello, ouch* and *OK* are interjections. They are often followed by an exclamation mark:

Blast! *I meant to go the supermarket this afternoon.*

Hello! *I didn't expect to see you.*

What you need to know about determiners

The term 'determiner' is used to refer to a small group of words that were traditionally classed as adjectives, but are now usually regarded as a separate class of word. The role of determiners is to allow you to be more specific about nouns: to indicate which thing or person is being referred to, and how many of them there are. Words such as *a, some* and *several* are determiners. Many words that function as pronouns can also function as determiners.

There are several different kinds of determiner, each of which has a specific use:

> ➤ articles
> ➤ demonstrative determiners
> ➤ possessive determiners
> ➤ quantifiers
> ➤ distributive determiners
> ➤ exclamatives
> ➤ interrogative determiners

Articles

The commonest determiners are the **articles**. The word *a* is known as the **indefinite article**, and the word *the* is known as the **definite article**.

The indefinite article is used when it is not specified which particular person or thing is being referred to:

*I picked up **a** book.*

***a** man wearing jeans*

An is used rather than *a* before vowels and also before words that are pronounced as though they begin with a vowel:

*I picked up **an** apple.*

***an** MP*

***an** hour*

> **!!!** You don't need to use *an* before a word beginning with *h* when the *h* is sounded. Writing *an hotel* or *an historic victory* is rather old-fashioned and is best avoided.

The definite article is used to specify a particular person or thing:

*I picked up **the** book.*

***the** man wearing jeans*

Demonstrative determiners

The demonstrative pronouns – *this, that, these* and *those* – can also
be used as determiners, when the noun has already been referred to:

> **Those** *notes have all been destroyed.*

> *Please bring* **this** *map with you.*

Possessive determiners

The **possessive determiners** are *my, your, his, her, its, our, your*
and *their*. They are related to the possessive pronouns, and like them
they indicate ownership:

> **My** *notes have all been destroyed.*

> *Please bring* **your** *map with you.*

Quantifiers

Quantifiers are words that indicate 'how much' or 'how many'. This
group of words includes *some, any, all, another, enough, several,
many, few, less, much, little, more, most, half, double, both* and *no*:

> *Could I have* **more** *cheese?*

> *There wasn't* **any** *petrol in the car.*

Distributive determiners

There are four **distributive determiners**, which are used to refer
to how things are shared or distributed between people. They function
as two pairs: *each* and *every*, and *either* and *neither*.

Each is used when referring to individual members of a group that
consists of two or more:

> **Each** *soldier was issued with ten rounds.*

> *She staggered up the steps, a box under* **each** *arm.*

Every is used when referring to a group that consists of three or more:

> **Every** *window was shattered by the blast.*

> *It is impossible to reply to* **every** *letter.*

Either is used for a choice between two alternatives:

Either date will suit me.

The game could have gone *either* way.

Neither is used to exclude both of two people or things:

Neither option is particularly attractive.

Exclamatives

The **exclamatives** *what* and *such* are used for exclamations, the kinds of things that are followed by an exclamation mark:

What rubbish!

She's *such* a liar!

Interrogative determiners

The **interrogative determiners** are *which, what* and *whose*. They come immediately before a noun as part of a question:

Whose socks are these?

Which wine is the least expensive?

What size do you take?

Five grammar rules for everyone

There are two types of grammar rules: ones that are important because they help you to write clearly, and ones that are obeyed for the sake of tradition. It is important to know about and follow the first; you can make up your own mind about the second type of rule.

The most important grammar rules are ones that indicate clearly the relationships between the different words in a sentence. If these relationships are clear to the reader, there should be no problem about the meaning of a sentence being understood.

RULE 1: DON'T CONFUSE THE PAST TENSE WITH PAST PARTICIPLE

We saw on pages 55–7 that verbs have a past tense and a past participle. In some cases the same form of the verb is used for both:

I *cut* my finger.

*The finger was **cut**.*

For some verbs there is more than one acceptable form that can be used for the past tense and past participle:

*I **burned** the leaves.*

*I **burnt** the leaves.*

*a pile of **burned** leaves*

*a pile of **burnt** leaves*

For some irregular verbs, there are different forms for the past tense and past participle. These should not be used interchangeably. Use the past tense form for main verbs; use the past participle as an adjective or in combination with an auxiliary verb:

*I **broke** my leg.*

*a **broken** leg*

*My leg was **broken**.*

Some past tenses and past participles are often confused. The table below shows some of the more easily confused ones. Make sure you get these right:

BASE FORM	PAST TENSE	PAST PARTICIPLE
begin	began	begun
bite	bit	bitten
go	went	gone
ring	rang	rung
see	saw	seen
show	showed	shown
shrink	shrank	shrunk
take	took	taken
wake	woke	woken

Check in a dictionary if you are not sure of the correct form of the past tense and the past participle.

RULE 2: MAKE SUBJECTS AND VERBS AGREE

The form of a finite verb depends on the subject of the verb. Make sure that the subject and the verb agree in **number** and **person**.

A singular subject is followed by a singular form of the verb, while a plural subject is followed by a plural form of the verb:

*Vikram **is** arriving today.*

*Vikram and Fiona **are** arriving today.*

Similarly, there must be agreement between the **person** and the verb. A first-person subject requires a first-person form of the verb, a second-person subject requires a second-person form of the verb, and a third-person subject requires a third-person form of the verb:

*I **am** arriving today.*

*She **is** arriving today.*

*You **are** arriving today.*

> The correct forms of verbs for each subject are shown on page 55.

Watch out for sentences in which it is not immediately clear what the subject is. For example:

In this country, only one in three children goes to school.

Here, it is only *one child* that goes to school, not *three*, so the verb should be singular.

There is a similar difficulty in this sentence:

A number of stolen paintings were recovered during the investigation.

Here it is the *paintings* that were recovered, not *a number*, and there were more than one of them, so the verb should be plural.

RULE 3: DON'T USE THE SUPERLATIVE TO INDICATE A COMPARATIVE

We saw on page 67 that adjectives have three forms: the positive (*big, beautiful*), the comparative (*bigger, more beautiful*) and the superlative (*biggest, most beautiful*).

The comparative is only used when comparing two things, and the superlative when comparing three or more. This is obvious if you think about a sentence such as:

I reckon Jack is taller than Jill. (not *tallest*)

This means that you should also use a comparative in a sentence such as:

I measured Jack and Jill, and he is the taller.

(Jack would only be *tallest* if, for example, you measured Joan as well.)

RULE 4: USE THE OBJECT FORMS OF PRONOUNS AFTER A PREPOSITION

We saw on page 73 that personal pronouns have a different form depending on whether they are the subject of an object:

	SUBJECT	OBJECT
FIRST PERSON SINGULAR	*I*	*me*
SECOND PERSON SINGULAR	*you*	*you*
THIRD PERSON SINGULAR	*he – she – it*	*him – her – it*
FIRST PERSON PLURAL	*we*	*us*
SECOND PERSON PLURAL	*you*	*you*
THIRD PERSON PLURAL	*they*	*them*

A preposition such as *between, for* or *from* should always be followed by the **object form** of the pronoun (i.e. *me, you, him, her, them*):

*There's some sort of feud going on between **them**.*

When a pronoun is one of two words that are governed by the preposition, take care not to use a subject pronoun:

*Between **you** and **me**, I think he's gone a little mad.* (not *between you and I*)

*The sweets were for **Roger** and **me**.* (not *for Roger and I*)

(If in doubt, try the phrase without the first item, and you should see that *between I* and *for I* are not right.)

RULE 5: WATCH OUT FOR 'DANGLING' PARTICIPLES

A 'dangling' participle occurs when a participle in an opening phrase does not relate, as it should, to the subject of the main part of the sentence.

> **Running** out of the house, **a car** knocked him over.
>
> **Being** a valued customer, **we** would like to make you a very special offer.

These examples are grammatically inaccurate because it is not the car that was running out of the house, nor is it those making the special offer who are the valued customer.

Sometimes the effect of a dangling participle can be highly comical, and this can undermine your credibility as a writer:

> **Cycling** down a road once used by Livingstone, **a leopard** suddenly appeared in front of her.

(Here the idea of a leopard on a bicycle is likely to cause a snort of derision, which may not be the effect you were hoping to create.)

> **Condemned** by many as a threat to world peace, **the minister** said that nuclear weapons had made a significant contribution to NATO.

(The minister may perhaps be seen by critics as a threat to world peace, but one imagines that the writer intended the opening phrase to refer to nuclear weapons.)

The problem can often be resolved by adopting a fuller mode of expression, using a subject and a main verb instead of a participle:

> As she was cycling down a road once used by Livingstone, a leopard suddenly appeared in front of her.
>
> Although many have condemned them as a threat to world peace, the minister said that nuclear weapons had made a significant contribution to NATO.

Five grammar rules for traditionalists

The following rules are often ignored in modern Standard English. However, there are a few people who still feel strongly about them. It is worth knowing about these in case you are writing a document that will be read by people who have strong opinions on this kind of thing.

RULE 1: DON'T SPLIT INFINITIVES

We saw on page 59 that the infinitive form of the verb consists of the word *to* and the 'base form' of the verb. It is often said that writers should always keep *to* and the base form together. Breaking this rule by putting an adverb in between is called 'splitting the infinitive':

> **to finally agree** *on a pay deal*

> **to needlessly destroy** *our cultural heritage*

The infinitive is a single word in many other languages, including Latin. Because Latin was for many years regarded as the model for good English, split infinitives have traditionally been considered as signs of bad writing.

There are occasions when a split infinitive seems clumsy:

> *She went quickly to her room* **to hurriedly get** *her hairdrier into action.*

The sentence can be reworked in order to express the meaning more elegantly:

> *She went quickly to her room and hurriedly got her hairdrier into action.*

In other cases, however, the close connection of adverb and verb requires them to stand close together:

> *He raised his other hand* **to gently caress** *her shoulders.*

Some modifying words such as *only* and *really* have to come between *to* and the verb in order to achieve the desired meaning:

> *Part of a personnel officer's job is* **to really get to know** *all the staff.*

> *You've done enough* **to more than make up for** *it.*

It is now usual to allow a split infinitive when the rhythm and meaning of the sentence call for it. However, it is a good idea to avoid the split infinitive when writing for people who are likely to have strongly traditional views about grammar.

RULE 2: USE *WHOM* RATHER THAN *WHO* FOR THE OBJECT OF A VERB

Traditionally, the pronoun *who* is used for the subject of a verb, and *whom* for the object:

> *The man* **who** *beat me was called Mike.*

> *The man* **whom** *I beat was called Mike.*

This distinction can sometimes sound quite formal or old fashioned. In less formal writing you can use *who* instead of *whom* for the object of the verb:

> The man **who** I beat was called Mike.

> a woman **who** he lived with for six years

The only time it is really necessary to use *whom* is when it comes immediately after a preposition:

> The person **to whom** I spoke was called Mike.

> a woman **with whom** he had lived for six years

RULE 3: DON'T CONFUSE *SHALL* AND *WILL*

The words *shall* and *will* can both be used in front of verbs to indicate the future tense and in expressions about permission.

Traditionally, when making statements about the future, *shall* is used after the first person of the verb (*I*, *we*), and *will* is used after any other pronoun or noun phrase:

> **I shall** go to the bank this afternoon.

> **You will** arrive at noon tomorrow.

> **The company will** discontinue production in October.

The opposite applies when expressing intentions, promises or threats. In these cases *I* and *we* are used with *will*, and *shall* is used after any other pronoun or noun phrase:

> **I will** not listen to such rubbish.

> **You shall** have a car for your birthday.

> **They shall** never enter this house again.

Nowadays, however, *will* is commonly used to express the future in all cases, including after *I* and *we*:

> **I will** go to the bank this afternoon.

> **We will** arrive tomorrow.

Similarly, *shall* is often used after *I* and *we* when expressing intentions, promises or threats:

*I **shall** look forward to it.*

*We **shall** not surrender to terrorism.*

RULE 4: USE A SINGULAR VERB AFTER A GROUP NOUN

As we saw on page 54, a group noun such as *army* or *committee* represents a single unit composed of a collection of individuals. There is some dispute about whether a group noun should be followed by a singular verb or a plural verb.

Many traditionalists insist on using a singular verb after a group noun when the noun itself is grammatically singular:

*the committee **has** decided*

However, it is increasingly common – and especially in British English – to allow group nouns to take a plural verb in places where the group noun seems to indicate a collection of individuals rather than a single body:

*the committee **have** decided*

A sensible approach is to make a 'policy decision' and then stick to it consistently throughout your writing. In particular, don't treat a group noun as both singular and plural in the same passage, and especially not in the same sentence:

*The team **does** not trust him and **it** (not they!) never will.*

RULE 5: DON'T END A SENTENCE WITH A PREPOSITION

Many traditionalists shudder at the idea of a sentence ending with a preposition, as in:

*He was looking for a table to put his books **on**.*

*Kurt is someone I have every confidence **in**.*

It is sometimes taught that a preposition should always come before the word or phrase it governs. If you want to follow this rule, you can move the preposition in front of its noun or phrase, and add *which* or *whom*:

*He was looking for a table **on which** to put his books.*

*Kurt is someone **in whom** I have every confidence.*

However, following this rule will sometimes produce absurd results, especially when the preposition is part of an idiomatic phrase:

*We don't have much **on which** to go.*

It is far more natural to write this as:

*We don't have much to go **on**.*

In fact, it is generally acceptable in modern English to use a preposition at the end of a sentence, and it is often more natural to write a sentence in this way.

Punctuation

Why we use punctuation

When we speak, we often hesitate, pause, repeat ourselves, stress particular words or syllables, and constantly change the volume and pitch of our voice to organize the string of words that emerges from our mouth. This generally sounds coherent as we hear it, but when it is written down it looks very odd:

> *these are these are very **affordable** items of jewellery and they're just they're (pause) basic **enhancements** (pause) to (pause) to **you** to your **hands** to your **appearance** to your **look** um actually the sort of the kind of ring that maybe if you like to wear **lots** and **lots** of rings maybe rings on every finger or **several** of your fingers and so you don't want um lots of really really **heavy** rings you like some of the lighter more **subtle** rings these are then when they're going to **come** into play*

We use these 'paralinguistic devices' (so called because they are used alongside or in parallel with words) because, even after selecting the right words from our vocabulary and arranging these words according to the rules of English grammar, we need to make sure we are communicating successfully.

When we write, we use punctuation marks as visual signals on the page in a similar way to the paralinguistic features in spoken language. There are two main ways that punctuation can act as a substitute for the paralinguistic elements of speech:

> ➤ We can distinguish between statements (*She's not coming.*), questions (*She's not coming?*) and exclamations (*She's not coming!*). In speech this would be done by changes in the pitch or tone of the voice, which can also be used to show feelings such as surprise, disappointment and anger.

> ➤ Punctuation also helps us to organize information into complete units of meaning. This allows us to distinguish between *I'm afraid I don't like dogs.* and *I'm afraid. I don't like dogs.* In speech this would be achieved by a brief pause.

The way that different punctuation can give completely different meanings to a piece of writing was clearly appreciated by the eighteenth-century MP and writer Richard Sheridan. When Sheridan was asked to apologize in writing for calling a fellow MP a liar, he cleverly gave the following reply:

> *Mr Speaker, I said the honourable member was a liar it is true and I am sorry for it. The honourable member may place the punctuation where he pleases.*

The punctuation marks

Punctuation marks can be divided into different categories depending on how they are used in writing.

Some punctuation marks indicate the boundaries between sentences:

- full stop
- question mark
- exclamation mark

Some punctuation marks indicate the boundaries between different areas within a sentence:

- comma
- semicolon
- colon
- dash

Some punctuation marks separate words or groups of words from their surroundings:

- quotation marks
- brackets

Some punctuation marks are used between and within words:

- hyphen
- slash
- apostrophe

Full stops

The full stop is the most basic punctuation mark and its main use is to mark the end of a sentence:

He lives in Glasgow.

Full stops can be used after abbreviations, although this is becoming less common in modern English and the trend is towards a more 'minimal' punctuation style (see page 284).

If a sentence ends with an abbreviation, you do not need a second full stop as well, though you can follow the abbreviation with any other punctuation mark:

The book covers spelling, grammar, punctuation, etc.

Does the book cover spelling, grammar, punctuation, etc.?

Ellipsis

You can use a series of three full stops to show that a sentence is incomplete or that something has been left out. This is also called an **ellipsis**.

You do not need a full stop in addition to this if the ellipsis comes at the end of a sentence:

There was an uncomfortable silence. We waited and waited ...

An ellipsis is often used in the middle of a quotation to show that some words have been left out:

As Davies points out, 'The facts ... speak for themselves'.

Question marks

Question marks are used instead of full stops to indicate that the sentence is a question rather than a statement or exclamation:

When will you arrive?

You don't expect me to believe that?

Do not use a question mark after statements that look like questions but are not, such as instructions and indirect questions·

Will everybody move out of the way.

He wants to know what's going on.

Exclamation marks

Exclamation marks are used instead of full stops to indicate that the sentence is an exclamation rather than a statement or question:

The film was brilliant!

So you've decided to change your shirt this week!

Exclamation marks are not generally used in formal writing. They tend to be used in less formal writing, such as personal letters, to emphasize feelings such as excitement, surprise, humour or urgency:

I can't wait!

Don't be late!

Exclamation marks are used in speech to emphasize strength of feeling:

'I hate it here!' she screamed.

Exclamation marks are used in notices, posters and advertising for emphasis and as a way of attracting attention:

DANGER!

KEEP OUT!

URGENT!

Note that commands do not have to end with an exclamation mark unless the command is particularly emphatic:

'Open the door.'

Nothing happened.

'Open the door when I tell you!'

The door swung open.

> **➡** In informal writing exclamation marks can sometimes be used more freely and creatively to show extra emphasis. See page 273.

Commas

The comma is probably the most common of all punctuation marks and it has a number of uses. Some of these are quite fixed, others depend more on the style of the writer and the potential for ambiguity in the text.

Commas are used in **lists** to mark off the different items:

He speaks German, Spanish, Russian and French.

In simple lists, it is usual to leave out the comma between the last two items in a list. However, if the items in the list are long or complicated and the lack of a comma could lead to difficulty, you can use a comma, known as a **serial comma**, before the last item:

Hollywood stars such as Charlie Chaplin, Ben Turpin, Harold Lloyd, and Laurel and Hardy

Commas are sometimes used in **numbers containing more than four figures**, although it is also possible to use a space instead (see page 345).

Commas were traditionally used in **addresses**, inserted at the end of each line and between the building number and street name, although this is becoming less common.

Commas are used in **informal letters** after the opening (*Dear David,*) and the close (*Yours sincerely,*) of informal handwritten letters, but are generally omitted from more formal letters and those that have been written using a computer.

A comma or a pair of commas is used to **separate the name or title of a person** who is being addressed directly:

Kirsty, can you give me a hand?

Come here, Alan.

Now, sir, how can I help?

Commas are used in **non-defining relative clauses** to mark off additional information about the preceding word (see page 76). This is an extremely useful distinction and the presence of a comma can change the meaning of a sentence:

Methanol is a form of alcohol which is highly toxic. (= methanol is highly toxic)

Methanol is a form of alcohol, which is highly toxic. (= alcohol is highly toxic)

a session on health and safety for committee members who had expressed a need for formal training (= some committee members had expressed an interest)

a session on health and safety for committee members, who had expressed a need for formal training (= all committee members had expressed an interest)

Commas are used to **separate the two parts of a sentence when the natural order has been reversed** for reasons of style, with the subject of the sentence being placed at the end:

Joining the Army in 1967, he rose rapidly through the ranks.

Suspicious of their motives, she refused to offer her support.

Commas are used **between adjectives that are being used to describe separate qualities of something**. As when commas are used in lists, no final or serial comma is generally required:

a huge, ugly, dimly lit, badly designed building

a grumpy, miserable, smelly, mean old man

However, if the adjectives are being used cumulatively to convey a single idea rather than to refer to distinct qualities, commas are not used:

a nice shiny red sports car

a great big hairy black dog

Commas are used to **mark the beginning or end of direct or quoted speech**, and between split quotations. Note that the comma at the beginning is outside the quotation marks, and the one at the end is inside:

Evans looked up and said, 'I wish you would leave me alone.'

'I have no complaints,' she purred.

'I'm going,' she announced, 'and you can't stop me.'

Commas can be used in pairs for **extra or 'parenthetic' information**, in the same way as brackets or dashes. Make sure to include both commas when you use them in this way:

His second novel, published last year, was a great success.

Mr Hurd, the Foreign Secretary, addressed the UN Security Council.

Commas can be used to **ensure that a sentence is not ambiguous**. Without a comma, the following sentences might lead the reader to 'trip up' and read the sentence inappropriately:

All morning, rolls and coffee were available. (morning rolls)

Outside, the car park was soon full. (outside the car park)

Remarkably, few people are aware of this. (remarkably few)

She felt sick, and tired of having to study. (sick and tired)

However, he chooses to interpret the results differently.
(however he chooses to interpret the results)

Commas can be used to **allow the reader to pause before continuing with a particularly long sentence**, indicating to the reader which groups of words are to be taken together, and allowing the text to be read more effectively:

If, when you study Napoleon's Russian strategy, you find a certain resemblance to the German campaign, you might appreciate one of the great ironies of modern European history, the fact that two great militarists were defeated by the weather and by their sheer ignorance of the basics of geography.

Semicolons

The semicolon occupies a position midway between the full stop and the comma. It is used **to show that a balance exists** between two parts of a sentence, either to connect or contrast:

No previous experience is necessary; all successful candidates will receive full training.

Some called him a genius; others claimed he was a fraud.

I will say no more about it; the matter is closed.

> **!!!** It is a common mistake of people who are not familiar with the use of semicolons to use a comma in this sort of sentence.

Note that conjunctions such as *moreover, furthermore, nevertheless* and *consequently* are often preceded by a semicolon:

> *She may have seemed a good prime minister; nevertheless, she failed to face the facts.*

> *He was a great writer; moreover, he had a sense of history.*

Semicolons may also be used in **lists** in order to avoid ambiguity if the items in a list are themselves composed of separate items:

> *There was an alpine garden of saxifrages, sempervivum and sedum; a herbaceous border of hostas, aquilegias and delphiniums; and at the far end a wall of fuschia and rhododendrons.*

Note that a semicolon is included before the final *and*:

> *Copies of the report have been faxed to our offices in Lagos, Nigeria; Nairobi, Kenya; and Harare, Zimbabwe.*

Colons

Like the semicolon, the colon occupies a place midway between the full stop and the comma. It is generally thought to be slightly stronger than the semicolon, and has a wider variety of uses.

Colons are used to **introduce material that explains or illustrates a previous statement**. It has the meaning *namely* or *that is to say*. In this role, colons are used throughout this book to introduce examples:

> *The tornado left a trail of devastation in its wake: buildings reduced to rubble, trees snapped like matchsticks, cars and buses strewn across fields.*

> *The following items were missing: a credit card, a driving licence and a watch.*

> *There is one thing we do need: patience.*

Colons are **used in the titles of books, films, etc** to separate a main title from a subtitle:

> *D H Lawrence: Man and Myth*

> *The Classic Serial: Brideshead Revisited*

Colons are used in a similar way to semicolons to **indicate balance**. Colons are specifically used when the two parts of a sentence are balanced against each other, and the second part contrasts with the first part rather than explains it:

Knowledge is one thing: the opportunity to use it is quite another.

To err is human: to forgive, divine.

Colons are used to **introduce direct speech or quoted material** in plays and scripts:

FIRST WITCH: *When shall we three meet again?*

RIPLEY: *Let go of her!*

It is also common for a colon to be used when **introducing a long quotation**:

I take my text for today's sermon from Genesis, chapter 2:

A colon can be used to **introduce direct speech**:

John suddenly shouted: 'Look out! He's got a gun!'

However, this is relatively rare, and it is more common to use a comma:

John suddenly shouted, 'Look out! He's got a gun!'

Colons are used **between numbers to indicate a ratio** in standard mathematical notation:

Girls outnumbered boys in the proportion 3:2.

Colons are also used in American English **after the salutation in a letter** in formal business correspondence (*Dear Sir:*) where in British English there would be a comma or, as is becoming increasingly common, no punctuation at all.

Dashes

There are two kinds of dash, the **em dash** or **em rule**, which is longer (—), and the **en dash** or **en rule**, which is shorter (–). The names are printing terms and come from the correspondence between the dash sizes and the letters *m* and *n*. Both of these dashes are longer than the hyphen (-).

Both the em dash and the en dash can be used in pairs for **extra or 'parenthetic' information**, in the same way as brackets or commas. In this use, the dash creates a more emphatic break than a comma, but does not separate information as emphatically as brackets:

> *The company has never been – and indeed may never be –*
> *profitable.*

When en dashes are used, a space is left around the dashes, but when em dashes are used there is no space:

> *She was – thankfully – unhurt.*

> *She was—thankfully—unhurt.*

The em dash can also be used to indicate that speech is broken off suddenly:

> *'What on earth are you—' he began.*

The en dash can also be used to express a range of figures:

> *a distance of 300–450 miles*

The en dash can be used to connect two terms of equal importance:

> *the Ali–Frazier fight*

> *the Paris–Dakar rally*

Quotation marks

Quotation marks, or quotes, are also known as **inverted commas**, as they look like commas that have been turned upside down. Like brackets, they should always be used in pairs. In general, single quotation marks (' ... ') are favoured in British English and double quotation marks (" ... ") in American English.

The commonest use of quotation marks is to **indicate direct speech**. They are used to enclose the actual words used by the speaker:

> *John suddenly shouted, 'Look out! He's got a gun!'*

> *'I was absolutely terrified,' said Frank.*

See pages 113–4 for more information on how to present direct speech.

Quotation marks may also be used to **highlight a word or phrase** that is different from the text around it. This might be, for example, because the word or phrase is less formal or is more technical, or because it is a humorous use of the word:

They want some time to 'chill out' after their exams.

We stopped at The White Horse for some 'liquid refreshment'.

See page 274 for the use of quotation marks to show humour or authorial opinion.

It used to be common to use quotation marks to **indicate a title** of a play, film, book or other work:

We went to see 'West Side Story' at the Lyceum.

However, this use of quotation marks is now less common, as computers allow you to put titles in italics or underline them.

Brackets

Brackets are pairs of marks that are used to mark off letters or words from the surrounding text. The commonest kinds of brackets are **round brackets** (...) and **square brackets** [...]. You may also come across **angle brackets** < ... > and **curly brackets** or **braces** { ... }.

Round brackets

Round brackets or **parentheses** are used to **enclose comments** that are not vital to understanding the text but contribute to it in some way. This achieves the same effect as commas or dashes, but marks a more emphatic separation:

This has caused a great deal of pain (both mental and physical).

The change (there was a 20% swing to Labour) led to his resignation.

I recommend the novels of Neil Gunn (1891–1973).

A bracketed sentence included as part of another sentence does not need a capital letter or a full stop, but a bracketed sentence that stands alone as a complete sentence needs both:

Norma Jean Mortensen took the stage name Marilyn Monroe. (She might have got nowhere under her real name.)

Round brackets can be used as **an economical way of showing**

alternatives – for example, if a word might be singular or plural:

the candidate(s) for the post of Treasurer

They are also used **around letters or numbers** that are included when listing items in a text:

He seemed (a) unaware of the problem and (b) unconcerned about the outcome.

The project must be (1) carefully researched and (2) adequately funded.

> **!!!** Some readers tend not to read any words that are contained inside brackets, because they assume that the information is not important. So beware of putting important information inside brackets – your readers may skip over it.

Square brackets

Square brackets are used around material that was not in the original text, but has been added by an editor or by another author:

He [St Stephen] was the first Christian martyr.

The word *sic* (meaning 'thus') is used in square brackets to show that misspelt or unusual material has been deliberately included:

As James Joyce put it: 'My patience are [sic] exhausted.'

Hyphens

The hyphen looks like a dash, but is shorter. It used in two ways:

> ➤ Hyphens between words show that the words form a compound and have a single meaning.

> ➤ Hyphens within words show when a word has been broken into two and spread over two lines of text.

Compound words that are always hyphenated

A **compound word** is formed from two or more existing words or from a word part (a prefix or a suffix) and a word. Often, the words or word parts eventually become fused into a single word, and the hyphenated version of the compound can be regarded as a halfway stage in this process.

There are many fused or solid compound words, but we are so familiar with these that we do not usually think about their separate elements. These words include *bedroom, football, landlord, postman, seaweed, teapot, upstairs* and *wheelbarrow*.

When compound words are hyphenated, there is a reminder that they are composed of separate words (*able-bodied, has-been, hanger-on, long-standing, passer-by, spin-off*). However, some words remain hyphenated even when they have become so familiar that we no longer think of them in terms of their component parts.

There are many words that can be used either hyphenated or in a solid form, and you may notice that dictionaries are not always in agreement about this. The trend in modern English is for words to be solid, where in the past even a word such as *today* would have been written as *to-day*. If in doubt, consult a dictionary. If you are still in doubt, make a choice and use your choice consistently. The following rules should help you to decide whether or not to use a hyphen:

➤ Compounds that consist of noun/adjective + present participle tend to be hyphenated (*long-lasting, meat-eating, money-saving*).

➤ Compounds that consist of noun + past participle tend to be hyphenated (*protein-derived, disease-ridden, oxygen-deficient*).

➤ Compounds that consist of adjective + noun tend to be hyphenated (*high-frequency, low-calcium, white-knuckle*).

➤ Compound words in which the first element ends with the same vowel as the beginning of the second element are usually hyphenated (*re-establish, anti-inflammatory*), although *co-operate* and *cooperate* are both acceptable.

➤ Compound words in which the first element is a prefix and the second element begins with a capital letter should be hyphenated (*non-Christian, anti-Semitism*).

➤ When written as words, numbers between 21 and 99 should be hyphenated (*fifty-six, eighty-nine*).

> Compounds that contain numbers should be hyphenated (*a ten-year lease, nineteenth-century poetry, pre-1066 Saxon culture*).

> Many place names involving names of rivers are hyphenated (*Berwick-upon-Tweed, Burton-on-Trent, Stratford-on-Avon*), although there are exceptions, such as *Newcastle upon Tyne*.

> Double-barrelled surnames are usually hyphenated (*Alec Douglas-Home, Vita Sackville-West*), although there are some exceptions, such as *Iain Duncan Smith*.

Compounds that are sometimes hyphenated

Hyphens are used to link groups of words when they **function as an adjective before a noun**:

a top-secret mission

an up-to-date assessment of the situation

a well-intentioned person

When such groups of words come **after a verb**, they are usually not hyphened:

The mission was top secret.

The report is completely up to date.

He is well intentioned.

Hyphens are also used when the second element of a compound has been omitted to save repetition:

the pro- and anti-whaling lobbies

a guide to nineteenth- and twentieth-century architecture

pre- and post-war economic developments

Using hyphens to split a word

When a word is too long to fit at the end of a line, it can be broken into two using a hyphen. Hyphens used in this instance are called **soft hyphens**, because they are not actually part of the word they break, as opposed to **hard hyphens**, which are integral to the spelling of a word.

If a document is produced using computer software, the spaces between words and between letters can be automatically expanded or contracted to create a straight edge down the side of a page of text. Text can also be wrapped, or allowed to flow from line to line and page to page. In many cases, therefore, there will be no need to use hyphens to split words.

If you do need to break a word using a hyphen, there are two important points to bear in mind:

> Only split the word at places that leave complete syllables (*keep- sake* rather than *ke- epsake*, *mile- stone* rather than *mi- lestone*).

> Try not to split the word in such a way that it creates unrelated words that could confuse the reader (*re- install* rather than *rein- stall*, *ther- apist* rather than *the- rapist*).

Slashes

The slash – also called the oblique or oblique mark – is becoming more common in printed text, partly because of the trend towards informality in text, and also because it figures so prominently in website addresses. In computing, in addition to the slash (/), the back-slash (\) is also used.

Slashes are used to **present alternatives** in a compressed form:

Tea/coffee will be available.

You will need money and/or a change of clothes.

Painter/decorator available for local work.

Slashes are frequently used when **presenting text in non-sexist language**:

If the manager is attending, will s/he please notify the office.

anyone offering a lift in his/her car

Dear Sir/Madam ...

A slash is also used:

> in some abbreviations, such as *c/o* (care of) and *a/c* (account)

> as an abbreviation for *per* (*80 km/hr*, *50m/sec*)

> ➤ as an abbreviation for *to* when referring to a specific period of time, such as the financial year or academic year (*my 1992/3 tax form, the 1998/9 graduation ceremony*)

> ➤ to connect two terms of equal importance in the same way as a dash (*the London/Birmingham train*)

Apostrophes

Apostrophes are used following nouns as a **sign of ownership or possession**, showing that something belongs to or is associated with a particular person or thing:

David's coat

my daughter's homework

the ladies' golf tournament

Apostrophes are used in **periods of time**:

a week's time

three years' experience

Apostrophes are used to **indicate that one or more letters are missing** from a word, often when that word is a contraction of two longer words:

I'm (= I am)

you're (= you are)

she's (= she is)

we're (= we are)

that'll (= that will)

mustn't (= must not)

they've (= they have)

Apostrophes also indicate contraction in the standard spelling of certain words apart from these common contractions.

o'clock (= of the clock)

ne'er-do-well (= never-do-well)

will o' the wisp (= will of the wisp)

In some expressions there are two apostrophes because a letter has been missed out in two places:

> *salt 'n' vinegar* (= and)
>
> *rock'n'roll* (= and)

Apostrophes are used to indicate informal words that are shortened from longer words:

> *a swamp full of 'gators* (= alligators)

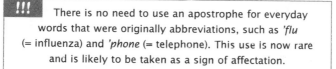

> **!!!** There is no need to use an apostrophe for everyday words that were originally abbreviations, such as *'flu* (= influenza) and *'phone* (= telephone). This use is now rare and is likely to be taken as a sign of affectation.

Apostrophes can be used in **dates** to show that a number is a contracted form:

> *the '45 Rebellion*
>
> *the summer of '67*

Apostrophes are sometimes used to **indicate a plural** of a very short word. This is not terribly logical and is widely disapproved of, but there are times when it helps to make the meaning clear:

> *There are two i's in the word.*
>
> *Mind your p's and q's.*
>
> *I'm going to one of my uncles do's.*

Rules for using apostrophes

There is often confusion about when it is necessary to use an apostrophe and where to place it. In fact, the rules are quite straightforward. The important principle is that when an apostrophe is used to show possession, you put it after the complete name of the person or thing that has the possession. If you would say the word with an extra *s* sound, then add an *s* after the apostrophe.

You use *'s* after a singular noun:

> *the dog's tail*
>
> *Friday's newspaper*

a full day's work

the bus's wheels

You also use *'s* after a plural noun that does not end in *−s*:

children's books

the people's favourite

women's rights

If something belongs to someone, the apostrophe comes after the owner's name:

Jack's bike

Lisa's book

Rover's lead

Where a number of named people possess something equally, only one apostrophe is necessary. Put it after the name of the last member of the group:

John, Paul, George and Ringo's haircuts

William and Mary's reign

You use an apostrophe alone after plural nouns ending in *−s*:

the dogs' leads

my parents' fault

a boys' school

in two hours' time

You also sometimes use an apostrophe alone after names or other words ending in *−s*:

Archimedes' principle

for goodness' sake

Mrs Jones' cakes

> **!!!** Using the apostrophe alone in this way is becoming more common as it is easier to say, although in the past you would always have added *'s*, as in *Charles Dickens's novels*.

Words such as *hers, ours, yours* and *theirs* do not have apostrophes, even though they show possession. This is because the idea of possession is integral to the meaning – it is not created by adding an ending to the name of the possessor:

> *Is that coat yours?*

> *Their house is bigger than ours.*

This rule also applies to the word *its* when it indicates possession:

> *one of its nine lives*

> *lying on its back*

But *it's* is used to indicate a contraction meaning *it is* or *it has*:

> *It's only two weeks until the holidays.*

> *It's been a long time since I was last here.*

!!! Many people find it difficult to remember whether to use *it's* or *its*. Remember: only use an apostrophe if you can substitute *it is* or *it has*.

Dealing with Special Information

The standard rules of grammar, spelling and punctuation will stand the writer in good stead for most tasks. There are, however, some things you might want to include in your writing that are not easily dealt with under these rules and require special attention. In this chapter, we shall look at how to deal with:

- speech
- quotations
- proper names
- abbreviations
- numbers
- dates
- lists
- foreign words and phrases
- words used in an unusual sense

Sometimes there are precise conventions governing the presentation of these things. However, sometimes the way that such information is presented might depend on your own choice, or on the preferred style of a particular organization or institution you belong to.

If the method of presentation depends on individual choice, it might be worth your while keeping a record of the decisions you make about particular issues in particular situations. That way you can be consistent, and make sure that the same style is used throughout your writing.

Organizations and institutions might actually have their own **house style guide** setting out a policy on such matters. In such cases it is important to follow the rules set out in that document.

If there is no style guide available, the guidelines set out below will help you.

How to deal with speech

When the actual words spoken are given, these are placed inside quotation marks:

> **'There has been an accident,'** he said.

> **'Is anyone hurt?'** she asked.

If the speech is merely reported, and the actual words are not given, then quotation marks are not used:

> *He said that there had been an accident.*

> *She asked if anyone was hurt.*

Any punctuation marks that belong to the quotation are included within the quotation marks:

> *'I am hurt,' said Jim, 'and I need help.'*

In this sentence, the comma after *hurt* is part of the speech, and so it is included within the quotation marks.

Punctuation that applies to the surrounding sentence stands outside the quotation marks:

> *'I think', said Jim, 'you should go and fetch help.'*

In this sentence, the comma after *think* is not part of the speech, and so it is not included within the quotation marks.

When a speech finishes before the end of the sentence, do not use a full stop at the end of the speech, but use a comma instead:

> *'That is a beautiful car,' said Hugh.*

When the end of a speech is also the end of a sentence, it is not usually necessary to put a full stop after the closing quotation marks:

> *Hugh shouted, 'Look out for the car!'*

If you have speech within a speech, use double quotation marks for the embedded quotation:

> *'They made us go round in circles,' said Mary, 'and we had to keep moving until a man shouted "Stop!" and waved his hands.'*

> In American English the preferred style is to use
> double quotation marks as standard, with
> single quotation marks for quotes within quotes.

The words of each new speaker should be placed on a separate line, in a new paragraph:

> *'There has been an accident!' said Jim, as he burst through the door, his coat dripping with rain.*
>
> *'Where?' asked Diane.*
>
> *'Down by the bridge. A car must have skidded on the wet surface.'*
>
> *'Is anyone hurt?' she asked.*

How to deal with quotations

Short quotations should be incorporated directly into the surrounding sentence, within quotation marks:

> *Shakespeare said that 'all the world's a stage'.*

> Unlike in speech, the final full stop is placed outside
> the quotation marks.

Longer quotations – ones that run to several sentences or several lines of text – should begin on a new line and be slightly indented. They should be preceded by a colon, but there is no need to use quotation marks:

> *This point is clearly made by Daniel, who asserts that: grammarians do not impose rules on a language; they merely collect from the language rules already in existence, and set them forth in an orderly way.*

Italics may be used to highlight particular words or phrases within a quotation. If the author is doing this, it is usual to add '(my italics)' at the end of the quotation:

> The report said that their activities "extended beyond what was acceptable and *could pose a threat to national security*" (my italics).

How to deal with proper names

It is usually worth trying get the presentation of proper names right, as it tends to cause offence if you get it wrong.

Capital letters are used at the beginning of a proper noun such as the name of a person or place:

*This is my friend **Mark Keiran**. He lives in **Milton Keynes**.*

Some words can be used both as proper nouns and common nouns. These words are written with capitals when they refer to the title of a specific individual, event, movement or institution, but not when referring more generally:

PROPER NOUN	COMMON NOUN
*a statement by the **Prime Minister***	*when she became **prime minister***
*the European **Parliament***	*the **parliaments** of Europe*
*when she joined the **Communist** Party*	*when she became a **communist***
***World War** II*	*those who fought in both **world wars***

You will sometimes see proper names written without capitals, for example when a company or organization wants its name to appear informal and contemporary – a name might even run words together without spaces, in the style of an e-mail address:

learn direct

creativescotland

The titles of books, periodicals, plays, films, albums, TV programmes, long poems and works of art are indicated either by italics or by quotation marks.

The first word and all significant words that follow it begin with a capital letter:

The Wind in the Willows

Beneath the Planet of the Apes

Foreign names and places may have different forms in English and the local language. Use the English forms where these are more familiar than the local names: it sounds less affected to write *Cologne* rather than *Köln* and *The Hague* rather than *Den Haag*. However, many local spellings have now become accepted as the standard English form. For example, *Mumbai* is now preferred to *Bombay* and *Beijing* is preferred to *Peking*.

Words such as *river, mountain, ocean*, etc are capitalized when they form part of a proper name:

> *the Ohio River*
>
> *the Pacific Ocean*

Many place names are not spelt with an apostrophe, even though you would expect there to be one:

> *St Albans*
>
> *Earls Court*

In other place names, however, the apostrophe is used:

> *Land's End*
>
> *St John's Wood*

Most place names that involve a preposition will be spelt with a hyphen (see page 106):

> *Stoke-on-Trent*
>
> *Weston-super-Mare*

> **!!!** Because the spellings of place names do not obey consistent rules, you should check the correct form of any unfamiliar ones before you use them in an important document.

How to deal with abbreviations

An abbreviation is a group of letters that represents a word or group of words. Abbreviations may be written using lower-case letters (*pm, mm, oz*), upper-case letters (*BC, EU, CNN*) or a combination of the two (*Hz, pH, BSc*).

There is often a question of whether to use a full stop after an abbreviation to indicate that letters have been omitted. In modern

British English, full stops are not generally used in the following cases:

➤ after shortened version of a word (*Dr, Mr, Prof*)

➤ after abbreviations of countries or organizations (*UK, EU*)

➤ after acronyms (*NATO, UNESCO, NASA*)

➤ after scientific symbols (*kg, cm*)

Full stops are optional but are becoming less common in these cases:

➤ after strings of letters representing words (*eg* or *e.g.; ie* or *i.e.; RSVP* or *R.S.V.P.*)

➤ after people's initials (*H.G. Wells* or *H G Wells*)

!!! In American English it is more common to see stops used after abbreviations.

If you want to create a plural form of an abbreviation, there is often a question of whether it is necessary to add the letter *s* or not. Use the following guidelines:

➤ Do not add an *–s* to metric units (*76cm, 786g, 500cc*).

➤ For most other units, it is normal to omit *–s* in modern usage, but some can have an *–s* (*100yds, 24hrs*).

➤ A few abbreviations can be pluralized by doubling the abbreviation instead of adding an *–s* (*pp* = pages).

➤ It is acceptable to use an apostrophe when creating a plural of a lower-case abbreviation (*p's and q's*).

➤ However, do not use an apostrophe to create a plural form of an upper-case abbreviation (*MPs, AGMs*).

How to write numbers

It is usual to write out the numbers between one and twelve in **words**, but to use **figures** for numbers from 13 onwards:

*She has **three** children.*

*a journey of **35** miles*

However, it is always better to spell a number if it comes at the beginning of a sentence:

Thirteen people turned up.

Always use figures when numbers are part of measurements (*16cm, 77˚C*), including percentages (*57%*) and times of day (*7.45pm*), as well as when expressing someone's age (*He was 75 yesterday.*).

Use words for birthdays and anniversaries:

his twenty-fifth birthday

Numbers that consist of more than one word are usually written with a hyphen:

twenty-one pounds and eighty-seven pence

Where possible, **fractions** should always be expressed as a single symbol (¾, 4¾) rather than a keyed sequence of characters (*3/4, 4 3/4*). When written out in full, fractions should be hyphenated:

three-quarters

four and three-quarters

The exceptions to this are:

➤ when referring to fractions that represent only one part, in which case you can write, for example, *a quarter* or *one quarter*

➤ when referring to combinations such as *half an inch* or *half a dozen*

When you need to write very **large numbers**, use commas to make them easier to read. To decide where to place the commas, count from the right and place a comma after every three figures:

a crowd of 23,678

a population of 167,983

2,569,746 square kilometres

Note that commas are not used after the decimal point:

6,574.5687

When writing a **sequence of numbers**, it is often not necessary to write all of the numbers in full. Use as few figures as possible and separate them using an en dash:

See pages 42–5. (rather than *42–45*)

The exceptions to this are:

➤ Numbers from 10 to 19 should always be written in full (*10–11, 13–17*).

➤ Measurements such as length (*21–27mm*), temperature (*42–48˚C*) and percentages (*73–79%*) should be written in full.

Use Arabic numerals (*1, 2, 3,* etc) rather than Roman numerals (*I, II, III,* etc) except in numbers that follow the names of monarchs, popes and the like, or in the numbering of volumes of books:

the reign of Henry VIII

A History of England, Volume IX

Lower-case roman numerals are used to indicate the preliminary pages at the start of a book:

See the diagram on page xxi.

> Some special conventions apply when numbers are used in the course of scientific writing. These are set out on page 345–6.

How to write dates

Write dates without commas and without a suffix after the number of the day:

13 November 1959

The British style for writing the dates in shortened form is to use the order day/month/year:

My date of birth is 13/11/59.

The American style is month/day/year:

My date of birth is 11/13/59.

If there is any possibility of confusion, write the month in words and the year in full:

My date of birth is 13 November 1959.

When referring to historical dates, it is usual to use small capitals when indicating whether a date is AD or BC:

AD *56*

700 BC

(The letters AD should strictly come in front of the number of the year, although in practice they are often used after the number.)

If you place AD before the number of the year, this means *in the year of our Lord*, and so you do not need the word *in*:

He was born AD *56.*

Some writers prefer to use the abbreviation CE (meaning *Common Era* or *Christian Era*) instead of the more formal Latin abbreviation AD (= *Anno Domini*).

1958 CE

When referring to **approximate dates**, use the Latin abbreviation *c.* (which is short for *circa*, meaning 'around'). Note that this only refers to the date that comes immediately after it, for example when giving the years of someone's birth and death:

c.1604– c.1683 (both dates are uncertain)

c.1604–1683 (date of birth is uncertain)

1604– c.1683 (date of death is uncertain)

When writing the names of **decades**, you can use figures (*the 1990s, the 90s*) or words (*the nineties*) but there is no need for apostrophes. It does not matter which option you choose, but try to be consistent in using the some form throughout your writing.

When writing the names of **centuries**, it is usual to use ordinal numbers expressed as figures:

the 21st century

If the century is being used as an attributive adjective, a hyphen is required:

19th-century architecture

An abbreviated form can be created by using a lower-case *c* to mean 'century' after the number, or by using an upper-case *C* before the number:

C19

18c–19c

19c architecture

When writing **sequences of dates**, follow the conventions for sequences of numbers as described on pages 118–9, using as few figures as necessary to indicate the meaning, and separating dates using an en dash:

1914–18

the reign of William IV (1830–7)

(However, in material that is part of something such as a chapter heading or title, write both dates in full.)

It is of course possible to use words to connect dates instead of an en dash, but do not combine words and en dashes:

1914–18

from 1914 to 1918

between 1914 and 1918

How to deal with lists

If you want to include a list in a piece of continuous writing, you can make the structure clear by:

➤ using an introductory wording that makes it clear a list will follow

➤ using a colon immediately before the start of the list

➤ separating each item of the list with commas or semicolons

➤ presenting each item in the list in an equivalent manner

The neatest way to separate the items on a list is to use commas, provided that commas are not already present in the text:

The ideal candidate should have the following qualities: exceptional creativity, a passion for promoting healthy eating,

> *experience in working as part of a team and the ability to work under pressure.*

If the items on the list are longer or more grammatically complex, it is better to use semicolons:

> *The committee made several recommendations: firstly, that a new post of Creative Director should be created; secondly, that the existing post of Managing Editor should be abolished; finally, that the company should seek to relocate to more suitable premises.*

For long or complex lists, rather than writing in a solid paragraph it is possible to separate the items, giving each a line of its own. This takes up more space, but makes the list much easier to read:

> *The successful candidate will require:*
> *a degree or other higher education qualification;*
> *the ability to speak persuasively to all levels of management;*
> *experience in research;*
> *energy, enthusiasm and commitment.*

With the increasing trend in modern English towards informality, simplicity and minimal use of punctuation, it is becoming usual to use bullet points to indicate the items on a list and use a very open punctuation style:

> *The ideal candidate should be:*
> ➤ *exceptionally creative*
> ➤ *passionate about promoting healthy eating*
> ➤ *highly experienced in working as part of a team*
> ➤ *able to work under pressure*

Another style is to use numbers or letters instead of bullet points. This style is appropriate when the items on the list are ranked in order of importance or when numbers will be useful for referring to the items at a later point:

> *Contestants will receive credit for:*
> *(i) technical ability*
> *(ii) artistic interpretation*
> *(iii) innovation*

How to deal with foreign words and phrases

If possible, avoid using foreign words and phrases in English. They tend to make your writing difficult to understand, and can appear pretentious.

The English language contains many words that have been borrowed from other languages including ones from French, Latin, Greek, Italian, Spanish, German and Dutch. However, most of these words have become 'naturalized' and are now regarded as standard English words. It is not necessary to give words such as *croissant* (which is originally French) or *zeitgeist* (which is originally German) any special treatment.

You may be able to tell when a foreign word has become naturalized because:

> ➤ It becomes pronounced in a more English-sounding manner.
> ➤ It becomes widely used in English sentences.
> ➤ It is listed in English dictionaries without italic letters or a label that indicates foreign status.

If a foreign word or phrase is not 'naturalized' and it is necessary to use it, it should be shown in the opposite typeface to the surrounding sentence: i.e. italic when the sentence is in normal 'roman' type, but in normal 'roman' type when the sentence is italic:

> *He administered the* coup de grâce.

If you need to give a translation, this should be in round brackets and in the same typeface as the surrounding sentence:

> *The principle of* caveat emptor *(let the buyer beware) is enshrined in law.*

The title of a film, piece of music or other art work may come from another language:

> *She used a quotation from* Le Misanthrope *to illustrate her point.*

If there is no recognized English title for the work, give any translation of the title in quotation marks:

> *He appeared in* La Verdad Sospechosa *('The Suspicious Truth').*

If there is a recognized English equivalent, treat the title of the translation as a work in its own right, and put it in the same typeface as the foreign title:

> *The publication of* Im Westen Nichts Neues *(All Quiet on the Western Front) caused a sensation.*

If you need to write French words, take care to show any accents correctly. French words might include grave accents (*père*), acute accents (*sauté*), circumflex accents (*bête noire*) or cedillas (*garçon*).

If you need to write German words, include umlauts (*Führer*). German nouns always begin with a capital letter.

If you need to write Spanish words, include tildes (*mañana*) and stress accents (*olé*).

Naturalized foreign words

Foreign words that have become naturalized in English may sometimes retain an accent from their original language. This often happens when the accent helps to show how the word is pronounced or helps to distinguish it from a similar word. The following are the most common examples you are likely to use:

à la	*dénouement*	*papier-mâché*
blasé	*divorcé(e)*	*pâté*
café	*emigré(e)*	*première*
cliché	*fiancé(e)*	*protégé(e)*
communiqué	*matinée*	*purée*
crèche	*mêlée*	*rosé*
déjà vu	*née*	

Foreign words that have become naturalized in English may also form plurals in the manner of their original language. Some of the more common foreign plural forms are listed on page 29.

Some naturalized French words have different masculine and feminine forms. Usually, the feminine form is created by adding an -*e* to the masculine form:

MASCULINE FORM	FEMININE FORM
blond	*blonde*
divorcé	*divorcée*
emigré	*emigrée*
fiancé	*fiancée*
protégé	*protégée*

How to show that a word is used in a special way

There are times when you may want to alert your readers to the fact that a word is being used in a special way. You can draw your readers' attention to the special use of a word by putting it in italics or by putting quotation marks around it.

You might wish to alert your readers to the fact that the word is being used in a way that is different from its standard meaning – for example, in a technical sense:

Our web pages have received over 5,000 'hits'.

You might wish to alert your readers to the fact that the word is being referred to *as a word*:

I strongly object to the use of 'traitor' in your letter.

You might think that the word is likely to be unfamiliar to your readers, but no alternative is available:

He bowls leg-breaks and 'chinamen'.

You might want to show that you do not fully approve of the word:

A kind of a sticky 'goo' came out.

Italics are always used in preference to quotation marks when you want to give special emphasis to a word:

The evidence only came to light after *the trial.*

Getting Information

The amount of information that anybody can carry around in their head is limited. It is therefore a good idea to know where you can turn to for help when you are writing. You should have access to works of reference, which can provide you with information and give you a definitive answer if you are not sure about the correct way of expressing something. These sources of help might include:

- a dictionary
- a thesaurus
- specialist reference books
- the Internet

If you do not have access to these at home, they may be available at a library.

In this chapter, we shall look at the sort of help that is available from these sources, and at the most effective ways of using them.

Getting help from dictionaries

At various places in this book you have been advised to check in a dictionary if you are not sure about a particular point. If you are serious about becoming a better writer, it is a good idea to get hold of a dictionary, as this will allow you to:

- check the correct spelling of a word
- look up the definition of a word in order to clarify its exact meaning

Many dictionaries have additional features, such as:

- information about the origin or 'etymology' of a word
- information about the correct pronunciation of a word
- examples of how a word is used in a sentence
- advice about how to use difficult words correctly
- tables and lists containing miscellaneous useful information, often collected at the back of the book

How to use a dictionary

Dictionaries have certain conventional ways of presenting information. You need to be aware of these if you are to use them effectively.

The words are arranged in **alphabetical order** from A to Z. If you are looking for something that is spelt with a hyphen or as two words, ignore the hyphen or the space. For example, you should look for *ad hoc* after *adhesive* rather than after *ad*.

Some dictionaries give a separate entry for every word. However, dictionaries sometimes put **words that are formed using suffixes** at the end of the entry for the word they are derived from, rather than giving every single word an entry of its own. So if you are looking for *efficiency*, you may not find it above *efficient* (where you might expect it to be), but tucked away at the end of the entry for *efficient*, along with *efficiently*.

Dictionaries often use a lot of **abbreviations** to indicate features such as **parts of speech** and **restricted-use labels**. Some common abbreviations used in dictionaries are *n* for *noun*, *sl* for *slang*, *Brit* for *British*, and so on. There should be a key to the abbreviations at the beginning of the dictionary, so you can refer to this if the meaning of an abbreviation is unclear.

Dictionaries use **different typefaces** to indicate different types of information. For example, main entry words might be in a bold typeface, whereas examples of how words are used might in an italic typeface. Once you become accustomed to how your dictionary uses the different typefaces, it becomes quite easy to find your way around the book and to recognize the different pieces of information in it.

Dictionaries have to use special systems of **symbols to show how a word is pronounced**. Sometimes these systems use symbols that may be quite unfamiliar, such as the symbols of the International Phonetic Alphabet. In other dictionaries the systems attempt to represent pronunciation using normal letters. As with the use of abbreviations, there should be a key to the system at the beginning of the dictionary. There may also be a key at the foot of each page of the dictionary.

A typical example of the different types of information contained in a dictionary and the way that the information is presented can be seen on pages 128–9.

Headwords are shown in bold letters at the beginning of each entry. Some may be abbreviations, and some may be cross-references to other entries.

Different meanings are shown in numbered senses.

Parts of speech, eg *noun, verb, adj, adv*, are shown. A change to a new part of speech is signalled by an arrow.

Examples show the ways in which the word can be used.

Usage panels give further information on aspects of English where there is frequent uncertainty.

campaign *noun* 1 organized action in support of a cause or movement 2 a planned series of battles or movements during a war ▸ *verb* 1 organize support: *campaigning against the poll tax* 2 serve in a military campaign

campanile /kampəneeleh/ *noun* a bell-tower

campanology *noun* bell-ringing ◇ **campanologist** *noun*

camphor *noun* a pungent solid oil obtained from a cinnamon tree, or a synthetic substitute for it, used to repel insects *etc*

campion *noun* a plant with pink or white star-shaped flowers

campus *noun* the grounds and buildings of a university or college

can¹ *verb* (**could**) 1 be able to (do something): *can anybody here play the piano?* 2 have permission to (do something): *asked if I could have the day off* ◇ **can but** can only: *we can but hope*

can, may Essentially, **can** denotes capability or capacity, and **may** denotes permission or opportunity. Because these two sets of meaning constantly overlap, the two words have become highly interchangeable, with **can** more versatile than **may** · *Hospital trusts attract more staff and can determine their own pay rates* · *You can do it when you come home from work.* In both these examples, **may** is also possible.
Both **can** and **may** are used to denote what is probable or habitual · *A quiet river on a summer's day may be a raging torrent in February* · *Things can go dreadfully wrong at this stage.* When capability or capacity is predominant, **can** is used · *I can't cope with life at the moment.*

can² *noun* a sealed tin container for preserving food or liquids ▸ *verb* (-**nn**-) seal in a tin to preserve ◇ **canned music** pre-recorded bland music

canal *noun* an artificial waterway for boats

canapé /kanəpeh/ *noun* a small piece of bread *etc* with a topping, served as an appetizer

canary *noun* (**-ies**) a songbird with yellow plumage, kept as a pet

canasta *noun* a card-game similar to rummy

cancan *noun* a high-kicking dance performed by women

cancel *verb* (**-ll-**) **1** put off permanently, call off: *cancel all engagements for the week* **2** mark for deletion by crossing with lines ◊ **cancel out** make ineffective by balancing each other

cancer *noun* a malignant growth ◊ **cancerous** *adj*

candid *adj* frank, open, honest ◊ **candidly** *adv*

candida /kandidə/ *noun* an infection caused by a yeastlike fungus

candidate *noun* **1** an entrant for an examination, or competition for a job, prize *etc* **2** an entrant in a political election ◊ **candidacy** or **candidature** *noun*

🕘 From a Latin word meaning 'dressed in white', because of the white togas worn by electoral candidates in ancient Rome

candied *adj* cooked or coated in sugar

candle *noun* a stick of wax containing a wick, used for giving light ◊ **candlestick** *noun* a holder for a candle ◊ **candlewick** *noun* a cotton tufted material, used for bedspreads *etc* ◊ **not worth the candle** not worth the effort or expense needed

candour or *US* **candor** *noun* frankness, honesty

candy *noun* **1** sugar crystallized by boiling **2** *US* (**-ies**) sweets, chocolate ◊ **candyfloss** *noun* a mass of spun sugar

---

Pronunciation is shown for words that present difficulties.

The plural of nouns is given where there could be a problem.

Irregular verb forms are shown immediately after the verb.

Related words are often included in the entry.

Word histories give interesting information about the history of some words.

Phrases and idioms that include the headword are grouped at the end of the main entry.

Usage information labels tell you how and where a word is used (these are explained on pp viii-ix).

Tips for finding the word you want

There are ways to speed up how quickly you can find a word in a dictionary. The first and last words covered on each page of the dictionary are shown at the top of the page in what are called the 'running heads'. Following these running heads is the easiest way of keeping track of how far through the alphabet you are, and so getting quickly to the word you want.

Another useful technique is to think of the dictionary as having four quarters, approximately A–D, E–L, M–R, and S–Z. If you are looking for the word *catapult*, open the dictionary in the first quarter; if you are looking for *mysterious*, open it just past the middle. Then use the second and third letters of the word to home in on the page you need.

If you can't find the word you are looking for where you expect it to be, remember that dictionaries sometimes put words with suffixes at the end of the entry for the word they are derived from, and so think of any 'root words' that your word might be listed under. For example, if you can't find *defiant*, check under *defy*.

What sort of dictionary do I need?

There are many different dictionaries available, and these can vary greatly in size and style. Broadly speaking, the larger the dictionary, the more words it will cover. If you are thinking about buying a dictionary, you need to consider what level of coverage you require:

➤ Smaller dictionaries are cheap, and have the advantage of being easy to carry about in a bag or briefcase. However, they are not likely to cover every word you might need to look up.

➤ Medium-sized dictionaries – ones with more than 700 pages – should contain almost all the words you need to look up for general use. However, they may not contain some more technical or unusual words. This size of dictionary often allows information to be presented more clearly than in smaller dictionaries, where information has to be squashed in to save space.

➤ Some dictionaries are specially aimed at people who are learning English as a foreign language, and these can include a lot of information that is not needed by people who speak

English as their native language. As a result, these dictionaries often don't cover as many different words as their size might suggest.

➤ Very big dictionaries – ones with more than about 1400 pages – contain many rare and unusual words. So if you can afford to invest in one, it should seldom let you down. Their main disadvantage, apart from the expense, is that their size means that they are not easy or convenient to carry around with you.

Getting help from thesauruses

A thesaurus is a book that contains lists of **synonyms** – that is, words that have a similar meaning to another word. A thesaurus allows you to look up a common word and find a range of words that have the same or nearly the same meaning. Looking up a word in a thesaurus may help you to find a more exact term when writing an essay, a livelier phrase for a report, or a simpler expression for a letter. This will enable you to express what you have to say using the full range of words available to you.

A thesaurus is not the same thing as a dictionary. Synonyms listed in a thesaurus are not necessarily precise definitions of the word under which they are found, and there will be many subtle distinctions between the words. For this reason it is always advisable to use a thesaurus in conjunction with a dictionary.

How to use a thesaurus

There are two main ways in which a thesaurus can be arranged:

➤ Some thesauruses – notably the famous *Roget's Thesaurus* – are arranged by theme. These books have an index, and you need to look up a word in the index to know where to find synonyms for the word.

➤ More modern thesauruses are arranged in an 'A-to-Z' style, like a dictionary. If you are using an A-to-Z thesaurus, you can go straight to the word you are looking for without having to search in an index.

The lists of synonyms in a thesaurus might be arranged in alphabetical order, or they might be grouped so that the most common words or the ones closest in meaning to the entry word are shown first. You will need to get used to the style of the particular thesaurus in order to use it most efficiently.

Not every synonym of a word will be useful for your purposes, and so thesauruses often use **labels** to indicate that a synonym is restricted in use to certain occasions. A label might tell you that a word is only appropriate in informal contexts and so should not be used in business correspondence or formal writing. Similarly, it might point out formal or technical words that are not appropriate for more general use. A label might also indicate that a word is restricted to a certain regional variety of English, such as American or Australian English.

If the word you are looking up in the thesaurus can be used in a number of different senses, it is important for you to be able to tell which sense of the word each synonym applies to. In a themed thesaurus such as *Roget's*, the different senses of a word will appear in different parts of the book. In an A-to-Z thesaurus, the different senses of a word are usually numbered, and there may be a short definition or an example phrase indicating which sense of the word the synonyms that follow refer to.

A typical example of the way that the information is presented in a thesaurus can be seen on page 133.

What sort of thesaurus do I need?

If you want to use a thesaurus, the main choice is between one that uses alphabetical arrangement or a themed thesaurus that requires you to use an index. Most users find that alphabetically arranged thesauruses are easier and quicker to use. The main advantage of a thesaurus with a themed arrangement is that similar concepts are covered in adjoining entries, so if the entry for the word you look up does not contain a useful synonym, there might be something useful in an adjoining entry.

The arguments on pages 130–1 about the different sizes of dictionary also apply to thesauruses. Since the point of a thesaurus is often to

Headwords are shown in bold letters at the beginning of each entry.

Different meanings are shown in numbered sections, introduced either by a phrase in italics showing the word in use or by a key synonym in capitals.

Parts of speech, eg noun, verb, are shown by abbreviations.

Idioms and phrasal verbs are grouped alphabetically at the end of some entries. These are indicated by the symbol ◊.

Synonyms or alternative words are listed with the most commonly used ones before less frequent and more specialized terms, or arranged by shades of meaning.

Antonyms, words that mean the opposite of the headword, are introduced by the symbol ⊟.

Lists of related words are shown in panels after some entries.

Labels in italics indicate when words are restricted to certain areas of language.

frontier *n* border, boundary, borderline, limit, edge, perimeter, confines, marches, bounds, verge.

frosty *adj* **1** ICY, frozen, freezing, frigid, wintry, cold, chilly. **2** UNFRIENDLY, unwelcoming, cool, aloof, standoffish, stiff, discouraging.
⊟ warm.

froth *n* bubbles, effervescence, foam, lather, suds, head, scum.
➤ *v* foam, lather, ferment, fizz, effervesce, bubble.

frown *v* scowl, glower, lour, glare, grimace.
➤ *n* scowl, glower, dirty look (*infml*), glare, grimace.
◊ **frown on** disapprove of, object to, dislike, discourage.
⊟ approve of.

frozen *adj* iced, chilled, icy, icebound, ice-covered, arctic, ice-cold, frigid, freezing, numb, solidified, stiff, rigid, fixed.
⊟ warm.

frugal *adj* thrifty, penny-wise, parsimonious, careful, provident, saving, economical, sparing, meagre.
⊟ wasteful, generous.

fruit

Varieties of fruit include: apple, Bramley, Cox's Orange Pippin, Golden Delicious, Granny Smith, crab apple; pear, William, Conference, Asian pear; orange, Jaffa, mandarin, mineola, clementine, satsuma, tangerine, kumquat, Seville; apricot, peach, plum, persimmon, sharon fruit, nectarine, cherry, sloe, damson, greengage, grape, gooseberry, goosegog (*infml*), physalis, rhubarb, tomato; banana, pineapple, olive, lemon, lime, ugli fruit, star fruit, lychee, date, fig, grapefruit, kiwi fruit, mango, papaya, pawpaw, guava, passion fruit, avocado; melon, honeydew, cantaloupe, casaba, Galia, watermelon; strawberry, raspberry, blackberry, bilberry, loganberry, elderberry, blueberry, boysenberry, cranberry; redcurrant, blackcurrant.

help you to find an unusual word, there is probably an even greater advantage to be had from using a larger book in the case of thesauruses than is the case with dictionaries.

It is possible to get a combined dictionary and thesaurus, which offers two books in one. The main disadvantage of these combined books is that they are usually created out of two smaller books, so you may not get as wide a coverage of language as you would wish.

Getting help from other reference books

Besides a dictionary and a thesaurus, there are several other books that may be regular sources of help for a writer. Your local library should contain a reference section where you can go to consult these books (although they cannot usually be taken away). If you find that you need to consult a particular book regularly, it might be worth investing in your own copy.

Specialist dictionaries, covering subjects such computing, law, music and science, explain the meanings of words that might not be covered in a general dictionary. They are also likely to give more detail about the meanings of words than a general dictionary. These books are usually aimed at professionals and students in a particular subject. You can also get dictionaries that cover the language of a particular region and dictionaries of slang words.

More useful to the general writer is a **dictionary of quotations**, which allows you to look up the author and source of a famous quotation and check the exact wording. These books are also very enjoyable to browse through, and you can look up a particular word in the index and see all of the different quotations that contain it, which can be useful if you want an amusing quotation to liven up something that you are writing.

Another useful resource is a **biographical dictionary**, which allows you to look up a famous or historically significant person to find information about their life and achievements and check details such as birth and death dates.

A **directory** is a book listing the names of all the people in a certain group and giving information about them. They can be useful sources of up-to-date information about living people. We are all familiar with telephone directories, but there are also directories of other kinds. One of the most famous is *Who's Who*, which aims to list the most eminent and influential people in society.

Encyclopedias are useful places to go to look up factual information on a wide range of subjects. The largest, such as the *Encyclopedia Britannica*, run to many volumes, but it is also possible to get single-volume encyclopedias for home use. Encyclopedias are good places to look up information about the natural world, history, religion, art, and, by definition, just about any subject. You might need to be a little careful when looking up information about subjects such as sport and politics in an older encyclopedia, as this sort of information can quickly become out of date.

For completely up-to-date information you might consult a current volume of *Whittaker's Almanack*. This is an annual publication that contains detailed statistical information about the year ahead, including astronomical data and tide charts. It also contains detailed statistics about government, public bodies and current events.

An **atlas** is an essential source of information about geography. As is the case with encyclopedias, you may find that information in older books has become out of date as the names of places have changed and some countries have been reorganized or even broken up altogether.

Getting help from the Internet

Spending a lot of money on building up a library of reference books has now been rendered largely unnecessary by the arrival of the Internet, which allows you instant access to a vast amount of information.

The Internet is especially useful if you need information that is up to date. You are more likely to find current information online than in a library of books that were printed years ago. However, not all websites are regularly updated, and so some caution is required.

One thing to keep in mind when using the Internet for research is that, whereas the standard reference books can usually be relied on to give a definitive answer to a question, the accuracy of information that is posted on the Internet cannot be guaranteed. Of course, errors can also occur in printed works, but they are less common because printed works go through an editing and proofreading process. It is therefore advisable to use reliable websites provided by people who have reputations to maintain: organizations, companies, universities and academics. The type of organization that maintains a site on the Internet can be seen from the sequence of letters in its address:

> *.ac* or *.edu* indicates that the website belongs to a university or college.

> *.com* or *.co* indicates a commercial enterprise.

> *.gov* indicates a government department.

> *.net* indicates a network provider.

> *.org* indicates a non-commercial organization.

How to search the Internet

If you want to use the Internet to find information, you have to decide which of the various 'search tools' will best suit your purpose. There are three basic types of tool:

> search engines

> directories

> bots

Search engines

A search engine will search its database of web pages for a specific word and display a list of websites containing the word. The database is compiled by a program that trawls the Internet on the lookout for new sites. A search engine is therefore very comprehensive and useful for finding specific or obscure information.

Here are the addresses of some popular search engines:

> AltaVista – www.av.com

> Go – www.go.com

> Fast Search – www.alltheweb.com

➤ Google – www.google.com

➤ Lycos – www.lycos.com

Some search engines (for example, AltaVista and Google) also offer the facilities of a directory.

Directories

A directory is a selection of websites arranged according to subject. Unlike a search engine, the database of a directory is created by people rather than computer programs. As a result, you will find fewer sites featured. However, the sites in the directory's database will have been selected by the directory provider for their relevance and often a review of each site will help you to make your choice.

The sites in a directory are listed according to a branching system, starting with a general subject and branching into specific categories, which then sub-branch into even more specific categories. This means that you can quickly find sites on a topic that interests you, and you can also see related sites on similar topics. You can also save time by first narrowing down your search to a particular category and then using the search engine within that category alone.

Here are the addresses of some popular directories:

➤ Yahoo – www.yahoo.com

➤ About.com – www.about.com

➤ Open Directory – http://dmoz.org

There are also more specialized directories focussing on particular subjects. You can find these directories by looking in one of the following specialized directory guides:

➤ Directory Guide – www.directoryguide.com

➤ Gogettem – www.gogettem.com

➤ Search IQ – www.searchiq.com

Some specialized directories are called 'libraries'. These are useful for finding detailed information on specific subjects. Online libraries are generally compiled by experts, which makes them reliable and authoritative. A good starting point is the WWW Virtual Library at www.vlib.org.

Bots

A bot (short for 'robot') collects and compares up-to-date information from a number of search engines and directories, carrying out so-called 'metasearches'. These give you fewer sites to choose from than a search engine, but the sites are more likely to be useful to you.

Here are the addresses of some popular bots:

> MetaCrawler – www.metacrawler.com
> Search.com – www.search.com

Performing searches

The first step to get to the website you want might not involve using any of the above search tools, but simply consist of guessing an address. This often works if you want general information about a company, organization or individual.

Suppose you wanted information on a company named Huggle Helicopters plc. You could try typing 'www.hugglehelicopters.com' (or 'www.hugglehelicopters.co.uk' if it is a UK firm) or simply 'www.huggle.com' into the address bar (called the 'location field' in Netscape Navigator). If this does not produce a satisfactory result – perhaps because the company has an address that is nothing like its name or because it does not actually have a website – you will have to use a search tool.

Whether you are using a search engine, a directory or a bot, the searching process is similar. You type a keyword or keywords into the box provided and press 'return'. You can also type in various signs and symbols that will help you to narrow down your search:

> Type **AND** between two words to restrict the search to sites containing both words.
> Type **OR** between two words to restrict the search to sites that contain either one word or the other, or both.

➤ Type **NOT** in front of a word to restrict the search to sites that do not contain that word.

➤ Type **NEAR** between two words to restrict the search to sites where the two words are fairly close (say within 20 words of each other).

➤ Type a plus sign (+) between two words to achieve the same result as typing **AND**. This symbol can also be used in front of a so-called 'stop word' (a common word such as *the, of* or *how* that is normally ignored in the search, or a single letter such as the initial in a name) to ensure that the 'stop word' will be included in the search.

➤ Type a minus sign (–) between two words to achieve the same result as typing **NOT**.

➤ Put **double quotation marks** around a phrase to restrict the search to sites containing exactly that phrase rather than the individual words. You use brackets instead of double quotation marks in some search tools.

So, for example, typing in *"richard strauss" AND operas OR songs* will bring up websites about Richard Strauss' operas and sites about his songs, whereas typing in *"richard strauss" AND operas AND songs* will only yield sites mentioning both operas and songs.

However, the exact method of searching and the devices used for searches can vary from tool to tool. Some use the plus and minus signs, but some do not; some automatically include every word in the search, so AND and NOT do not apply. Each search tool should contain instructions under a heading such as 'Help' or 'Search tips' or 'Refine your search'. It is well worth spending a few minutes reading these instructions to make sure you use the tool efficiently. You will usually also be given the option of an advanced search, which will allow you to restrict your search even more.

Refining your search

Suppose you want to find a summary of the plot of Charles Dickens' novel *Hard Times*. If you go to a search engine and simply type in *hard times* and press 'return', one of two things may happen. Either you will get literally thousands of web pages containing occurrences of the word 'hard' plus all sites containing occurrences of the word 'times' (whether occurring in the same site or not) or you will get all sites containing both words (though not necessarily occurring together). In other words, your search will have been interpreted as either *hard OR times* or *hard AND times*, depending on the search engine. You need to refine your search.

A good refinement would be to type in *"hard times"*. This will ensure that the words appear in the website together and in the correct order. However, this refinement will still return sites mentioning the phrase *hard times* in any context (for example in a discussion of economic recession). Some further means of restricting the search is needed.

Your next stage might be to think of a word or phrase connected with the novel that is unlikely to appear in any other context. This can then be searched for at the same time. For example, type in *"hard times" AND "charles dickens"* and the sites you get will mention the novel and the novelist only. Even now, however, there will probably be too many sites to allow you to retrieve the precise information swiftly.

You want a summary of the plot of the novel, so you can narrow your search down even further by typing: *"hard times" AND "charles dickens" AND "plot summary"*. By now, the search engine should be returning sites that promise the information you want.

One problem with using a search engine when looking for information is that the search engine simply searches for words without being aware of their context. Consequently, you may find that some sites thrown up by your search provide literary essays in which the words *plot summary* occur or refer to the novel *Hard Times* in passing without actually being about Charles Dickens' novel.

If a search engine does not take you to a suitable website, you may find using a directory to be of more value. For example, to find sites on Charles Dickens, you could go to a directory, click on 'Literature' (or the closest thing to it: 'Arts' or 'Humanities') and by clicking on ever more specific categories, you will probably come to Charles Dickens and a selection of recommended sites on the novelist.

Tips for quick and successful searching

The following tips should help you to retrieve the information you require quickly:

> Speed up your search by restricting your search to the UK Web (this is usually an option in search engines). On the other hand, if you cannot find what you want, it may be because you are restricting your search to the UK Web instead of taking advantage of the whole of the World Wide Web.

> Speed up your search by restricting it, if appropriate, to one language.

> If you are unsuccessful with one search engine, try a different one. Some engines search more web pages than others or have a different database.

> If one keyword does not yield the result you want, try a different keyword related to the same subject.

> If you have a lot of searching to do, you need to be patient. Some sites can take a long time to download.

> The amount of time it takes to access a website is affected by the number of people using the Internet at any one time. If it takes a long time to move from one website to another, you might be better to try again later when the system may not be so busy. It is a good idea to avoid times of peak use in the USA. Mornings are a good time for UK users, since this is when most of the USA is asleep.

> If you do not want pictures on websites, then switch to 'text only'. It will make it faster to download pages. To switch off pictures in Microsoft Internet Explorer, click on 'Tools', then 'Internet Options', then 'Advanced', then 'Show Pictures'.

> Add especially helpful sites to your 'Favourites' menu (in Internet Explorer) or 'bookmark' them (in Netscape Navigator), so that you can easily return to them by clicking on the 'Favourites' or 'Bookmarks' menu on your toolbar.

> Print out or save to disk any web pages you are really interested in.

Confusing Words

A good writer needs to be aware that the English language contains a number of traps. These include words that are easily confused, or words that are widely used incorrectly.

The next two chapters of the book point out some of the most common of these traps. This chapter lists groups of words that are easily confused, while the next chapter lists words whose correct use is disputed.

After you have looked through the lists, you should have an idea of the words you need to be especially careful about using. It is not necessary for you to memorize all of the approved usages: if you are aware that a certain word causes difficulties, you can always look it up here to refresh your memory before you use it.

accord, account

Of one's own accord refers to willingness or initiative:

> *I had been doing a little searching **on my own account**.*

On one's own account refers to benefit or advantage:

> *She had undertaken of **her own accord** not to tell anyone else.*

However, the two often overlap in meaning and are frequently confused or used imprecisely.

adherence, adhesion

Both of these words have the meaning 'sticking', but they differ slightly in their use.

Adherence is used for figurative senses:

> *his **adherence** to the strict letter of the law*

Adhesion is used for literal senses:

> *For heavier paper and cardboard, this type of glue gives better **adhesion**.*

adjacent, adjoining, contiguous

All of these words share the meaning 'next to', but notice the difference in meaning. *Adjacent* things are beside or next to each other, but they may not be in direct contact with each other. *Adjoining* or *contiguous* things touch each other, usually by having an edge or boundary in common.

adopted, adoptive

Adopted is generally used when referring to a child:

> her **adopted** son, Rory

Adoptive is used when referring to people who adopt a child:

> **adoptive** parents

It is also correct, though rare, to use *adoptive* to refer to the child.

adverse, averse

Adverse means 'unfavourable' or 'hostile':

> an **adverse** reaction to her new film

Averse means 'reluctant about' or 'opposed to':

> not **averse** to negotiating with the management

affect, effect

Affect is always a verb and has two main senses. The first sense means 'to influence, make a difference to':

> The changes won't **affect** the staff in this branch.

> I'm glad to say that none of us will be directly **affected**.

The second sense is rather formal and means 'to pretend':

> Though she **affected** indifference, I knew she was really very upset.

Effect can be a noun or a verb. As a noun it means 'result, consequence':

> What **effect** will these changes have on this branch?

*I was still suffering from the **effects** of the journey.*

The verb effect is more formal and means 'to cause, to bring about':

*His aim was to **effect** a radical change in the party structure.*

allusion, delusion, illusion

An *allusion* is an indirect reference to something:

*I understood this to be an **allusion** to his past life.*

A *delusion* is a false belief that is created in your own mind:

*He suffers from the **delusion** that he's attractive to women.*

An *illusion* is something that creates a misleading appearance or a false belief:

*The high ceiling and white walls create the **illusion** of space in what is, in reality, quite a small room.*

ambiguous, ambivalent

In strict usage, *ambiguous* refers to the meaning and significance of things, whereas *ambivalent* refers to people's emotions:

*Note the **ambiguous** sentences at the beginning of her new book.*

*Somali men tend to be very **ambivalent** in their attitudes towards these women.*

However, *ambivalent* is often used in informal language where you might expect *ambiguous*.

amoral, immoral

Amoral means 'having no morality':

*We live in a more impersonal, **amoral** and uncertain modern world.*

Immoral means 'violating a morality':

*It is **immoral** to be rich when so many people are starving and homeless.*

ante-, anti-

When the prefix *ante-* is attached to the beginning of a word, it carries the meaning of 'before':

ante*cedent*

ante*diluvian*

ante*natal*

The prefix *anti-* is more common. When this prefix is attached to the beginning of a word, it carries the meaning of 'against or opposed to' and 'opposite to':

anti*biotic*

anti*clockwise*

anti*social*

appraise, apprise

Appraise means 'to evaluate':

*They decided to stop and **appraise** the situation.*

Apprise means 'to inform':

*The judge had not been properly **apprised** of her wishes.*

However, *appraise* is sometimes used in informal language where you might expect *apprise*.

aural, oral

Aural means 'relating to the ear', or 'listening':

*an **aural** test*

Oral means 'relating to the mouth' or 'spoken':

***oral** hygiene*

*practising her accent for the **oral** part of the exam*

avoid, evade

Avoid is neutral in meaning; *evade* implies an element of personal effort often involving cunning or deceit. Typically you *evade* more seriously unwelcome things such as arrest, detection, identification, taxes and (quite often) the truth:

> *The drop in revenue was largely due to efforts to **evade** the poll tax.*

> *For once they managed to **evade** the searchlights and dodge the guard-dogs.*

You can *avoid* these things too, but more usually you *avoid* things that are more routinely unwelcome and more easily dealt with:

> *What can I do to **avoid** catching head lice?*

> *It is best to **avoid** continuous hard braking.*

Note that *tax avoidance* is legal, and *tax evasion* is illegal.

beside, besides

Beside means 'next to, at the side of':

> *We settled down **beside** a roaring fire.*

Besides means 'in addition to, other than':

> *There were four other candidates **besides** Katia.*

between, among

Between is used to describe the relationship of only two people or things, which are often named or given a number:

> *The estate was divided **between** Hugh and George.*

> *I want to share the money equally **between** my two sons.*

> *The sugar is on the top shelf, **between** the rice and the coffee.*

Among or *amongst* is usually used when there are more than two people or objects, especially when these are not named individually:

> *They came upon a little house **amongst** the trees.*

> *Share the sweets **among** your classmates.*

> *The jar is on the top shelf, **amongst** the other food containers.*

However, it is also now common and quite acceptable to use *between* for more than two people or things when they are named individually:

*I want to share the money **between** John, Peter and Louise.*

biannual, biennial

Biannual means 'happening twice a year', whereas *biennial* means 'happening every two years'.

can, may

Essentially, *can* denotes capability or capacity, and *may* denotes permission or opportunity. Because these two sets of meaning constantly overlap, the two words have become highly interchangeable, with *can* being more versatile than *may*:

> *Hospital trusts attract more staff and **can** determine their own pay rates.*

> *You **can** do it when you come home from work.*

In both these examples, *may* is also possible.

Both *can* and *may* are used to denote what is probable or habitual.

> *A quiet river on a summer's day **may** be a raging torrent in February.*

> *Things **can** go dreadfully wrong at this stage.*

When capability or capacity is predominant, *can* is used:

> *I **can** cope with life at the moment.*

> ***Can** you see the point I am trying to make?*

canvas, canvass

Canvas is a strong fabric:

> ***canvas** shoes*

Canvass is a verb meaning 'to ask for votes or support':

> *They were **canvassing** for the Liberal Democrats.*

censer, censor, censure

A *censer* is a container in which incense is burnt:

*acolytes carrying **censers***

A *censor* is a person who examines books, letters or films and decides whether they contain any harmful material that must be deleted or that makes them unsuitable for publication etc. *Censor* is also a verb:

*His letter had been so heavily **censored** that only 'Dear Alice' and his signature could be read.*

Censure is criticism or blame. It can also be a verb:

*A civil servant was **censured** for leaking the story to the press.*

ceremonial, ceremonious

Ceremonial is an adjective and a noun and means '(for, involving or suited to) a formal ceremony':

ceremonial *robes*

*the **ceremonial** of the investiture*

Ceremonious is an adjective and means 'excessively formal or polite':

*He swept his hat from his head with a flourish and gave a low **ceremonious** bow.*

childish, childlike

Both these words mean 'of or like a child' and are applied to adults. Notice that *childish* is a term of disapproval, but *childlike* is usually used in an approving or neutral way:

*That was a really **childish** thing to do!*

*She has a **childlike** quality that makes her ideal for the part.*

*He was **childlike** in his naivety.*

classic, classical

The noun and adjective *classic* describes a work of literature or art of high quality and lasting value:

*that **classic** of Russian literature, 'War and Peace'*

*a **classic** Hitchcock movie*

As an adjective, *classic* is also used to refer to something that is typical of its kind:

> *one of the* **classic** *signs of drug dependency*

> *a* **classic** *example of a mixed metaphor*

Other adjectival senses of *classic* include 'simple and elegant':

> *a variation of the* **classic** *little black dress*

The plural noun *classics* refers to the study of ancient Greek and Latin:

> *Nowadays, a smaller percentage of university students study* **classics***.*

Classical is an adjective and means 'of or relating to classics or to ancient Greece or Rome':

> *a* **classical** *education*

> **classical** *Greek drama*

Classical is also used to refer to music that is serious and formal rather than light or modern and to a style of art and architecture:

> *a* **classical** *composer*

Classical can also refer to a method that was once regarded as being orthodox but has now been overtaken:

> **classical** *economic theory*

comical, comic

Both words have the meaning 'causing laughter', and they are largely interchangeable:

> *Her long body would have looked* **comical** *as she ran back and forth.*

Only *comic* still has a direct association with comedy:

> *He had a solo spot with a* **comic** *song.*

comparable, comparative

Comparable means 'of the same kind, of the same scale, to the same degree, etc':

*You won't find wine of **comparable** quality throughout Italy.*

Comparative means 'judged by comparing with something else':

*In the periods of **comparative** calm between bombardments, they tried to get some much-needed sleep.*

complacent, complaisant

Complacent means 'self-satisfied or confident in your own abilities':

*It's dangerous to get too **complacent** in today's cut-throat market.*

Complaisant means 'willing to do what others want, especially in a cheerful relaxed way':

*Her father rarely allowed her to have her own way; it was her mother who was the **complaisant** one.*

complement, compliment

A *complement* is something that completes or perfects:

*A dry white wine is an ideal **complement** to fish.*

Complement can also be a verb meaning 'to enhance or complete':

*The curtains **complemented** the wallpaper.*

(In grammar, *complement* denotes a word or phrase added after the verb to complete the predicate of a sentence.)

A *compliment* is an expression of praise or regard:

*My **compliments** to the chef.*

Compliment can also be a verb meaning 'to praise':

*She was **complimented** on account of her good work.*

confidant, confident

A *confidant* is someone in whom one confides:

*She has no close **confidant** to whom she can turn for advice or help.*

Confident means 'having a strong belief in one's abilities, assured':

*She was **confident** she would win.*

consequent, subsequent

Consequent means 'following as a result':

> *the heavy rain and **consequent** flooding*

Subsequent means 'following afterwards', but does not imply 'as a result':

> *the heavy rain and **subsequent** earthquake*

contagious, infectious

There is often confusion between *infectious* and *contagious*: an *infectious* disease is spread through the air, while a *contagious* disease is spread by touch, although when used figuratively, of laughter for example, they mean the same thing.

continual, continuous

Continual means 'constantly repeated or very frequent':

> *How can I be expected to concentrate when there are **continual** interruptions?*

Continuous means 'never stopping':

> *We've had three weeks of **continuous** rain.*

council, counsel

A *council* is a group of people who organize, control, take decisions or advise:

> *a **council** of ministers*

Counsel is a rather formal word meaning 'advice':

> *his wise **counsel***

Counsel also means 'a lawyer or lawyers':

> *a Queen's **counsel***

definite, definitive

Definite means 'certain' or 'clear, not vague':

> *I can't give you a **definite** answer until next week.*

Definitive means 'authoritative, that cannot be improved upon':

> *This is regarded as the **definitive** work on language development in young children.*

dependant, dependent

Dependant is a noun and means 'a person who depends on another for money, food, etc':

> *As a young man without **dependants**, he was free to spend his money as he pleased.*

Dependent is an adjective:

> *He's still **dependent** on state benefit.*
>
> *a clinic where drug- and alcohol-**dependent** celebrities go for treatment*

> **!!!** There is a similar distinction between *confidant* and *confident*.

deprecate, depreciate

Deprecate means 'to express disapproval at':

> *He **deprecated** her mistaken but well-meaning enthusiasm.*

Depreciate is often used in a financial context, meaning to fall in value:

> ***depreciating** assets*

However, both words are used to mean 'disparage or belittle':

> *constantly **deprecating** her attempts at writing poetry*
>
> *She always **depreciated** her own work and praised that of others.*

derisive, derisory

Derisive means 'showing derision':

> A **derisive** note was back in Luke's voice.

Derisory means 'deserving derision':

> This show in fact attracted a **derisory** 9000 or so paying visitors.

desert, dessert

A *desert* is a place where there is little rainfall:

> the Sahara **desert**

Deserts can also mean the 'things that a person deserves':

> He got his just **deserts**.

A *dessert* is a sweet dish served at the end of a meal:

> We had apple pie for **dessert**.

> **!!!** A quick way of remembering which is which is to think that *sugar* and *spice* are often found in a *dessert*.

disc, disk

The word for a thin flat circular object is usually spelt *disc* in British English and *disk* in American English.

However, in the context of computers, the spelling *disk* is always used, even in British English:

> Insert the **disk** into the appropriate drive.

discreet, discrete

Discreet means 'not saying or doing anything that may cause trouble or embarrassment':

> This is a very delicate matter; can we rely on you to be **discreet**?

Discrete means 'separate, not connected or attached to others':

> *On closer examination, we find that the pattern is formed from thousands of **discrete** dots of colour.*

distinct, distinctive

Distinct means 'clearly or easily seen, heard, etc':

> *a **distinct** smell of alcohol on his breath*

Distinctive means 'characteristic':

> *the **distinctive** call of the peewit*
>
> *He has a **distinctive** walk.*

doubtful, dubious

Doubtful means that doubt exists in someone's mind:

> *She fixed a **doubtful** gaze on the whiskery young protester.*
>
> *It was **doubtful** if Miss Angus liked anyone very much.*

Dubious means that doubt is likely or justified by a situation or circumstance:

> *The story sounds **dubious**.*
>
> *Everyone's position was **dubious** in some respect.*

economic, economical

Although there is some overlap in meaning, *economic* is more closely associated with *economics*, and *economical* has a less specific sense related to the general sense of *economy*:

> *Consultation will focus on the **economic** and diplomatic issues.*
>
> *It may be **economical** to use a cheaper form of fuel.*

effective, effectual

Although there is a broad overlap in meaning between these words, each has distinct senses, which ought to affect the choice of which one to use.

Effective means 'successful, likely to be successful':

> *The only **effective** way of maintaining a weed-free border is to cover the soil with black polythene or old carpet.*

It also means 'impressive, powerful':

> *Despite his small stature, Mussolini was an **effective** speaker.*

A further sense refers to something, such as a law, coming into operation or force:

> *a new tax allowance, **effective** from January 2000*

Finally, *effective* means 'in reality, even if not in name or in theory':

> *The old king is very frail. His eldest son is now the **effective** ruler, though he hasn't yet been appointed regent.*

Effectual means 'actually successful':

> *The measures introduced by the last government to control welfare spending proved to be **effectual** in some areas but not in others.*

elder, eldest, older, oldest

Elder and *eldest* can only be used when referring to the relative age of the members of a family, and the adjective is preceded by its noun or a determiner such as *the*, *my* or *his*:

> *This is my **elder** brother, John.*

> *My brother Peter is the **eldest**.*

In all other instances, use *older* or *oldest* instead:

> *Carbon-dating shows that this is the **older** of the two skeletons.*

> *Peter is **oldest**.*

electric, electrical, electronic

Electric is used to describe something that produces or is produced by electricity, or that is operated by electricity:

> *an **electric** battery*

> *an **electric** kettle*

Electrical is more general and means 'of or concerned with electricity':

> an **electrical** generator

> **electrical** goods

Electronic refers to devices, such as computers, that use small electrical circuits:

> **electronic** mail

> an **electronic** flash unit

elicit, illicit

Elicit means 'to draw facts, a response, etc from somebody, often with difficulty':

> I finally managed to **elicit** an answer from him.

Illicit means 'unlawful' or 'not allowable':

> **illicit** gambling activities

enquiry, inquiry

Both of these words can mean 'a request for information'. However, only *inquiry* is used to talk about a formal investigation into events:

> a major **inquiry** into government finance

evoke, invoke

These words share the meaning 'to call up' but their specific meanings extend this sense so that there is a distinction between them.

Evoke means 'to cause or produce' or 'to bring into the mind':

> The withdrawal of financial support **evoked** an angry response from community leaders.

> The scent of lavender **evoked** memories of winters spent at her grandmother's house while her parents toured the provinces.

Invoke means 'to call up a spirit' or 'to use or bring into operation':

> The shaman **invokes** the spirits of their ancestors.

> When challenged about the benefits of treatment in such cases,

*doctors often **invoke** their sworn duty to preserve life.*

*If our case fails in the national courts we shall **invoke** the European Declaration on Human Rights.*

farther, further

Use either *farther* or *further* when there is an actual physical distance involved:

*I can't walk any **farther** / **further**.*

Use *further* when the meaning is 'additional' or 'beyond this point':

*I would like to make one **further** point.*

fewer, less

Use *fewer* with plural countable nouns. Countable nouns are nouns that can be made into plurals, because they apply to things that can be split up into units and counted:

*There are **fewer** apples on the tree this year.*

*If **fewer** people smoked there would be **fewer** cases of heart disease.*

Use *less* with uncountable nouns. Uncountable nouns do not have a plural form, because they apply to things that cannot be split up into units and counted:

*There is **less** fruit on the apple tree this year.*

*If fewer people smoked there would be **less** heart disease.*

Less is also used for specific amounts of money:

*He earns **less** than twelve thousand pounds a year.*

Less is also preferred for other specific quantities:

*He lives **less** than three miles away.*

*We have twenty-four hours or **less** to reach the injured climber.*

See page 53 for a full explanation of countable and uncountable nouns.

fortuitous, fortunate

Fortuitous means 'happening by chance':

> *Their meeting was entirely **fortuitous**.*

Fortunate means 'lucky':

> *Consider yourself **fortunate** that you weren't badly hurt!*

You will occasionally find *fortuitous* used to mean 'fortunate', a use that is encouraged when the thing described involves both random chance and good luck:

> *It was **fortuitous** that they arrived just as we were leaving.*

However, you are recommended to use *fortunate* if that is what you mean.

hanged, hung

The normal past tense and past participle of the verb *hang* is *hung*:

> *She **hung** the apron over the back of a chair.*

> *Curtains could be **hung** from a pole across the wall.*

When the verb refers to killing by hanging, the correct form of the past tense and past participle is *hanged*:

> *He was later **hanged** for his part in a bomb plot.*

> *An unidentified man has **hanged** himself in his cell.*

Hung is increasingly used in this sense also, but in formal English it is better to use *hanged*.

historic, historical

These words do not mean quite the same thing. *Historic* refers to fame or importance in history:

> *Today will be remembered as a **historic** day in boxing.*

> *the conversion of **historic** barns into houses*

Historical is a less judgemental word that refers to something as a fact or to its connection with history:

> *The **historical** fact is that the settlement of 1688–1701 failed to settle everything.*

*Some people think of Sherlock Holmes as being a **historical**
figure.*

Note that you can use either *a* or *an* before both words; *a* is now more
usual.

immigrate, emigrate

To *immigrate* means 'to enter a country in order to live there'. A person who does this is called an *immigrant*:

*There are many Irish **immigrants** in the USA.*

To *emigrate* means 'to leave a country in order to settle in another
one'. A person who does this is called an *emigrant*:

*My parents **emigrated** from Turkey.*

imminent, eminent

Imminent means 'about to happen'. It is often used in a negative context:

***imminent** job losses*

Eminent means 'distinguished':

*an **eminent** lawyer*

incredible, incredulous

Incredible means 'unbelievable':

*The whole episode was quite **incredible**.*

Incredulous means 'showing disbelief, not believing':

*'You cannot be serious!' he screamed, his voice **incredulous**.*

ingenious, ingenuous

Notice that the spellings of these words differ by only a single letter,
though their meanings are quite different.

Ingenious means 'very clever' or 'cleverly made':

*That's an **ingenious** contraption you've built there.*

Ingenuous means 'innocent, open, frank':

> *On closer examination, the girl had a pleasing appearance,* ***ingenuous*** *but not foolish.*

intense, intensive

Intense means 'very great, extreme', or 'very deep or strong':

> ***intense*** *cold*

> *There's* ***intense*** *competition for places on that course.*

> *an* ***intense*** *blue*

Intensive means 'concentrated, thorough' or 'taking great care or using much effort':

> *an* ***intensive*** *training programme*

> *an* ***intensive*** *search*

junction, Juncture

A *junction* is a place where two things join:

> *a railway* ***junction***

> *Turn left at the* ***junction*** *of Great George Street and Cranworth Street.*

A *juncture* is a particular point in time or in a sequence of events:

> *At this critical* ***juncture***, *nothing should be said or done that would jeopardize the negotiations.*

laudable, laudatory

Laudable means 'deserving praise':

> *There is nothing that is not* ***laudable*** *and praiseworthy in this scheme.*

> *It was all very* ***laudable*** *bringing culture to the masses.*

Whereas *laudatory* means 'expressing praise':

> *The paper continued to write* ***laudatory*** *pieces about the embattled Mr Young.*

lay, lie

These two verbs are commonly confused because their meanings are close and their forms overlap.

Lay is a verb in its own right, meaning 'place':

*Many individual units had begun to **lay** down their arms.*

It is also the past of *lie*:

*When she reached her room Lucy **lay** on the bed to review the situation.*

You are recommended not to use *lay* as a main verb when you mean *lie*.

Another cause of confusion is the closeness in form of *laid* and *lain*. *Laid* is the past and past participle of *lay*; but *lain* is only the past participle of *lie*:

*He paused, then **laid** a hand on her shoulder.*

*After waking he had **lain** and thought of the day ahead.*

liable, likely, apt, prone

These words all have similar but slightly different meanings, so care should be taken to use them in the correct context. Note also that *liable to*, *likely to* and *apt to* must be followed by the verb in the infinitive. *Prone to*, on the other hand, can be followed by a noun, a verb in the infinitive, or the *-ing* form of the verb.

Is liable means 'runs the risk of, will probably' and usually conveys the idea that there will be unpleasant consequences, especially for the subject of the sentence. Usually this is the result of some previous action or event:

*People who play with fire are **liable** to get burnt.*

Is likely means 'will probably' and is correctly used to refer to something happening in a particular set of circumstances, or at a particular place or time:

*Since he doesn't drink, he isn't **likely** to want to go to a pub.*

*If you don't hurry up, you are **likely** to miss the beginning of the play.*

Apt and *prone* both mean 'tending to or in the habit of', but *prone* should only be used of people. *Prone* is also preferred when referring to the unpleasant aspects of a person's character or to a tendency for bad or unpleasant things:

> *These tiles are **apt** to break if you use tile clippers to cut them.*

> *Elderly people are **prone** to falls, often because of arthritic joints or dizziness.*

> *Nahum was no longer so kind or considerate, and he was **prone** to strange moods.*

libel, slander

Libel is defined as 'any false or malicious defamatory publication or statement'. This includes writing, print, broadcasting and pictures.

Slander is similar, but applies to spoken words (not broadcast), looks, signs and gestures.

luxuriant, luxurious

Luxuriant has nothing to do with luxury, but means 'growing strongly or vigorously; abundant, prolific':

> *The heavy rains have brought **luxuriant** vegetation to these normally arid islands.*

> *his **luxuriant** beard*

Luxurious means 'of or relating to luxury or riches':

> *It is one of the most **luxurious** health clubs in the country.*

magic, magical

The adjective *magic* generally means 'relating to magic', and *magical* can have this meaning too:

> *The stone was believed to have **magical** properties.*

However, only *magical* can mean 'enchanting, as if caused by magic':

> *It was a **magical** experience.*

mitigate, militate

Mitigate means 'to make less serious':

> *That was wrong of me, but it in no way **mitigates** your own actions.*

Militate means 'to have a strong influence or effect', and is usually followed by *against*:

> *This is certainly a problem that **militates** against the widest acceptance of the language.*

observation, observance

Observance relates to *observe* in the sense 'to obey or follow' and is used mainly about laws, rules, rights and principles, especially religious principles:

> *He advocated a more meticulous **observance** of the canons of Islam.*

> *strict **observance** of the Sabbath*

Observation relates to senses of *observe* meaning 'to notice' or 'to watch', and is used more generally:

> *From our **observations** it is clear that the guidelines for use were rarely followed closely.*

> *Accuracy depends to a large extent on vigilance and **observation**, as well as concentration.*

Observation also has the special meaning 'remark':

> *The newspaper article made one telling **observation** about him.*

of, have

Of and *have* can sound similar in speech. In writing, always use *have* as a verb after words such as *should, could* and *would*:

> *I could **have** done it better.* (not *I could of done it*)

> *If only they would **have** come sooner.* (not *If only they would of come*)

partly, partially

These words are often used indiscriminately to mean 'in part':

> *A blow on the head left him **partially** deaf for the rest of his life.*

> *About half the population is wholly or **partially** dependent on food aid.*

> *Redpath was a good policeman **partly** because he was also a sensitive and humane man.*

Both are found in conjunction with words such as *because, due to, explains, filled, obscured, open, responsible, successful* and *true*.

Partly is used more often when it is paired, either with itself or with *and also* or *but also*:

> *Poor productivity is to be blamed **partly** on bad management of the workforce and **partly** on lack of investment.*

> *It is **partly** a personal and **partly** a property tax.*

> *The film was a big success, **partly** because of its openness about sex, but also because of the leading actors.*

Partly is also used more often when followed by an adjective or participle that is itself further qualified:

> *The house is **partly** built of stone.* (which refers to a completed house)

> *The house is **partially** built.* (which refers to an uncompleted house)

> !!! In general prefer *partly*; use *partially* only when there is a special sense of incompleteness.

passed, past

Passed is the past form of the verb *pass*:

> *I **passed** him in the corridor.*

Past is an adjective, preposition, adverb or noun:

> *dwelling on **past** miseries*

> *He stayed on **past** his stop.*

*The ball whizzed **past**.*

*our country's glorious **past***

peremptory, perfunctory

Peremptory means 'that must be complied with', 'allowing no denial or discussion' or 'arrogantly abrupt, imperious':

*They have the same force as an order of the court although they are not **peremptory**.*

*The voice on the telephone was sharp and **peremptory**, but I didn't hear too well what it said.*

Perfunctory means 'done merely as a duty or routine, without genuine care or interest':

*He gathered his few possessions together and left with only the most **perfunctory** of farewells.*

practicable, practical

Both words mean 'able to be done, used, etc', and a plan (for example) can be said to be *practical* or *practicable*. But *practical* has the further connotation of 'efficient, sensible, useful' and is therefore more judgemental; it can also be applied to people, whereas *practicable* can not:

*It is perfectly **practicable** to make the journey by car.*

*They stood by to offer advice and **practical** assistance.*

*He was clever enough, but somehow he wasn't **practical** with it.*

presume, assume

These words are sometimes used synonymously, but there is a distinction between them that is valuable enough to be observed.

To *presume* means 'to suppose (something to be the case) based on the facts available':

*We had heard nothing for months, so **presumed** he was dead.*

To *assume* means 'to accept something is so, to take for granted':

*I just **assumed** that someone would meet me at the airport.*

165

prevaricate, procrastinate

Both words are to do with failure to deal with a matter or to answer a question immediately or promptly, and they are sometimes confused.

If you *prevaricate*, you respond to a question but avoid a direct or truthful answer, and you are therefore not being totally honest.

If you *procrastinate*, you don't deal with the matter at all but put it off to some later time.

principle, principal

These words have different meanings.

Principal is an adjective as well as a noun. As an adjective, it means 'main or most important':

> He gave as the **principal** reason for his resignation lack of co-operation from colleagues.

As a noun, it means 'person in charge':

> Professor Hill took over as **principal** of the college.

Principle is a noun meaning 'rule' or 'theory':

> the **principles** of English grammar

> I'm not going to sacrifice my **principles** for money.

proceed, precede

Do not confuse *proceed* meaning 'to go on or forward' with *precede* meaning 'to go before'.

purposefully, purposely

Purposefully, which means 'with purpose', refers to a person's manner or determination:

> He stood up and began to pace **purposefully** round the room.

Purposely, which means 'on purpose', refers to intention:

> Earlier estimates had been **purposely** conservative.

refute, rebut, repudiate, reject

If you simply deny an argument or allegation, you *reject* or *repudiate* it:

> The Prime Minister **rejected** the accusation the following day.

> He **repudiated** the suggestions as unwarranted.

If you *refute* or *rebut* the argument or allegation, you produce a reasoned counter-argument or proof:

> He had **refuted** criticisms of his work with patience and gentle good manners.

> Wilson was hard put to **rebut** all these complaints.

You will sometimes see and hear *refute* used in the simpler sense of 'deny'. It is worth avoiding this use because it can give rise to ambiguity: your readers won't know whether *refute* means reasoned proof or just emphatic denial.

seasonable, seasonal

Seasonable means 'appropriate to the season, opportune'; *seasonal* is a more neutral word relating to the seasons of the year.

sensual, sensuous

These words are often used synonymously, but people who are precise about language insist on a distinction between them.

Sensual relates to things that please the senses, especially with reference to sex and the human body:

> Select a sophisticated, **sensual** scent to match your little black dress.

Sensuous relates to seeing and hearing things of beauty:

> The shadowy interior is a **sensuous** mix of gilt and candle wax.

specially, especially

Specially means 'for a special purpose':

> I made this cake **specially** for your birthday.

Especially means 'particularly, above all':

> *I like making cakes, **especially** for birthdays.*

stationary, stationery

Stationary is an adjective meaning 'not moving'.

> **stationary** *traffic*

Stationery is a noun meaning 'writing materials'

> *a shop selling **stationery***

> A quick way of remembering which is which is to think
> that *stationery* includes *writing **paper**.*

there, their, they're

Their means 'belonging to them':

> *They can do what they like in **their** own home.*

There means 'at, in, or to that place':

> ***There** they can do as they please; it is their retreat from the world.*

They're is the short form of 'they are':

> ***They're** moving their desks over there.*

> **!!!** A good way of remembering which is which is to think
> that *there* includes the word *here* in it, so that is the correct
> spelling when you are writing about a place.

to, too, two

These words all sound alike, but are spelt differently.

To is the most common of the three. It can be a preposition or adverb:

> *writing **to** his parents*
> *going **to** the shops*
> *pulled the door **to***

Too means 'also' or 'to a greater extent than is required':

> *You can come along **too**.*

> *We were **too** tired to carry on.*

Two is the number:

> ***two** o'clock*

> *dinner for **two***

> **!!!** A good way of remembering which is which is to think that *too* has an extra *o* at the end of it, so that is the correct spelling when you are writing about extra or more things.

---

uninterested, disinterested

Uninterested means 'not interested, not taking an interest':

> *She seemed quite **uninterested** in anything I had to say.*

> *He's **uninterested** in sport.*

Disinterested means 'impartial, unbiased':

> *What we need is a **disinterested** third party who can judge the issue fairly.*

who, whom

Who used for the subject of the verb:

> ***Who** told you?*

In strict usage, *whom* is used for the object of a verb and after a preposition:

> ***Whom** did you tell?*

> *To **whom** do I have the pleasure of talking?*

> ➡️ See pages 89–90 for a fuller explanation.

---

whose, who's

Whose is correctly used to mean both 'of whom' and 'of which':

> the boy ***whose*** *father is a policeman*

> the book ***whose*** *pages are torn*

Note that *who else's* is more common than *whose else*, because *who else* is regarded as a unit and *whose else* is more awkward to say.

Note also that *who's*, which is pronounced the same way as *whose* and is sometimes confused with it, is a contraction of *who is* or *who has*:

> ***Who's*** *there?*

> *I'm looking for the person* ***who's*** *taken my pen.*

your, you're

Your is the possessive form of 'you':

> *Are those* ***your*** *CDs?*

You're is the short form of 'you are':

> *Come on, Isabel,* ***you're*** *next.*

> **!!!** Try to avoid using the
> shortened form *you're* in formal writing.

Controversial Words

The words discussed in this chapter of the book should set alarm bells ringing in your head. They are all words that have some warning or controversy attached to them, and some of your readers may have strong views about the way they are used.

In some cases, all that is required is that you take care to use the word accurately and grammatically. In other cases, the word is more problematic, and you are recommended to use an alternative word or to rephrase the sentence rather than use a word in a way that many people think is incorrect.

aggravate

The principal meaning of aggravate is 'to make worse':

> He **aggravated** a groin strain.

The use of *aggravate* to mean 'to make someone angry' is often regarded as incorrect, although it is well established, especially in spoken English:

> She finds his continuous whistling extremely **aggravating**.

ago

Ago follows the noun it refers to. It is usually followed by *that* and not *since*:

> It is months **ago** that I last saw her. (not *since I last saw her*)

In this sort of sentence, you are recommended to use either *since* or *ago* alone, but not both:

> It is months **since** I last saw her.

> I last saw her months **ago**.

anticipate

The use of *anticipate* meaning 'expect' or 'foresee' is often regarded as incorrect, although this is in fact an established meaning that carries stronger connotations of forestalling or preventing than 'expect' does:

> I **anticipate** wet weather this afternoon.

comprise

When you write that A *comprises* Bs, you mean that Bs are the parts or elements of A:

> The village school **comprises** one old building dating back to 1868 and two modern buildings.

Because it means the same as *consist of*, it is sometimes confused with this and followed by 'of', but this use is ungrammatical:

> The instructions **comprised** two sheets of A5 paper. (not comprised of two sheets)

data

When referring to collected information, especially in electronic form, *data* is increasingly treated as a singular noun, since a unified concept is often intended:

> The data **is** entered by a keyboarder.

When the composite nature of the information is important, it is often used as a plural:

> As more data **accumulate**, it may turn out that there are differences.

> The data **were** easily converted into numerical form.

However, in these examples the singular is also possible:

> As more data **accumulates**, it may turn out that there are differences.

> The data **was** easily converted into numerical form.

different

In current British English, *different* is followed more or less equally by *from* or *to*:

> He was, in fact, totally **different from** Keith.

*James looked very **different from** the last time she had seen him.*

*This is very **different to** the ideal situation.*

*The next day was Christmas Eve, but it was no **different to** any other day.*

Note that the verb *differ* is never followed by 'to'.

In American English, but much less in British English, *different* is commonly followed by *than*, especially when a clause follows:

*It was all very **different than** they had imagined.*

do

The use of *do* as a substitute for *have* in sentences such as *I have a more demanding job than you do* is sometimes regarded as poor style, and is best avoided in formal contexts.

dozen

Although *dozen* is singular, it is often followed by a plural verb, and general plurality rather than exactness of number is usually implied:

*There **were** a dozen or more people in the room.*

The same applies to *half a dozen*, which is similarly inexact in reference:

*Lying on the beds **were** half a dozen prisoners.*

former

Former contrasts with *latter* (see page 175); unlike *latter* it is invariably used to refer to one of only two things. This is not for any grammatical reason but because it would be awkward to refer back across several things in reference to the first of them.

good

The use of *good* as a substitute for the adverb *well* is not acceptable in Standard English:

He did well in his exams. (not *He did good*)

have

There is no need to add an extra *have* after *had* in sentences such as:

> If he **had** done it, I would have been very angry. (not If he **had have** done it)

> If they **had** told me earlier, I would have been able to prevent it. (not If **they had have** told me)

> → See also the comment on page 163 about the confusion of *of* and *have*.

hopefully

Some people object to the use of *hopefully* to mean 'it is to be hoped':

> **Hopefully**, it was all over now and he'd be able to take a spot of leave.

This objection stems from the fact that *hopefully* originally meant 'in a hopeful manner':

> The hungry children looked **hopefully** at the cake.

Occasionally, this can cause ambiguity:

> They were **hopefully** attempting a reconciliation.

You are recommended to avoid the disputed usage of *hopefully* if you are talking to someone who is likely to be precise about the use of language.

infer

Infer means 'to conclude from the facts':

> I **inferred** from his comments that he was a friend of Monica.

The use of *infer* to mean 'to imply or suggest' is widely disapproved of. Use *imply* or *suggest* instead, especially if you are writing to someone who is likely to be precise about the use of language:

> I didn't mean to **imply** that you were wrong. (not I didn't mean to **infer**)

kind

Kind gives rise to a difficulty when it is followed by *of* with a plural noun and needs to be preceded by a demonstrative pronoun (*this*, *that*, *these* or *those*). To avoid difficulty, use *this kind of* + singular noun, or *these kinds of* + singular or plural noun:

> *This kind of **component** is much smaller and more reliable than a valve.*

> *Those are the kinds of **assumptions** being made.*

> *Those are the kinds of **assumption** being made.*

> **!!!** Note that the same difficulty arises with the word *sort*.

latter

Latter is often used in contrast with *former* to refer to the second of two choices (when *former* refers to the first):

> *Do I have to choose between goat's cheese and chocolate cake? Sometimes I prefer the **latter**, sometimes the **former**.*

> *He and Mr Doran – the **latter** complaining mightily about his lumbago – pushed the boxes to the back of the table.*

More loosely, especially in speech, it refers to the last of several choices:

> *The story is reported in the Express, Guardian and Telegraph. The **latter** also has extensive photo coverage.*

It can also be used to mean more or less the same as *later*:

> *An upturn in profits was recorded in the **latter** part of the decade.*

> *It will not be long before her name appears in the **latter** stages of the world's leading tournaments.*

literally

Careful writers do not use *literally* unless they mean that what they are writing is to be understood in a straightforward literal way:

*They'd put glue on the soles of his boots, so he was **literally** going nowhere.*

*For ten years, the spring water has been **literally** going down the drain.*

The colloquial use of *literally* merely for emphasis is widely regarded as being incorrect, especially when used with an idiomatic expression that is not intended to be understood in a literal way. Do not say *The police have literally gone through the whole place with a fine toothcomb* if that is not literally the case.

majority

Strictly, *majority* should only be used with reference to several things that could be numbered or counted:

*The **majority of our customers** leave a generous gratuity.*

*The **majority of perennials** flower during this period.*

It should not be used when referring to things that are not countable, such as substances and concepts:

*He spent **most of** his working life as a schoolteacher.* (not **the majority of** his working life)

Note that in the examples above *majority* takes a plural verb, although it is a singular noun.

media

When referring to newspapers and broadcasting, *media* is still more commonly treated as a plural noun:

*The media **are** highly selective in **their** focus on sexual violence.*

Occasionally, however, it is used as a singular noun, especially when a unified concept is intended:

*These people have fears which the media **has** played on shamelessly over the years.*

*This may lead the media to slant **its** coverage.*

neither

Neither may be followed by a singular or plural verb, although a singular verb is usually regarded as more correct:

*Neither of us **likes** the idea very much.*

*Neither of the old women in the house **was** in bed.*

*Neither of them **was** drunk.*

Note that *neither* should be paired with *nor*, not with *or*:

*He possessed **neither** arms **nor** armour.*

none

When *none* refers to a number of individual people or things, it can be followed by a singular or a plural verb – rather like a collective noun – depending on whether the individuals or the group as a whole are intended:

*The hotel is half a mile from the beach and none of the rooms **overlook** the sea.*

*None of us **has** time for much else but the work in hand.*

public

Public can be treated as a singular or plural noun; the phrase *members of the public* is often used in order to reinforce the plural:

*The public **welcome** the way we are treating teachers as a professional body.*

*You can hardly blame manufacturers for turning out what the public **seems** to want.*

*Most members of the public **understand** this fact.*

unique

Unique is commonly qualified by words such as *absolutely, completely, more, most, very*:

*The atmosphere in the cathedral is **completely unique**.*

*Surely no one ever had a **more unique** or peaceful environment in which to work.*

Some people object to this, regarding *unique* as something absolute in itself. Avoid (in particular) using *more*, *most* and *very* with *unique* when writing or speaking to people who are likely to be precise about the use of language:

> *The atmosphere in the cathedral is **unique**.*

> *Surely this was a **unique** and peaceful environment in which to work.*

what

Take care not to add a *what* after *than* in comparative constructions such as:

> *He can play faster than I can.* (not *than what I can*)

What should only follow *than* when it means 'that which' or 'the things which', as in:

> *Those are better than what we saw in the shops yesterday.*

Ambiguity

One of the most fascinating yet infuriating features of language is that the same group of words can sometimes be capable of several different interpretations. If a statement can have more than one meaning, it is said to be **ambiguous**. Ambiguous wording can mean that your message is misunderstood, or that people do not take it seriously.

In this chapter we are going to look at some of the ways that ambiguity can arise, how it can cause problems and how to avoid it.

Comedy and confusion

Many jokes rest on the fact that a sentence can be understood in two different ways. For example, the sentence *Your majesty, the peasants are revolting* may be understood to mean either that the inhabitants of the countryside are staging a rebellion against their monarch, or that they have disgusting personal habits.

It is easy to imagine the writer of a comedy exploiting this ambiguity by having a messenger relay the news of a rebellion, only for the monarch to misunderstand the sentence and reply, *I know, they never wash and they have no dress sense.*

But sometimes comedy is the last thing a writer wants to achieve. Careless use of language that creates unintentional comic effect can undermine a serious message:

> *Don't leave medicines around for children to find – keep them locked in a cupboard.*

Common sense tells us that the writer means that medicines, rather than children, should be kept locked in a cupboard. However, the fact that the grammar of the sentence allows us to 'misread' the sentence might distract the reader, and so the warning might not be taken seriously.

On some occasions, ambiguity serves not only to undermine a serious message, but to obscure the writer's intention·

> *Take two tablets or two capsules three times a day.*

Does this mean that you can take either tablets or capsules on any occasion, or that you should take only one or the other and not mix them at all? The consequences of misunderstanding here could be severe.

Of course, ambiguity does not always result in illness, death or costly legal action, but even if all it does is raise a smile, it takes the reader's attention away from the writer's message, and undermines the reader's confidence in the writer.

Some common sources of ambiguity

In spoken communication, it is often possible to ask the speaker to clarify anything that seems ambiguous; but in writing, the reader needs to be able to make sense of the text as it stands.

There are a number of elements of language that can create ambiguity. Some of the commonest problems relate to:

> ➤ unclear reference
> ➤ sloppy punctuation
> ➤ words with multiple meanings

Once you become aware of these, they become much easier to avoid in your writing.

Unclear reference

Sentences can become ambiguous when one word might equally refer to either of two different things, as in the following sentence:

> *If your baby finds fresh fruit too hard, try boiling it in a little water.*

The ambiguity here occurs because there are two nouns, *baby* and *fresh fruit*, and the pronoun *it* could in theory be referring to either of these. Although common sense tells us that we should not try boiling babies, the ambiguity creates an unfortunate and unwanted distraction.

The reference of a particular word can be especially unclear when a sentence contains:

> lists
> subordinate clauses
> negatives
> emphasizing words

Lists

It is often unclear whether an adjective or adverb is intended to be applied to one item in a list or every item in the list:

We need large envelopes and sticky labels.

They laughed and sang noisily.

Do we need large envelopes and large sticky labels, or large envelopes but sticky labels of any size? Did they laugh and also sing noisily, or did they laugh noisily and sing noisily? Whatever the answer might be, it is best to try and be clear about it so that there can be no room for misunderstanding.

The ambiguity can often be avoided by repeating a word, or by changing the word order:

They laughed and they sang noisily.

Noisily, they laughed and sang.

Subordinate clauses

Sentences that include **subordinate clauses** (see pages 231–4) can give rise to ambiguity because the subordinate clause may apply to more than one part of the main clause.

If a subordinate clause is added to a **simple sentence** (see page 224), there is not usually a problem in working out the meaning:

Although she was tired, Janet did not complain.

However, there may be an ambiguity when there are two items in the main clause and the subordinate clause might logically apply to either or both of them:

Janet told Ruth that she had to see the manager.

In this sentence it is not absolutely clear whether it was Janet or Ruth who had to see the manager. The context will often make this sort of thing clear, but if it does not you need to think about reworking the sentence to avoid the ambiguity.

If a subordinate clause is used with a **compound sentence** (see page 231), there is often a confusion about whether the subordinate clause refers to one part or both parts of the compound sentence:

As the report recommended, we have looked into the problem, and we have made a number of cutbacks.

In this sentence it is not clear whether making cutbacks was part of the report's recommendations or not.

Ambiguity in such cases can often be avoided by splitting up a long sentence into shorter, simpler sentences:

As the report recommended, we have looked into the problem. We have consequently made a number of cutbacks.

You could also rework the sentence more thoroughly to make the meaning absolutely clear:

We have carried out both of the report's recommendations: we have looked into the problem, and we have made a number of cutbacks.

See also pages 87–8 for the problem caused by 'dangling' participles in subordinate clauses.

Negatives

Ambiguity can arise when a negative might apply to more than one part of the sentence, as in the following example:

We didn't buy the shares because they were going down.

There are two possible ways that this can be interpreted: (1) We didn't buy the shares, because their value was declining (and this would have represented a bad investment); (2) We did buy the shares, but not because their value was declining (and the fact that we sold them and made a tidy profit when the price recovered is merely a coincidence).

Negatives often cause a problem when they come at the beginning of a sentence:

She had no make-up and earrings.

The ambiguity can avoided by delaying the negative, so that items that are not to be read as negatives stand before the negative word:

She had earrings and no make-up.

If a negative does apply to two different items, you may need to repeat the negative to make this clear:

She had no make-up and no earrings.

Or you could make it clear that the negative refers to both items by using *or* instead of *and*:

She had no make-up or earrings.

Emphasizing words

Words such as *only, even, already, nearly* and *almost* can cause ambiguity when it is not clear which word they emphasize. In informal spoken English, the speaker's intonation usually makes the meaning clear, and so the positioning of the emphasizing word is not essential to the meaning. However, in written English it is advisable to place these words immediately before the word they emphasize:

*They speak **only Welsh** at home.*

The reader is entitled to interpret the sentence differently if the word *only* is placed elsewhere:

*They **only speak** Welsh at home.* (= They speak Welsh but do not read it).

*They speak Welsh **only at home**.* (= They speak Welsh at home but nowhere else).

> **!!!** Remember that these words can create ambiguity, and be prepared to rephrase a sentence if it helps to make the meaning clear.

Sloppy punctuation

Punctuation ought to remove ambiguity from written language. By indicating which parts of a sentence are to be read as units, it helps to avoid the problem of unclear reference. (For guidance on how to use punctuation correctly, see pages 93–111.)

However, if punctuation is used carelessly, it can make the writer's intention unclear.

Commas

The following sentence was part of a letter of complaint submitted by a nurse about her superior:

She is making my life hell, so I resign.

The nurse's intention was to state that her superior was trying to make her resign by making her life difficult. Unfortunately, the reader believed that the nurse was using the comma to mark a pause between two factual statements, and drew the conclusion that the nurse was offering her resignation as a consequence of her superior's behaviour.

The writer's intention could have been made slightly clearer by omitting the comma so that the sentence contains only one statement:

She is making my life hell so I resign.

In fact, the problem could be avoided more easily by spelling out the message more fully:

She is making my life hell in an attempt to force me to resign.

Another common way that commas are misused is after a word such as *which, where, who* or *when*:

We stopped at the first village, where there was a post office.
(= We stopped at the first village, and the first village had a post office.)

Without the comma, the meaning is completely different, suggesting that we stopped at the first village that happened to have a post office:

We stopped at the first village where there was a post office.

Hyphens

Hyphens should help to avoid ambiguity by making it clear to the reader which words are to be read as units:

samples of iron and sulphur-rich compounds (= iron compounds and sulphur-rich compounds)

samples of iron- and sulphur-rich compounds (= iron-rich compounds and sulphur-rich compounds)

samples of iron-and-sulphur-rich compounds (= compounds rich in iron and sulphur)

Be careful to use hyphens correctly to join particular elements together. There is a significant difference between *a group of ten-year-old children* (children who are all ten years old) and *a group of ten year-old children* (ten children who are each one year old).

Hyphens can also help to avoid ambiguity by distinguishing between similar words. You can use a hyphen in words that contain the prefix *re-* to distinguish a word meaning 'to do the verb again' from another word:

WORD FORMED WITH PREFIX	SIMILAR WORD
to *re-lay* a carpet	to *relay* a message
to *re-cover* furniture	to *recover* one's composure
to *re-form* a band	to *reform* the tax system

Words with multiple meanings

When a word has several different meanings it is usually clear from the context which particular meaning is intended. However, this is not always the case:

The same thing happened to me only five years earlier.

Because *only* has more than one meaning, this sentence could be understood to mean: (1) the same thing happened to me, *except that* it happened five years earlier than it happened this time; (2) the same thing happened to me, but it happened *a mere* five years ago.

Sometimes a word can have exactly opposite meanings:

They fought with the English at Waterloo.

Does *with* here mean that they fought *against* the English or *on the same side as* the English? Unless the surrounding information makes this clear, the reader will be left to guess.

It can be difficult to notice when multiple meanings give rise to an ambiguity. However, be particularly careful about:

➤ words used in a metaphorical sense

➤ adjectives ending in *–ing*

Metaphorical senses

Words are used in **literal senses** or in **metaphorical senses**. The **literal** sense is what the word actually 'means':

*He **sailed** his boat into the harbour.*

*The weather forecaster said that there would be a **storm**.*

A word may also be applied as a **metaphor** to describe something it does not actually apply to:

*He **sailed** into the boardroom.*

*Her statement caused a **storm** in the business world.*

If you are using a word in a metaphorical sense, take care that the literal meaning is not also applicable:

*I **ran into** my old geography teacher last week.*

Did the writer literally run into the teacher, or are they using *run into* as a metaphor for 'meet'?

If there is a danger of confusion between the literal and metaphorical sense of a word, you can make it clear which sense is intended by inserting *literally* or *metaphorically speaking*:

*I **literally** fell off my chair in amazement.*

*This table is, **metaphorically speaking**, on its last legs.*

Adjectives ending in *–ing*

Words ending in *–ing* can usually be used with nouns in two ways: either to give more specific information about the use of the noun (*a recording studio, walking boots, a carving knife*), or merely to describe the noun (*a growing boy, a depressing experience, a smoking gun*).

In speech, you can tell the difference between the two uses, because words used in the first way are stressed, whereas words used in the second way are not. But in writing, where there is no stress to help us, this can lead to ambiguity: is *a singing class* a class for singing or a class that is singing? The context will usually make the answer clear, but beware of places where it does not.

Tips for avoiding ambiguity

Although the common sense of your readers will often be sufficient to resolve potential misunderstandings, you should not assume that this will always be the case. Even if your readers are able to make sense of something that is ambiguous, text that contains a lot of double meanings can be difficult to read, can distract attention from the content, and can undermine the credibility of the writer.

Here are some tips for avoiding ambiguity:

> Be aware of the potential for ambiguity to creep into written language – keep in mind the common causes of ambiguity described above.

> Use simple sentence structures wherever possible.

> Be prepared to spell out details if this will make your meaning clear.

> Don't rely on your readers to know what your intentions are.

> Always re-read what you have written, trying if possible to look at it from your readers' point of view, anticipating how it may be possible to 'misread' it.

> Show your writing to someone else; a second (or even a third) pair of eyes often sees things that you have missed.

Slang, Jargon and Clichés

One of the tricks of being a good writer is knowing which words belong in which places. There are some words and phrases that are widely used but are best avoided when you are writing in Standard English. These include slang words, jargon and clichés.

These may have their place in certain contexts: a creative writer wanting to capture the atmosphere inside a hospital or a school might well use such words. However, they are not appropriate for more formal writing, such as a report or a business letter.

Slang

Slang exists on the fringes of Standard English. It often originates from groups of people who are outside the mainstream of society or see themselves as being different in some way. Slang is associated with, among others, young people, jazz musicians, rappers, computer hackers and drug users. Many regions also have their own forms of slang.

Sometimes words that originate as slang eventually become accepted into the standard vocabulary of English. For example, the words *snob* and *donkey* were once considered slang words, but are now perfectly standard.

Most dictionaries will indicate if a word is considered as slang, and so you can always look a word up if you are not sure whether it suitable to be used in Standard English.

Although many slang words are widely understood (such as *gob* for 'mouth', *fag* for 'cigarette' and *dosh* for 'money'), these produce a highly informal style when used in writing. Using them in a formal letter or report would show that you did not appreciate what sort of language the situation requires.

A good writer will use the right language in the right situation. In an informal conversation you might say:

> *He tried to **nick** a **tenner** from the till and **scarper**, but his friends **shopped** him to **the Old Bill**.*

If you are writing a formal document, however, you should use standard words in place of slang:

> *He tried to **steal** a **ten-pound note** from the till and **run away**, but his friends **reported** him to **the police**.*

Journalese

Journalese is the name given to the style of language that is used in newspapers, especially in tabloid newspapers. It saves space by compressing meaning into fewer words, aiming to stress the immediacy and drama of a situation. Some features of journalese are:

➣ omission of articles and pronouns, so that *Jimmy Knapp, the leader of the striking railway workers* can be changed to *Jimmy Knapp, leader of the striking railway workers* or even *striking railway workers leader Jimmy Knapp*

➣ use of short, punchy, emotive words, so that every investigation or enquiry becomes a *probe*, everyone who is criticized or condemned is *slammed*, everything referred to or nicknamed is *dubbed* and every incident or situation becomes a *crisis*

➣ use of exaggerated language to make situations seem more dramatic or important than they really are (*The teenage superstar was left in agony after a titanic battle.*)

➣ use of the present tense, especially in headlines, to give a sense of immediacy (*City youth plunges to death.*)

➣ focusing on aspects of a story that may not be strictly relevant, but are believed to be of interest to readers (*Father of three Johnson, 31, who works as a dancer in the fashionable Red Rock nightclub ...*)

➣ shortening of people's full names, or use of nicknames (*Fergie backs Becks after injury scare.*)

➣ use of puns and phrases that are already familiar from proverbs, catchphrases, song lyrics, film titles and the like

This style of writing works in journalism because it grabs the reader's attention and gives a dramatic presentation of events. However, the use of condensed, dramatic language can sometimes obscure the writer's meaning, and the use of sensational language may not be appropriate for other forms of writing.

It might make good newspaper copy to write:

> *Daring thieves swooped on the fashionable store, which numbers several top Hollywood stars among its clients.*

However, a person writing a report for an insurance company would do well not use emotive words or introduce irrelevant details:

> *There was a break-in at the store.*

Jargon

Jargon might be defined as informal language that is used by a particular group or profession. It consists of words and phrases that are not part of the standard terminology of a subject, but are used to communicate information quickly and easily between members of the group. Jargon may contain informal expressions for long-winded technical terms, and it may also contain expressions for everyday words.

Jargon exists in most professions and pastimes. It is particularly common in business:

> *We may consider **getting into bed with** the Germans on this project.*

> *We need to find ways of **pushing the envelope**.*

> *Our new employees are on a **steep learning curve**.*

> *This calls for **blue-sky thinking**.*

When people who are familiar with the intricacies and fine distinctions to be made in a particular field get together, they often slip into jargon. However, for the general reader, this sort of language can be meaningless.

If you are writing a formal document for specialists, prefer official technical terms to jargon words.

If you are writing for a more general readership, use Standard English if you are able to. If you do need to use technical terms, you can make life easier for your readers by either explaining what the terms mean as you mention them, or else by supplying a separate glossary with definitions of technical terms.

Buzz words

Buzz words are words that suddenly become fashionable among certain groups of people because using them is thought to be a sign of being up to date or well informed.

Some buzz words can refer to something genuinely original that happens to be suddenly popular, such as a new form of technology. In such cases, you should not be apologetic about using them.

However, buzz words can often be used as a way of making something that is commonplace sound impressive, as in the following sentence:

> *We are planning to bring a new initiative on stream to build on our existing methodology for continuous quality improvement and package best practices and innovations into an effective knowledge management system.*

The 'hit list' below includes some words that are often used to make simple concepts sound more impressive. Avoid these words if they are not strictly applicable:

best practice	*in-depth*	*package*
challenging	*initiative*	*parameter*
constructive	*interactive*	*scenario*
deliverable	*interface*	*stakeholder*
dichotomy	*joined-up*	*syndrome*
dimension	*meaningful*	*synergy*
dynamic	*ongoing*	*track record*
facility	*on-stream*	*workshop*

Clichés

A **cliché** is a phrase or expression that has been used so often it has lost any freshness it once had.

Some similes have been used so often that they have become clichés:

as bright as a button

as bold as brass

as flat as a pancake

to drink like a fish

Some metaphors have been used so often that they have become clichés:

a baptism of fire

the long arm of the law

take the bull by the horns

Some quotations and proverbs have been used so often that they have become clichés:

All that glisters is not gold.

Beggars can't be choosers.

the blind leading the blind

Some idiomatic turns of phrase have been used so often that they have become clichés:

to add insult to injury

last but not least

when all is said and done

Some adjectives have been used so often with certain nouns that they have become clichés. In such cases, the adjective adds little to the meaning. Omit it altogether if you cannot find a more original alternative:

*a **burning** question*

*a **gaping** hole*

*a **graphic** description*

Expressions become clichés because they originally had a certain appeal. The problem is that they have become – if you will pardon the cliché – victims of their own success. Using an expression that has been used thousands of times before shows a lack of originality. Writing that contains a lot of clichés can therefore come across as being insincere and impersonal, and this is often the reverse of the effect you want to create.

Another problem with clichés is that they often contain metaphors that are not appropriate to the situation you are writing about. This can result in illogical or absurd statements:

If they do make bungee jumping illegal, they'll just drive it underground.

When our backs are against the wall, we turn around and start fighting.

> **!!!** Check your writing for clichés and consider removing or replacing any phrase involving a common figure of speech.

Sensitive Language

Sometimes language can seem like a minefield. Even apparently innocent language can have unwanted effects if it is used without sensitivity. Language can reinforce unhelpful stereotypes, promote negative opinions and patronize people. On the other hand, sensitive use of language can have the opposite effects, helping to break down unhelpful stereotypes and promote positive images.

Areas where sensitive language is required

Language is most likely to be considered as offensive or derogatory when it implies a judgement about other individuals or about groups that other individuals belong to. The following subjects each present their own problems to the writer, and we shall discuss each of them in detail:

- gender
- race and nationality
- religion
- physical and mental capability

In addition to these, you should apply the general principles of sensitive language when dealing with the subjects of:

- age
- sexuality
- marital or family status
- political beliefs

General principles

Sensitive use of language is a complicated and emotive area. There are no fixed rules about what is acceptable and what is inappropriate, and people often disagree. However, the following general principles may be helpful:

- Some traditional ways of referring to people may reinforce ideas that are unhelpful and are often incorrect, for example with regard to the roles of men and women in society or the lifestyles and values of minority ethnic groups.

➤ On the other hand, well-intentioned attempts to avoid insensitive language can sometimes interfere with the clear or direct expression of meaning, and can appear ridiculous if taken to extremes.

➤ People usually prefer to be regarded as individuals rather than as members of a particular group, and often it is not relevant to refer to people's race, gender or physical capability.

➤ There are often differences between the ways people refer to themselves, and the ways that they like to be referred to by others. It is a good idea to respect the right of people to choose how they should be referred to. Bear in mind that a group may use a term itself, but might still regard this term as offensive when applied to it by others.

➤ Ideas about what is appropriate might vary from country to country or region to region, and also change over time, so that terms that were at one time considered acceptable might now be regarded as offensive.

Gender

You risk offending many of your readers if you use language in a way that implies that there is only one gender, or that one gender is superior to the other. It probably goes without saying that you should avoid crude generalizations based on stereotypical portrayals of men and women. However, the subject of gender also poses some more subtle problems for writers.

It can be easy to use words in ways that reinforce stereotypes about the roles that men and women play in society. This can happen when language reflects ideas about gender roles that are now regarded as old-fashioned. If you wish to avoid perpetuating gender stereotypes, there are a number of things you can do:

➤ When talking about a person's occupation, prefer neutral terms to gender-specific terms:

GENDER-SPECIFIC NAME	PREFERRED TERM
air steward / air stewardess	flight attendant
barman / barmaid	bartender
cameraman / camerawoman	camera operator
chairman / chairwoman	chairperson
headmaster / headmistress	head teacher
policeman / policewoman	police officer
postman / postwoman	postal delivery officer
spokesman / spokeswoman	spokesperson
weatherman / weathergirl	weather forecaster

➤ Avoid using titles that imply that an occupation is done by only one gender:

GENDER-SPECIFIC NAME	PREFERRED TERM
clergyman	cleric or minister
doorman	commissionaire or porter
dustman	refuse collector
fireman	firefighter
foreman	supervisor
patrolman	patrol
salesman	sales representative
taxman	tax collector

➤ Avoid using words ending in *-ess* when referring to a woman's occupation, especially when there is a neutral alternative available. Many of these words (such as *manageress* or *directress*) suggest that there is something unusual about a woman holding a particular role.

➤ Avoid referring to women as though they are doing men's jobs (*a lady doctor*), or referring to men as though they are doing women's jobs (*a male model*).

➤ Be careful about using words that reinforce stereotypical images of the sexes, such as writing that men *converse* while women *gossip*, or that a woman is *hysterical* while a man is *angry*.

➤ Use the same criteria when talking about men and women: if you define a man in terms of his career (*photographer Andrew Logan*), you should define a woman by the same standard, rather than by physical appearance (*stunning redhead Andrea Logan*) or age and family circumstances (*35-year-old single mother Andrea Logan*).

➤ Bear in mind that some readers may object to the word *man* or words containing *man-* being used to refer to men and women in phrases such as *the benefits that science has brought to man*. It is usually possible to find an alternative:

GENDER-SPECIFIC TERM	ALTERNATIVE TERM
man	*people, humanity, the human race, humankind*
man-hours	*working hours*
mankind	*humankind*
man-made	*artificial, synthetic*

Gender also presents a problem to writers because some traditional grammatical forms treat the masculine gender as the normal or natural form, or imply that it can be used to include both genders. Many people object to the use of masculine pronouns (*he, his* or *him*) in sentences that refer equally to men and women, as in:

*Every applicant should include **his** curriculum vitae.*

*Anyone can learn a foreign language if **he** wants to.*

Some people prefer to use the plural words *they, their* and *them* (which imply no specific gender) in such situations. This usage is now quite common, although some people still regard it as ungrammatical:

*Every applicant should include **their** curriculum vitae.*

*Anyone can learn a foreign language if **they** want to.*

Other people prefer to use *he or she, his or hers* and *him or her*, but this can be clumsy, especially when these phrases have to be repeated frequently:

*Every applicant should include **his or her** curriculum vitae.*

*Anyone can learn a foreign language if **he or she** wants to.*

Perhaps the best solution is to rewrite the sentence in such a way that the problem is avoided altogether. The problem can often be avoided by using the word *a* instead of a pronoun, or by using a relative clause:

*Every applicant should include **a** curriculum vitae.*

***Anyone who wants to** can learn a foreign language.*

The problem can also be avoided by making the subject of the sentence plural:

*All **applicants** should include **their** curriculum vitae.*

*All **people** can learn a foreign language if **they** want to.*

Race and nationality

The subject of race and nationality is another area that requires sensitive treatment. Again, it is not just a question of avoiding crude stereotypes and deliberately offensive terms. Sensitive language should also involve:

> being aware of appropriate terms to refer to people's race or racial origin. For example, *Afro-Caribbean* is preferred to *West Indian*, and *British Asian* (rather than *Indian*, *Pakistani* or *Bangladeshi*) is preferred for British citizens whose families originate from the Indian subcontinent. In the United States, terms such as *African American* and *Chinese American* are preferred, and *Native American* or *American Indian* is used to refer to the members of the various nations (as opposed to *tribes*) that lived there before the arrival of Europeans.

> using positive terms rather than defining people by what they are not. Terms such as *non-white* are best used only when the context makes them relevant.

> not describing people in terms of qualities that reinforce stereotypes about their race or nationality (for example referring to a Chinese person as inscrutable, a German as efficient or a Scot as thrifty). Even when these qualities are positive, they fail to consider people as individuals and may cause offence.

> using the names people give themselves rather than those that have been given them by people who colonized their land. For

example, *Inuit* is now preferred to *Eskimo*.

➤ taking care to use terms relating to race and nationality accurately. Inaccurate use of such terms can give the impression that the writer could not care less about the people about whom he or she is writing, so take care to observe correct distinctions. For example, people who are Scottish, Welsh or Irish may not be impressed if you use *English* when you are actually referring to the whole of the British Isles.

Certain inaccurate uses of terms relating to race are particularly likely to cause offence:

➤ *Immigrants* are people of a different nationality who have come to a foreign country to settle in it; this term does not refer to people who were born in that country but happen to be of a different racial group from the majority of the population.

➤ *Black* does not refer to everyone who is not white.

➤ *Ethnic minorities* are not necessarily equivalent to *non-whites*. In many parts of the world, white people are an ethnic minority.

Religion

Most of the points mentioned about referring to race and nationality also hold true when referring to religion. In addition, you should be aware of the following:

➤ Religions (*Islam, Judaism, Christianity*) are usually spelt with a capital letter, as are religious denominations (*Protestant, Catholic, Sunni, Shia*), religious festivals (*Easter, Ramadan, Diwali, Passover*) and religious texts (*the Bible, the Upanishads*).

➤ Most Muslims prefer the spellings *Makkah* and *Quran* to *Mecca* and *Koran* when referring respectively to the holy city and the sacred book of Islam.

➤ Avoid assuming that members of a particular racial group share the same religion. For example, not all Asians are Muslims.

Physical and mental capability

Some of the language traditionally used when referring to people with disabilities has associations of passivity, pity and limitation. It often causes disabled people to be seen in terms of their disability rather than be treated as individuals. There are a number of things you can do to avoid this:

> Beware of describing people solely in terms of a disability, as though that defined their personality. It is preferable to talk of *a person with a disability* or *a disabled person* rather than *a cripple* or *an invalid*. Similarly, it is preferable to talk of *people with epilepsy* or *deaf people* rather than *epileptics* or *the deaf*.

> Many disabled people dislike being referred to as *handicapped* on the grounds that a handicap is created by external surroundings or by other people's attitudes (for example a building without a lift for a wheelchair user, or discrimination in the workplace) and not by the disability itself.

> Avoid inaccurate or outdated language. Where a recognized medical term exists, such as *cerebral palsy* or *Down's syndrome*, it is advisable to use it.

> It is preferable to refer to someone as *using* a wheelchair rather than being *confined to* it, or to write that someone *has* a particular disability rather than *suffering from* or being *afflicted by* it.

> Although the word *challenged* is common in North America as part of compounds that refer to particular disabilities (for example, *visually challenged* to mean *blind* or *partially sighted*), it tends to be avoided in British English because it has become a way of making fun of the idea of political correctness (as in the use of *intellectually challenged* to mean *stupid*). The terms *differently abled* and *special* can also attract ridicule for the same reason.

Part Two

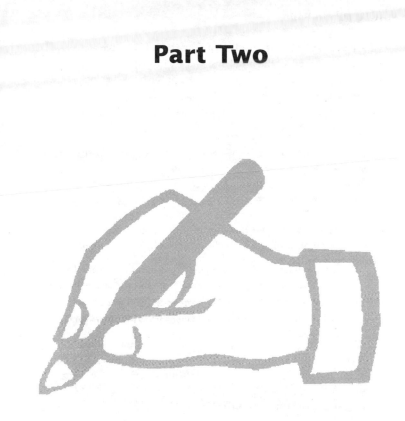

Putting
Pen to Paper

Once you have an understanding of the basics of language and an awareness of some of the problems, you are in a position to write with more confidence. In the second part of the book, we look at the actual process of writing, and what happens when we **put pen to paper**, or – as is becoming increasingly common – start typing on a computer keyboard.

This part of the book can be divided into three sections. Firstly, we analyse the process that should go into creating a written document, looking at each stage in detail. This involves **research and preparation**, **planning**, **drafting** and **composing**. We take a special look at how this process is affected by the opportunities offered by **word-processing** packages. As the final stage in this process, we look at the skills involved in **checking and proof reading** a written document.

Next, we go inside the process of composing written text, and look in detail at the ways of constructing **sentences** and **paragraphs**, and at the importance of creating a coherent **overall structure**.

Finally, we look at ways of making your writing more fluent and persuasive by paying attention to the style and tone of your writing. We look at the importance of **establishing your own writing style**, and at various techniques for **engaging your readers' interest** and **getting the point home**.

This part of the book, therefore, establishes all of the important principles behind good writing. These principles will then be put in practice in the final part of the book.

The Writing Process

Thinking before writing

When you have an informal conversation with someone you know well, you probably speak instinctively and naturally, without needing to plan in advance what you want to say. However, if you are speaking to people whom you do not know – especially in a more formal setting – it is usual to think in advance about who is going to be present, what you are going to say and how you are going to say it. This is true whether you are in a small-scale setting such as an interview, or a larger setting, such as when giving a presentation or making a speech.

The same is true of writing. If you are writing a short note or e-mail to a personal friend or close colleague, you will probably write it fairly quickly, and you will not take a lot of time thinking about it before you start it. On the other hand, if you are writing something longer and more formal, it makes sense to be more systematic in the way you go about it. This holds true whether it is going to be read by a single person or by a large number of people.

Your attention please ...

There are two reasons why more formal writing demands more attention:

> When you write, the information you give needs to be as complete and coherent as possible. Remember that – unlike a face-to-face conversation – your readers are not able to ask questions if something is unclear.

> When you write, you are judged on the basis of your writing in the same way that you are judged on your manner, appearance and presentation skills when you speak. Just as you would think about your appearance and your manner before going into a public or professional situation and make sure that you do your best to create a favourable impression, it follows that you should likewise think about the way you come across when you write.

203

To create a favourable impression through your writing, it helps to adopt a systematic approach. In this chapter we are going to divide the writing process into separate stages, and examine these stages one by one.

Some questions before you start

To focus your mind, before starting out on a piece of writing or perhaps even before making any notes, ask yourself the following questions:

> **What am I writing?** Are you producing a particular kind of document that needs to conform to a certain format or style, such as a report, agenda, set of minutes, letter, e-mail or fax?

> **Who am I writing this for?** Will the people who are going to read this expect it to be presented in formal or informal language? Will they be familiar with all of the technical terms that you might wish to use? What do they need to know that they might not know already?

> **Why am I writing it?** Do you want to provide information, argue a point of view, ask for advice, make a complaint or give instructions? Do you have a single intention or several different intentions? Either way, it is best to be clear from the start about what you are setting out to do.

> **How am I going to present it?** Once you know what you are writing and why you are writing it, you should be able to form some ideas about the type of language you need to use and your manner of presentation. For example, is a lengthy explanation required, or will a quick summary be sufficient? Do you want to fill the page with long, solid paragraphs, or will it look tidier if you leave lots of white space? Do you want to present information using tables or lists with bullet points?

> **What response do I want?** Do you want to receive an acknowledgement, a specific piece of information, or an apology from the person to whom you are writing? Do you need to make this clear in what you write?

Getting started

Once you have answered these questions, you should have a clearer idea of what it is you are setting out to do. You are now ready to make a start, but that does not mean that you should immediately start filling pages with words. The process of writing can be divided into four stages:

> ➤ research
> ➤ planning and thinking
> ➤ drafting
> ➤ revising

If you are writing a short document, or if you are writing about a subject with which you are very familiar, you may not always need to go through each of these stages. However, for a longer formal document you will almost certainly need to adopt this step-by-step approach.

Research

If you do not have all of the information that you need immediately to hand, you will need to do some **research**. You may be able to find out a lot from using reference books and the Internet (see pages 126–41) or you may need to go to a library to find books or articles on the subject. Besides reading, research might also include:

> ➤ personal interviews
> ➤ surveys
> ➤ scientific experiments

Your research may involve uncovering **factual information**, but may also involve finding out about various **ideas and theories** that other people have come up with about the topic.

Even if the points you intend to make are very familiar to you and your readers, there is still a good reason to put in some research. Your points will be more convincing if you can provide well-organized **evidence** to support them, and your research can provide documentation, statistics and quotations to help you.

Your research will only be of use to you if you can use it when you come to start writing, so you need to **make a record** of the things you find out. You do not need to write out everything in full: often, you might be able to summarize quite long passages of information using just a few well-chosen words. However, you do need to record enough detail to allow you to go back and check things later if necessary. Keep a list of your sources of information (for example books, magazines or websites). It is best to make a note of titles, authors, publishers and publication dates so that you can display this information in your final document if necessary (either in footnotes or in the form of a bibliography).

Some tips for successful research

> Try to make a decision early on about the type of information you are looking for, how detailed it needs to be and how much of it you need.

> Do not try to read every word of every book or article on the topic. Look at the contents page at the front of a book and the index at the back of a book to get a quick idea of what information the book contains.

> Make a decision at an early stage about whether a book or article seems likely to be useful to you. If it does, use an appropriate reading technique to extract information. (The techniques you might use are discussed below.)

> When you look things up, make written notes of facts and figures rather than trusting your memory.

> Keep your notes in a systematic manner in a single place. Index cards are a useful way of doing this.

> If you come across a quotation that you think you may want to use in your writing, copy it down word for word to save you having to look it up again.

> If a book belongs to you, you might want to make notes or underlinings on the page, and use highlighter pens to mark important passages.

> In case you want to revise or check anything later, it is useful to make a note of the chapter and the section number and page number each time you copy or summarize anything. If

the pages are large or the text is very dense, you might also make a note of the line number. All of this might sound time-consuming, but it will pay off when you start writing.

Different reading techniques

Most skilled readers use a variety of different techniques to extract information from books and articles. The technique they use may depend on the nature of the text that they are reading and on what sort of information they are looking for. The technique may even change as they progress from one part of a text to the next: they may read important passages slowly, but rush quickly through passages that do not appear to contain information that is relevant to their needs.

There are three ways of reading that may be appropriate when you are doing research:

> skimming

> scanning

> submarine reading

Skimming

When you **skim** or **skim read**, as the name might suggest, you are skimming over the surface of the text and reading at speed. For example, if you flick through a magazine or newspaper or glance at a television guide, you are usually skim reading, quickly 'getting the gist' rather than taking in every detail.

This is an extremely useful way of gathering information, especially in our culture, where we are surrounded by print and do not need to (or have enough time to) read everything closely. As you skim through a text, you can make notes of any passages that require more thorough examination.

Scanning

Another way of reading text rapidly is to **scan** the pages. In this case, however, you are looking for specific information, rather than trying to get an overall impression of the contents. You scan when you are looking up someone's phone number, or trying to find a word in a

dictionary or using the index of a book to find out about a particular
subject.

The difference between **skimming** and **scanning** can be seen if you
think about two possible approaches to looking at the contents page of
a book or a report. If you want to form an impression of what is there,
you would quickly skim through the contents page; if you are looking
to see if a specific item is included, you would scan the page.

Submarine reading

Submarine reading is so called because this is what you do when
you become completely immersed in a text. You read through it
carefully, and might do a number of other things while taking in the
subject matter, including analysing what is being said, comparing it
with other things you have read, agreeing or disagreeing with it, re-
reading parts you do not understand and noting missing or incorrect
information. This kind of reading demands full concentration. You
might read in this way when checking a contract, consulting an
instruction manual or reading an article about a subject that particularly
interests you.

Submarine reading is effective, but also time-consuming. A good
approach is to skim through a text to identify important passages, and
then adopt the 'submarine' approach for these selected passages.

Planning

Whether you are writing a one-page letter or a lengthy report, it needs
to have a clear and coherent structure, which means it needs to be well
thought out from the start. By the time you have thought about your
objectives and completed any research, you should have a clear idea of
what it is you are setting out to do. You now need to draw up a plan of
how to do it.

Your plan needs to have a clear structure, allowing you to introduce
information and ideas in a logical order. There are many possible
approaches. However, most plans will start with three clearly
identifiable parts:

➤ an introduction, in which you state what you are intending to do and why you are doing it

➤ a main body containing information, arguments and evidence

➤ a conclusion, in which you summarize what you have previously said, and state clearly any conclusions or recommendations

➡ The subject of establishing a suitable structure for your writing is dealt with in more detail on pages 245–54.

Converting research notes into a plan

Within this general structure, you need to arrange the particular things you want to say in your document. This can be done in a few easy stages:

➤ Write down all of the arguments or points that you have assembled during the course of your research. At this stage, all you need is a brief note of each point.

➤ Try to collect these arguments into groups under a series of general headings.

➤ Now try to fit the general headings together into the most logical order. If there are arguments for and against something, group all of the arguments for it together, then group all of the arguments against it together. Do not bounce backwards and forwards between the two.

➤ Make sure that the order you have come up with fulfils your original goals. If there are any obvious gaps in the order, you may need to go back and do more research to fill these in.

It is a good idea to start with a simple outline and move on to something more complex, fleshing out the bones only once you have built the skeleton. Do not be afraid to cross things out and move them around as you develop your plan – that is what this stage of the process is all about.

Lateral thinking

If you find it difficult to organize your thoughts, put aside the approach mentioned above, and see instead whether any more 'lateral' ways of organizing your material emerge from the material itself. Here are a few techniques you might try:

➤ Write a key word or underlying idea in the middle of a large sheet of paper, then write related words and ideas all over the sheet, drawing lines from the centre to related items, as well as between related items, to form a web or network of connected ideas. This might lead to something like this:

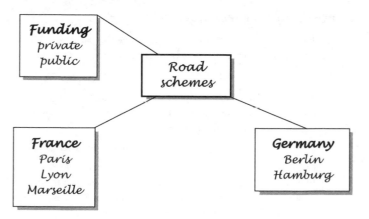

➤ Write single words or ideas on index cards and lay them out on the floor, arranging related items into groups or piles.

➤ Use question words such *who, why, where, when* and *how* to generate possible ideas for approaches to the topic. Imagine the questions your readers would ask you if they had the opportunity to speak to you in person.

Once you have decided what the key ideas or points are, assess their relative importance, and decide in what order you want to deal with them. There may be several different ways of arranging your material. What is important is that your plan covers all of the material and that it provides a clear structure for what you have to say.

Your final plan may look something like this:

> **Introduction:** *difference between public and private funding*
>
> 1. *Theoretical advantages of*
>   a) *public funding*
>   b) *private funding*
> 2. *Public funding*
>   a) *Case studies: Paris, Marseille, Hamburg*
>   b) *Do case studies bear out the theory?*
> 3. *Private funding*
>   a) *Case studies: Berlin, Lyon*
>   b) *Do case studies bear out the theory?*
>
> **Conclusion:** *summary of advantages and disadvantages of each system*

Having established a basic plan, you may wish to expand this into a more detailed plan, or you may wish to move on immediately to your first draft of the document.

Traditionally, at this early stage writers used pen and paper to create a plan, adding notes and crossing things out as they went. However, word processors now make it easy to put down a mass of ideas, and then re-order them by dragging blocks of text around the screen to build up a structure. Whichever method you are using, do not be afraid to change your mind – it is better to make alterations to your plan early rather than at a later stage when things are more settled and difficult to change.

Drafting – getting started

Once you have come up with a plan that meets your aims for your document, you are ready to start writing. You are now confronted with one of the most off-putting sights for a writer: a blank sheet of paper, or an empty computer screen. It is a good idea to get over this stage as quickly as possible, so make a start without assuming that the first thing you write will necessarily still be there in your final version. The important thing is to get started – it is far easier to make changes once you have something to work with, rather than wasting time staring anxiously at an empty screen and wondering what to do!

Drafting – filling out the plan

Once you make a start writing, you should find that the preparation work you have done pays off and the writing begins to flow more easily.

Keep in mind the following points as you write:

➤ Follow the plan you have drawn up. It would be a shame to waste all the work that went into producing it, and the plan will help you to organize your ideas.

➤ Do not think you have to complete a paragraph before moving on. If you get stuck, go on to the next one and come back later. You will then be able to look at it with fresh eyes and perhaps see what needs to be changed. If you are really stuck, delete the whole paragraph and start again.

➤ It is likely that new ideas and insights will occur to you as you write. If new ideas present themselves, do not be afraid to 'go with the flow' and change what you are doing to take account of them – provided that they can be accommodated within your plan.

➤ Try to deal proportionately with the various different points and arguments. Don't spend a long period on a single point and then skirt around other points that are more important.

➤ Think about the people who will be reading the document and try to make life easy for them. If people are going to use the document to retrieve information, think about making it easy to scan by using headings, lists and tables. If people are going to read it as a continuous piece, make sure that it is divided up into manageable paragraphs and that there is a coherent and logical structure.

➤ If you make a statement or express an opinion, back this up with evidence in the form of facts and figures or quotations. However, use facts and figures selectively and appropriately. Don't overwhelm your readers with them.

Revising and reworking

Once you have finished a single complete version of your document, you have the opportunity to change and improve it. It is usually more helpful to produce something that is complete but imperfect and then revise that, rather than wasting time trying to produce something that is perfect first time.

Check that all of the points in your plan have been covered in a logical order, and that everything that you have included is in fact necessary to your argument.

Check also that you deal with each issue clearly, and that you move smoothly from one point to the next. If you have not done this, add extra material to explain, introduce or summarize where necessary, as this will make your work more polished.

Once you are satisfied with the overall structure and content, you can concentrate on getting the introduction and the conclusion right. You may find that what you originally said in your introduction is no longer valid because you have made changes during the writing process. Now is the time to get it right.

If you are happy that your document is well organized and coherent as a whole, you can turn your attention to the details: check the 'five Cs', making sure your writing is:

> **Correct** – so that there are no errors in facts, spelling, grammar, punctuation, appropriate style and sensitive use of language.

> **Consistent** – so that things are expressed in the same way each time you refer to them, and you have followed the same style and the same layout throughout.

> **Clear** – so that language is easy to read, information is easy to understand, and text is attractively laid out, with plenty of space and enough headings to help your readers, but not so many that they interrupt the flow of the document.

> **Complete** – so that all of the relevant material is included, including explanations of unfamiliar terms and abbreviations, any background information and acknowledgement of your sources.

➤ **Concise** – so that the language and the amount and level of information are presented in the simplest and most direct way possible.

➡️ The subject of reading your final document to make sure that it is correct is dealt with in more detail on pages 219–22.

Using a word processor

Even if you have planned and drafted your writing by hand, it is most unusual nowadays not to use a word processor to produce the final draft of any formal written work. As well as producing a well-finished, professional-looking final result, word processors also have a number of functions that can make life easier when working with text:

➤ **Copy and paste** allows you to duplicate any area of your text quickly and simply, so that if a heading or passage needs to be repeated you can make sure it appears in exactly the same way each time. It also useful if you want to write a passage that differs only slightly from something you have already written. Simply copy and paste the first passage, and then alter it to produce the second.

➤ **Undo** and **redo** changes material and changes it back, so you can compare different versions of your work or undo errors – for example, if you have deleted or changed material by mistake.

➤ **Find and replace** locates every instance of a particular word or phrase and replaces it. This can be useful for ensuring that your work is consistent and allows you to deal with all occurrences of a particular error at once. For example, it will enable you find every occurrence of the word *Peking* and change them all to *Beijing*. You need to be careful, however, that you do not accidentally change something that you really wanted to leave unaltered (for example, you would not want to change *Peking duck* to *Beijing duck*). Another pitfall of this feature is that it can create changes to the layout of the text without you being aware of it. For example, the amount of text on a line or on a page may be altered.

➤ **Autocorrection** is a feature that detects errors and makes changes without the need for you to do anything. This sounds attractive, but bear in mind that sometimes you might wish to write something that the computer has been programmed to change. The autocorrection feature can also remove responsibility by leading authors to stop thinking about what they are writing, which is never a good thing.

➤ **Letter wizards** and the like are tools for laying out and formatting documents. As with the autocorrection feature, too much reliance on them can remove awareness and responsibility from users, tending to make them passive and more dependent on the computer to make decisions.

Some tips for word processing

The following tips are valid for Word 97 and Word 2000.

You can let Word **check your spelling and grammar** as you write:

➤ Click on 'ABC' on the standard toolbar; or click on 'Tools' on the menu bar, then 'Spelling and Grammar'; or simply press 'F7'.

➤ On the 'Spelling and Grammar' dialogue box, click on 'Options'.

➤ Click on 'Check Spelling' as you type and/or 'Check Grammar' as you type.

➤ Click on 'OK'.

➤ A red wavy line will now appear under a word whose spelling is doubtful. Right-click on the wavy line to get a shortcut menu allowing you to accept Word's suggestion by clicking on it, or to add the word you typed to the checking dictionary. Similarly, a green wavy line will appear under grammatical queries.

If you find the wavy lines distracting:

➤ Proceed as above, but click on 'Check Spelling' as you type and/or 'Check Grammar' as you type, so that the tick is removed.

➤ You can then check the whole text after you have written it by clicking on 'ABC' on the standard toolbar; or by clicking on 'Tools' on the menu bar, then 'Spelling and Grammar'; or simply by pressing 'F7'.

> **!!!** The spelling and grammar checks are not infallible. The best method is to use these checks to suggest possible errors, which you can then check using your own knowledge of spelling and grammar and correct if you wish. In any case, you should still read the final version of your document to check for errors, as explained on pages 220–1.

You can **stop the spelling check** from operating in a passage containing specialized terminology (where it would query too many spellings), while keeping it for the rest of the text:

➤ Highlight the passage in question.

➤ Click on 'Tools' on the menu bar, then 'Language', then 'Set Language'.

➤ Choose 'No Proofing' in the dialogue box.

➤ Click on 'OK'.

You can use the **thesaurus** function to find a synonym to replace a word you have used too often or to find a word that you cannot quite remember but whose sense you know:

➤ Put your cursor on the word you want a synonym for, or type in a rough synonym for the word you cannot remember and put your cursor over this.

➤ Click on 'Tools' on the menu bar, then 'Language', then 'Thesaurus'; or simply press 'Shift + F7'.

➤ Click on the appropriate meaning in the box on the left.

➤ Click on a synonym in the box on the right.

➤ Click on 'Replace' to insert the synonym in the text.

You can use the **AutoText** function to generate phrases or sentences that you use frequently by typing in an abbreviation:

> Highlight the text that you want to store.

> Click on 'Insert' on the menu bar, then 'AutoText', then 'AutoText'.

> Click on the 'AutoCorrect' tab.

> In the 'Replace' box, type an abbreviation that is not likely to be used in any other context.

> Click on 'Add'.

> Click on 'OK'.

Now, whenever you type that abbreviation, the whole phrase or sentence will appear.

Sometimes a page break will leave a line or just a few words of a paragraph on one page and the rest of the paragraph on the other page. You can prevent this happening by **overriding page breaks**:

> Click anywhere in the paragraph that you want to keep together.

> Click on 'Format' on the menu bar, then 'Paragraph'.

> Click on the 'Line and Page Breaks' tab.

> Click on 'Keep lines together'.

> Click on 'OK'.

Using a **table** is a neater and easier way of presenting information than using tabs:

> Put the cursor where you want your table to be.

> Click on 'Insert Table' on the standard toolbar.

> Choose the size of table from the grid displayed.

> Make alterations at any stage by clicking on 'Table' on the menu bar.

> If you do not want to display the lines in the table, click on the 'Outside Border' options on the Formatting toolbar and select 'No Border'.

You can easily add neat **captions** to your tables, diagrams etc:

> Click on the object you want to add a caption to.

> ➤ Click on 'Insert' on the menu bar, then 'Caption'.

> ➤ Type in your caption in the dialogue box.

> ➤ Select the position from 'Options'.

> ➤ Click on 'OK'.

You can ask the computer to **count the number of words** in a document:

> ➤ Highlight the text you want to count, unless you want to count all of the words in the document.

> ➤ Click on 'Tools' on the menu bar.

> ➤ Click on 'Word Count'.

You can **customize your menus and toolbars** by adding commands ('Save', 'Paste', 'Bold', etc) to any menu or toolbar that you want:

> ➤ Click on 'Tools' on the menu bar, then 'Customize', then the 'Commands' tab.

> ➤ In the 'Categories' dialogue box, click on the menu currently containing the command you want. The commands available are shown in the box on the right.

> ➤ If you want to add the command to a menu, click on the menu outside the box where you want to add the command.

> ➤ Choose the command from the dialogue box and drag it to the menu outside the box or to the toolbar where you want it to go.

> ➤ To remove a command, drag it on to the desktop.

> ➤ Click on 'Close'.

You can display **formatting marks**, such as spaces, tabs and paragraph marks on the screen:

> ➤ Click on 'Tools' on the menu bar, then 'Options'.

> ➤ Click on the 'View' tab.

> ➤ Click on the formatting marks (called 'nonprinting characters' in Word 97) that you want to see on screen.

> ➤ Click on 'OK'.

Checking the Finished Document

Your last chance

Once you have finished writing your document, and you have printed it out and are holding it in your hands, you need to look over it again to make sure everything is in order before you hand it over or send it off to the person or people who will read it.

It is important that you do this – it is the last chance you will have.

You will already know about the 'five Cs' (Correct, Consistent, Clear, Complete, Concise), and they apply here for two reasons:

> Everything needs to be in good order so that you can get your message across effectively to your readers or reader.

> You need to create a favourable impression so that your written work attracts comments for the right reasons rather than the wrong reasons, or is not remarked on at all because there is nothing to find fault with.

To make sure we make the most of this opportunity, we can separate the final check into two stages: **looking** and **reading**.

Looking at your work

Although you have been looking at what you have written for some time on a computer screen, it needs to be checked on paper as well to make sure it looks and reads the way it is meant to. The way something looks on a monitor and the way it looks on paper are not always as similar as you might expect. Documents can acquire a whole new identity when the density of the ink, the sharpness of the printing, the texture, brilliance and thickness of the paper, and the varying light conditions of the real world come into play. Fonts, size of type, headings, spaces and blocks of text all may look different when you are holding a piece of paper in your hands rather than staring at a screen.

To get a feel for this, try holding your document at arm's length and staring hard at it – try taking your glasses off or deliberately blurring your vision, so all you get is a visual impression rather than being able to read what the words actually say. Word processors have a 'full page view' that is similar to this, but there is no substitute for the real thing. When all you see is black marks on a white surface, you can decide whether or not those black marks are well arranged, rather than thinking about what they mean. It may even be a good idea to print early versions of your writing to get an idea of the way it looks, so that you can make any alterations to the layout before you have gone too far.

To check for consistency of layout, try holding the document at arm's length and flicking through it. Again, this will allow you to focus on what things look like rather than what they say.

Reading your work

On pages 207–8 we looked at a range of reading techniques that can be used to extract information from a text. When it comes to checking a written document for errors, a very different style of reading is appropriate. When you are reading to extract information, you get used to ignoring the smaller details in order to focus on the overall meaning. But when you are checking a document for errors, these details become extremely important.

It is a good idea to read through your document at least twice, looking at it in different ways. The first time you read through your work you can skim through it quickly to make sure it is properly organized and succeeds in meeting its aims. When have done this, you can **proofread** it to check for spelling mistakes and inconsistencies in grammar or punctuation.

Limitations of computerized spelling checks

A word processor with a spelling check function may help to identify some keying errors and simple spelling mistakes. However, it will not pick up cases of a correct word being used in the wrong place. For example, if I had just typed *the right word in the wrong plaice*, a spelling check would not detect that *plaice* was an error – even though I did not intend to write about the fish – because the computer recognizes it as an acceptable word.

Moreover, a spelling check cannot identify nonsense, as *ice cream juggernaut over the green horizon drinks furry mandolin* will confirm.

Finally, spelling checks and grammar checks are also only as good as the programming behind them, and sometimes make suggestions that are simply wrong.

For all these reasons, you should always read your finished document carefully yourself.

Proofreading

When you are **proofreading**, you read through a text with the sole intention of checking spelling, punctuation and grammar, and alphabetical and numerical order. At this stage you should not be thinking about whether the information is factually accurate or clearly expressed. In fact, professional proofreaders might even read a book backwards so that all they see is a succession of words rather than a coherent text.

Successful proofreaders tend not to assume that a document will be correct, and focus actively on looking for mistakes. Proofreading therefore requires you to be more alert and critical than usual, and to keep this up for quite a long period of time. Because this level of concentration can be difficult to maintain, people sometimes experience a kind of 'word blindness' when trying to proofread. This is especially true when they are looking at their own work. Because they are so familiar with it, they tend to picture it in the way they expect it to look, rather than the way it actually is.

To overcome the problems associated with proofreading your own work, it is a good idea to get someone else to proofread it, as a fresh pair of eyes will often see things that you miss.

However, the ultimate responsibility rests with you, and you should always read through the document yourself as well. It is advisable to take a break between the end of the writing process and the start of the proofreading process so that you can give your eyes and brain a rest and allow yourself to switch from 'write mode' to 'proofread mode'.

Proofreading tips

Proofreading involves actively looking for mistakes in the way that something is written, rather than passively absorbing information from the text, so remain aware of:

> ➤ words that you find difficult to spell – it is a good idea to keep a list of these

> ➤ easily confused words (see the list of these on pages 142–70)

> ➤ the sequence of any numerical ordering

> ➤ the sequence of any alphabetical ordering

> ➤ the numbering of pages

> ➤ consistency in the way that words with optional spellings are written

> ➤ consistency in the way that punctuation marks are used

To make things easy for yourself, it is worth keeping a list of your 'policy decisions' on matters of style and layout, as well as noting down decisions you make about optional spellings. For example, if you decide to spell words such as *specialize* with *-ize* rather than *-ise*, make a note of this and apply your policy consistently throughout the document.

A good way of checking the consistency of spellings in your document is to use the 'Find' function on a word processor. (In Word, click on 'Edit', then 'Find'; or simply press 'Control + F'.) This will allow you to check whether the document contains any spellings you have decided not to use. For example, you might search for the word *specialise*, and change this to *specialize* wherever it occurs, or you might search for letters *ise* and check in each case whether you need to change the spelling to *ize*.

Constructing Sentences

The preceding chapters have looked at the process of creating documents in a general way. However, even when we know what we are going to write in general, we still have to go through the detailed process of getting our ideas down on paper, shaping sentences out of words, and paragraphs out of sentences. The next three chapters look at how to express ideas in well-formed sentences and paragraphs and how to create a satisfactory overall structure for your writing.

What is a sentence?

Sentences are the basic units for expressing meaning. For our purposes we can define a sentence as a group of words that:

> ➤ makes sense by itself
> ➤ contains a finite verb (see pages 60–1)
> ➤ begins with a capital letter
> ➤ ends with a full stop or its equivalent (a question mark or exclamation mark)

Sentences, clauses and phrases

Sentences may contain clauses and phrases. It is important to establish the difference between a **sentence**, a **clause** and a **phrase**.

A **clause** is a group of words that includes a **subject** and its related **finite verb**. A clause may or may not constitute a complete sentence:

I like mushrooms.

when we arrive

A **phrase** is simply any set of words that expresses a single idea. A phrase forms part of a sentence, but it does not constitute a clause:

a box of mushrooms

was sleeping

along the ground

Clauses can be classified as **main clauses** and **subordinate**

clauses. A clause that can stand as a sentence in its own right is called a **main clause**:

she will come tomorrow

they walked home

A clause that cannot stand as a sentence in its own right is called a **subordinate clause**:

if time permits

after the party finishes

A sentence must contain a main clause, and may also contain one or more subordinate clause:

She will come tomorrow.

She will come tomorrow if time permits.

If time permits, she will come tomorrow after the party finishes.

Phrases can usually be classified according to what function they perform in a sentence – in other words, what part of speech they act as. We have already seen (on pages 69–70 and 78) that adverbs and prepositions can often exist as phrases rather than single words.

A **noun phrase** is a group of words that acts as a noun:

the boys hanging about on the street corner

a big red sports car

A **verb phrase** is a group of words that acts as a verb:

will be looking for

is running

Simple sentence structure

It is possible to analyse sentences into five basic components:

> subject
> verb
> object
> complement
> adjunct

The subject

The **subject** of a sentence is the thing around which the action revolves. The subject identifies a person or thing and then the rest of the sentence says something about the subject.

The subject is usually a noun or a pronoun:

***Sam** is a brilliant musician.*

***She** plays the violin.*

The subject may be a phrase rather than a single word:

***My cousin Ken** is arriving tomorrow.*

***Making baskets** is tougher work than you might think.*

The subject typically comes at the beginning of the sentence. In questions, however, the normal word order is reversed, and the subject comes after the verb:

*Aren't **you** cold?*

*Isn't **she** from New Zealand?*

The part of the sentence that comes after the subject and says something about the subject is called the **predicate**:

*Cats **make good companions for retired people**.*

*He **is arriving this afternoon**.*

The main verb

A sentence must contain a finite verb – that is, a verb that relates to the subject and says what the subject is doing:

*Hot air **rises**.*

*Jack and Jill **went** up the hill.*

The main verb may consist of a phrase rather than a single word:

*The girls **were eating** pizza.*

*I **was just about to phone** you.*

The main verb must have a tense, indicating whether the action took place in the past, is taking place in the present or will take place in the future:

*He **arrived** yesterday.*

*He **is arriving** now.*

*He **will arrive** tomorrow.*

There must be **agreement** between the subject and the main verb (see pages 85–6).

The object

A sentence can be complete if it contains no more than a subject and a main verb. However, many verbs require an **object**, which indicates the person or thing that receives or is affected by the action of the verb. (These verbs are called 'transitive verbs'. See the discussion on page 60.)

The object is a noun or a noun phrase. It usually comes directly after the main verb:

*He thumped **the table**.*

*They made **a funny noise**.*

Some verbs can have two objects, a **direct object** and an **indirect object**. The **direct object** is the person or thing that the verb directly affects – the thing being written, being blown, etc:

*I wrote Charlie **a letter**.*

*She blew me **a kiss**.*

The **indirect object** is the thing or person that the direct object is directed at, done to or done for. The indirect object typically comes before the direct object:

*I wrote **Charlie** a letter.*

*She blew **me** a kiss.*

If the indirect object is removed, the sentence can still stand alone and will still make sense, but feels less complete:

I wrote a letter.

She blew a kiss.

The complement

A complement is any word or phrase used to complete the meaning of a sentence. They often come after 'linking' verbs such as *be* or *become*:

> He is *a very nice man*.

> It grew *dark*.

The complement says something about the subject of the sentence:

> I am *a student*.

> She looks *ill*.

The adjunct

Adjuncts are phrases that act as adverbs to say something about the manner, place, time or extent of the action.

Adjuncts may consist of a single adverb or of a phrase:

> She ran *quickly*.

> She ran *as fast as her legs could carry her*.

Some verbs require an adjunct to complete the meaning:

> He was behaving *foolishly*.

> This contraption goes *round and round*.

The adjunct can come at the start of a sentence:

> *Foolishly*, he tried to escape.

> *In actual fact*, the film was brilliant.

Active and passive sentences

In a typical sentence, the verb describes what action the subject is doing or what state the subject is in. Sentences that have this relationship between the verb and its subject are said to be in the **active voice**:

> Elephants destroyed the field of maize.

> The hotel serves breakfast until nine o'clock.

However, it is possible to turn some 'active' sentences around, so that the person who is actually performing the action is not the grammatical subject of the verb. For example:

The field of maize was destroyed by elephants.

Breakfast is served until nine o'clock.

In these examples, the word that was previously the object has become the focus of the sentence, and the form of the verb has changed (see pages 58–9 on the forms of verbs used in such sentences). Sentences that are written from this point of view are said to be written in the **passive voice**.

The difference between the two types of sentence is that active sentences focus on the person performing an action whereas passive sentences shift the focus to the object of the action.

This shift of focus can be made for various reasons. Because passive sentences can allow the doer of an action not to be mentioned, they can be useful when the identity of the doer is not relevant or is not known. One common reason for using a passive sentence structure is that it allows you to avoid naming whoever is responsible for something:

The report has not been circulated.

Five glasses were broken.

In contrast, active sentences can sometimes seem rather blunt and tactless:

Frank has not circulated the report.

You have broken five glasses.

However, remember that active sentences are less complex, and so are easier to understand. That is why they are recommended when attempting to write plain English (see pages 17–18).

Statements, questions and commands

We have seen that a sentence can end with a full stop, a question mark or an exclamation mark. These three punctuation marks can be connected with the expression of three different types of sentence.

The full stop is used when a sentence is a **statement** of fact or opinion. Statements can be positive or negative:

They have three children.

I am waiting for the plumber.

I do not wish to take part in your survey.

The question mark is used when a sentence is a **question**. Questions can be classified as **closed questions** or **open questions**. **Closed** or **polar questions** require a 'yes' or 'no' answer:

Can't he come?

Open or **non-polar questions** call for a fuller answer and begin with a word such as *what, who* or *where*:

Why can't he come?

Alternatively, questions can take the form of statements with a **tag question** such as *haven't I?, didn't they?* or *isn't it?* added:

We all know what they are up to, don't we?

An exclamation mark is used when a sentence gives a **command**:

Tell me another one!

Commands do not have a subject for their main verb. This means that a sentence expressing a command can consist of a single word:

Stop!

Note that not all sentences that are commands require an exclamation mark:

Sit down.

Have a rest.

Let me get you a drink.

Moreover, not all sentences with an exclamation mark are commands. Sometimes a sentence that is a statement of fact or opinion can end with an exclamation mark to indicate an exclamation of surprise:

You finally made it!

We've been waiting for ages!

These three types of sentence are sometimes defined in terms of the 'moods' of their verbs:

> ➤ Statements are written in the **indicative** mood.

> ➤ Questions are written in the **interrogative** mood.

> ➤ Commands are written in the **imperative** mood.

The subjunctive

There is also a fourth 'mood', the **subjunctive**. This is used when expressing wishes, doubts, recommendation or uncertainty. Verbs that are represented in the subjunctive indicate things that do not actually happen, but might happen, could happen or would happen in certain hypothetical situations.

The subjunctive is often disregarded in modern English. When it is used it can sound rather formal and stilted.

The **present subjunctive** uses the base form of the verb by itself (*retire, send*) in the third person singular of the present tense, instead of adding *−s* to the base form (*retires, sends*):

*It is not necessary that he **retire** at sixty.*

*He insists that she **send** a reply at once.*

Similarly, the base form of the verb is used for the present subjunctive in irregular verbs:

*She asks only that she **be** left alone.* (not *is left*)

The **past subjunctive** uses *were* or *were to have*:

*I'd be careful if I **were** you.*

*She treated him as if he **were** a servant.*

*If only he **were to have been** in the team.*

Longer sentences

Writers are often encouraged to keep sentences short and simple. However, there are times when you are not able to express what you want to say precisely in very simple sentences. Moreover, if you were to use only short, simple sentences in your writing, the effect would be repetitive and tedious:

> *The threat of nuclear war has receded. This has reduced global tension. This has led to discussions between the superpowers. The superpowers have agreed to ...*

In order to express yourself accurately and fluently you need to vary the length of sentence and use **compound sentences** and **complex sentences** where appropriate.

Compound sentences

A **compound sentence** is essentially two or more simple sentences joined together by a conjunction, usually *and* or *but*:

> *The threat of nuclear war has receded **and** this has reduced global tension.*

> *The threat of nuclear war has receded, **but** this has not reduced global tension.*

Each section of the sentence joined by the conjunction has now become an independent **clause**. If the conjunctions were removed, the clauses would function as independent sentences.

When the subject of both clauses is the same, it is not usually repeated in the second clause:

> *Jeffrey followed in his father's footsteps and became a vet.*

> *They offered her a large bonus, but never delivered it.*

The clauses may be linked by a semicolon rather than a conjunction:

> *Jeffrey followed in his father's footsteps; he became a vet.*

> *They offered her a large bonus; however, they never delivered it.*

Complex sentences

A **complex sentence** contains a main clause and one or more **subordinate clauses**:

> *Although the threat of nuclear war has receded, global tension has not been reduced.*

Note that the subordinate clause cannot function as an independent sentence:

> *although the threat of nuclear war has receded*

However, the main clause can function as an independent sentence:

> *Global tension has not been reduced.*

The main clause forms the heart of a complex sentence. If the information in a subordinate clause is moved into the main clause, the nature and emphasis of the sentence alters:

> *Although the threat of nuclear war has receded, global tension has not been reduced.*

> *The threat of nuclear war has receded, although global tension has not been reduced.*

Compound-complex sentences

A **compound-complex sentence** is a combination of a compound sentence and a complex sentence. It contains two or more main clauses and one or more subordinate clause:

> *Now that the threat of nuclear war has receded, global tension has been reduced and the superpowers have started discussions.*

This sentence is composed of a subordinate clause (*now that the threat of nuclear war has receded*), linked to a main clause (*global tension has been reduced*), which is itself combined with a second main clause (*the superpowers have started discussions*).

You can go on and on adding clauses to make a sentence even more complicated. However, the more clauses a sentence contains, the more difficult it may be for your readers to interpret it, and there is a greater likelihood of ambiguity.

Types of subordinate clause

Subordinate clauses are useful because they are a way of supplying your readers with additional information about the main clause. They often anticipate a question that your readers might ask and answer it. There are a many different types of information that can be contained in a subordinate clause.

Clauses beginning with *in order to, so that* and *in case* answer the question 'What for?' and indicate the **purpose** of an action:

> *I put the plant on the windowsill **so that it would get more light.***

> *I'm taking an umbrella **in case it rains**.*

Clauses beginning with *because, since* and *as* answer the question 'Why?' and indicate the **reason** for an action:

> ***Since you are going into town**, would you post a letter for me?*

> *I'm taking an umbrella **because it is pouring down**.*

Clauses in which *that* picks up on the word *so* followed by an adjective or adverb answer the question 'How much?' and indicate the **result** of an action:

> *She speaks so quickly **that nobody can understand her**.*

> *The rain was so heavy **that I could not see**.*

Clauses beginning with *as if, like* and *just as* answer the question 'How?' and indicate the **manner** of an action:

> *Mix in the eggs, **just as recipe says**.*

> *He fell down **as if he had been shot**.*

Clauses beginning with *when, after, before, until* and *once* answer the question 'When?' and indicate the **time** of an action:

> ***After he left**, she burned all his letters.*

> *Kevin didn't seem very happy **when he came in**.*

Clauses can answer the question 'Where?' and indicate the **place** of an action:

> ***Everywhere we went**, we saw homeless people.*

> *I can't find my keys **in the place where I left them**.*

Subordinate clauses beginning with *although, while* and *however* introduce a **qualification** of the statement made in the main clause:

> *She carried on reading, **although she was quite tired**.*

> *I mean to get my revenge, **however long it takes me**.*

Subordinate clauses can also indicate **conditions** attached to the statement made in the main clause:

> *If nobody stops him*, he will kill us all.

> *Unless they arrive soon*, they'll miss the best part.

Subordinate clauses can indicate **comparisons**:

> It is almost as hot today *as it was yesterday*.

> He is happier now *than when he lived in Canada*.

> Another important type of subordinate clause is the relative clause, which is discussed on pages 75–6.

Punctuation of subordinate clauses

Readers rely on the position of commas to navigate their way through complex sentences. Make sure that commas mark transitions between clauses and do not break up clauses incorrectly.

Clarify the meaning by using a comma to mark the end of a subordinate clause when it comes before a main clause:

> *Although it was late, we decided to continue.*

> *In order to improve, we must practise every day.*

Use a comma to mark the beginning of a subordinate clause when it comes after a main clause and merely comments on it, rather than completing its meaning:

> *He is determined to succeed, whatever his critics may say.*

> *The train was late, just as it had been the day before.*

Do not use a comma to mark the beginning of a subordinate clause when it comes after a main clause and completes its meaning. A comma is not required when the subordinate clause begins with *that, to, because, than* or *so that*:

> *They told me that it was a long way to the village.*

> *She was tired because she had been up since dawn.*

Tips for writing sentences

This chapter has provided you with a lot of information about the mechanics of sentence construction and the different types of sentences. This should help you to recognize when a sentence is not complete, and to use the full range of different types of sentence structure available.

These are the most important points to keep mind:

➤ Write complete and correct sentences: every sentence should contain a main verb.

➤ Make sure that the subject and the main verb agree: a singular subject requires a singular verb, while a plural subject requires a plural verb.

➤ Usually, only one point should be covered in each sentence. If a sentence consists of two unconnected points, then split it into two sentences.

➤ If a sentence you have written seems awkward, see if it works better if you rearrange the component parts. Search for the word that is the focus of the sentence and put this at the start. the rest of the sentence should then fall into place.

➤ Use the appropriate punctuation mark at the end of the sentence.

➤ Use a comma when there is a pause between one clause and another.

➤ If you want to link two complete sentences to create a compound sentence, use a conjunction or a semicolon. Don't link sentences together with a comma.

➤ Remember that there are many different ways of expressing information. If you are not happy with what you have written, think about how you might rework it. Could the sentence be split into two simpler sentences? Would it work better as a question? Are any of the words redundant? Or are more words required to make the meaning clear?

➡ See the advice on page 244 about varying the structure of sentences to increase the effectiveness of your writing.

Constructing Paragraphs

Why do we use paragraphs?

It is customary to arrange the sentences in a written document into paragraphs. These consist of sentences grouped together in blocks. A new paragraph is marked off from the preceding text by beginning on a new line, and is either set in (or 'indented') from the left-hand margin or else preceded by a space (as in this book).

Paragraphs are more artificial units than words or sentences. However, the decision about when to begin a new paragraph should not be a random one.

So, what is a paragraph? A paragraph is best thought of as expressing a single idea or chunk of thought within a longer argument, description or narrative. This thought is usually developed over several sentences, but sometimes in just one. Paragraphs give the writer a useful way of organizing a complex text into a series of smaller, more manageable units. They also give your readers a route through the text, signalling where it is appropriate to pause and 'draw breath' before moving on to the next idea or chunk of thought.

A paragraph ending should therefore be regarded as a kind of punctuation mark. It signals a pause that is stronger than that of a full stop.

How long should a paragraph be?

The number of sentences or the number of lines in a paragraph is not fixed. Each paragraph should be long enough to express and develop one key idea. If you move on to a new idea, move on to a new paragraph.

However, try to keep your paragraphs short – under ten lines is a useful rule of thumb. This keeps you focused on the key idea that you are trying to communicate and it makes the text easier to read as well. If a paragraph seems very long, check to see if there is more than one key point that can be taken and used as the core for another paragraph.

On the other hand, make sure that each paragraph contributes something. If it fails to do so, combine it with the previous one or the next one, or remove it altogether.

A particularly important point can be broken down into different aspects and spread over two or more paragraphs – one aspect for each paragraph – in order to make it easier to digest. But never do the opposite: do not jam two ideas into one paragraph if they have nothing in common. Deal with them in two separate paragraphs.

In practice, most paragraphs are three sentences or more long, since this is usually what is required to develop a point convincingly. Too many short paragraphs will probably mean that the ideas are not fully developed, and that you are moving from subject to subject, giving the impression of 'bittiness'. Nevertheless, an occasional short paragraph of two sentences or even one sentence can be effective as it will stand out from the others and so draw attention to itself.

If you are writing for the Internet or producing advertising copy, you may take a more extreme approach and compose in paragraphs each consisting of only one or two simple sentences. This approach works well if all you have to express is a series of facts, as it makes it easy for your readers to take things in. However, it does not allow you to develop complex arguments.

The components of a paragraph

There are various ways of ordering sentences effectively in a paragraph. The way you go about this will depend on the information you want to communicate and the effect you want to create. However, a well-constructed paragraph will contain some, and possibly all, of these components:

> link to the previous paragraph
> topic sentence
> supporting sentences
> concluding sentence

Links to the previous paragraph

When you start a new paragraph, it is often helpful to show your readers how the point you are now presenting relates to what you have already written.

This might be done by a single word:

> ***However***, *not all of the results are quite so encouraging.*

> *It is, **moreover**, notoriously difficult to predict expenditure.*

> ***Next***, *we come to the various social factors.*

The link to the previous paragraph might also be achieved by a phrase or a subordinate clause. A linking phrase can mention or summarize the contents of the previous paragraph:

> *Despite these apparently impressive figures, ...*

> *Besides these insignificant gestures, ...*

> *Notwithstanding all the problems mentioned above, ...*

> *Although opinions of this sort might suggest approval, ...*

The link to the previous paragraph might even take the form of an introductory sentence, which summarizes or comments on the preceding paragraph and prepares for the key idea of the new paragraph:

> ***This demonstrates the advantages of the system***. *The disadvantages are not so numerous. ...*

> ***So far, so good***. *But we must also consider the economic factors. ...*

> A full explanation of linking devices is given on pages 252–3.

Topic sentences

The topic sentence tells the reader what key idea is being focused on in the paragraph.

A topic sentence will often be the first sentence of the paragraph, and it may include a link to the previous paragraph:

> *Although opinions such as these might suggest approval,*
> ***everyone involved is in fact aware of the scheme's***
> ***drawbacks.***

In this example, the topic sentence begins with a link to the previous paragraph, and goes on to establish the key idea of the new paragraph. Here, the subject of the paragraph is the scheme's drawbacks, which the writer will go on to discuss in the following sentences.

The topic sentence may come after an introductory linking sentence:

> *This demonstrates the advantages of the system.* ***However, the***
> ***system is not without its flaws.***

In this example, the paragraph begins with a summary of the previous paragraph, and the key idea of the new paragraph is established in the second sentence. Here, the subject of the paragraph is the flaws of the system, which the writer will go on to explain in the following sentences.

The topic sentence may even come towards the end of a paragraph, after a series of sentences which build up to it. It could even come right at the end of the paragraph, acting as a conclusion in its own right:

> *The film stars of the future will work long hours without*
> *complaint. They won't demand a private trailer, vegan catering*
> *or three personal assistants. Even better, there won't be any*
> *expensive contracts to negotiate, because* ***these actors will be***
> ***entirely generated by computer.***

In this example, the paragraph begins with a series of statements about computer-generated actors. The key idea that the actors of the future will be generated by computer is only established at the very end of the paragraph. Postponing the key idea like this can create suspense, and so make a piece of writing more interesting. Because of the delay in establishing the topic, this paragraph reads more like a puzzle than the other examples. Although this technique can be very effective in an introductory or concluding paragraph, it forces the reader to work harder, and so should be used sparingly if you are developing an argument.

Supporting sentences

Once the topic of the sentence has been established, the other sentences in the paragraph give you the opportunity to be more specific and to go into more detail.

Supporting sentences often provide illustrations and examples:

> *Experienced business travellers therefore make optimum use of the journey time.* **They prepare thoroughly for each trip, ensuring that everything is organized in the office before they depart, and that they will have everything they could possibly need with them when they go. The experienced traveller always travels with a notebook computer and a spare set of batteries for it.**

In this example, the topic is established in the first sentence: this paragraph is about making optimum use of time on a business journey. The second and third sentences support the topic sentence by giving examples of how experienced travellers use their time efficiently.

Supporting sentences may also be used to list a series of arguments:

> *Why Saint Valentine's Day became the day to pursue the object of your desire is not clear.* **The custom may be linked to an old idea that birds start to look for a mate on this date. It is unlikely that there is a direct connection between romantic love and any of the early Italian saints named Valentinus, despite legends that have grown up to the contrary. One theory suggests that the early Church replaced ancient love festivals with the feast of Saint Valentine, but the old associations remained.**

In this example, the topic is established in the first sentence: this paragraph is about the disputed origins of Saint Valentine's Day customs. The supporting sentences list three suggestions as to why these customs may have become associated with this day.

Supporting sentences may also explain in more detail the idea established in the topic sentence:

> *The term 'Fascist' comes from the Italian political party formed by Benito Mussolini.* **The Italian Fascists took as their emblem the 'fasces', a bundle of rods bound around an axe, which in ancient Roman times was carried before a magistrate as a symbol of his power. The sticks**

symbolized the magistrate's power to punish by beating, and the axe his right to carry out executions.

In this example, the topic is established in the first sentence: this paragraph will explain the origin of the term 'Fascist'. The supporting sentences go beyond the statement in the topic sentence and show not only how the word came into English from Italian, but also how the word originally came to be used in Italian.

Concluding sentences

The final sentence of a paragraph offers you the opportunity to take stock. You may wish to make a comment or draw a conclusion based on the points made in the paragraph:

*Various explanations have been offered to account for this custom. It may be linked to an old idea that birds start to look for a mate on this date. It is unlikely that there is a direct connection between romantic love and any of the early Italian saints named Valentinus, despite legends that have grown up to the contrary. Another theory suggests that the early Church replaced ancient love festivals with the feast of Saint Valentine, but the old associations remained. **None of the explanations is completely satisfactory.***

You may also wish to lead your readers towards a new but related topic to be taken up in the next paragraph:

*The early part of the 1986 season was marred by a series of injuries. He broke a finger in May, causing him to miss two weeks. Shortly after his return, he strained a calf muscle. Then, in July, he was sidelined by a knee problem. **It was not until August that his form began to improve.***

You may be able to combine these two ideas by drawing a conclusion and also preparing for a new but related topic:

*Initial results were promising. Congestion at peak times was reduced, revenue increased and waiting times were shortened. **All of this would seem to suggest that the experiment was successful, were it not for one crucial point.***

Paragraphs that do not require a topic sentence

Paragraphs that are based around a topic sentence and supporting sentences are extremely useful when you are developing a chain of thought. The structure allows you to make a point and to develop it, and then move on to the next point. Use this structure if your aim is:

➤ to analyse

➤ to argue

➤ to assess

➤ to discuss

This will usually be the case if you are writing an essay, a report or a business proposal.

However, it is not always appropriate to structure a paragraph around a topic sentence. There are times when the statements you make will be self-evident and require no explanation or justification. Paragraphs do not generally require a topic sentence and supporting sentences when your aim is:

➤ to give a straightforward description

➤ to report a sequence of events

➤ to explain the steps in a process

This might be the case if you are telling a story or giving a set of instructions. In the following example, each sentence is of equal importance:

> *On entering the village, you will see a church on your right. Just after the church, turn left onto Birdston Road. Continue along this road for a quarter of a mile. Then, just after you pass a pillar box, turn right onto Redmoss Road. The hotel is on the left-hand side, opposite the Village Hall.*

Fluency

Whatever the structure of your paragraph, you should aim to make your writing fluent and interesting.

Meaning has to flow naturally from one sentence to the next, only stopping when the end of the paragraph is reached. If there is a jump in thought between one sentence and the next, use a linking word (such as *for*, *but*, *so*, *therefore*, *however*) to indicate the direction of the argument:

> *When sanctions were lifted, foreign capital started flowing into the country. **However**, the economic outlook remains gloomy. The government is **therefore** pursuing a number of initiatives aimed at increasing output.*

If a linking word or phrase is insufficient to show the way that the argument is progressing, you may need to add a sentence to bridge the gap:

> *Government support has fallen off sharply. **This means that we are facing a significant shortfall in revenue**. We shall therefore be opening five new shops to raise funds.*

A full explanation of linking devices is given on pages 252–3.

Fluency is also aided by maintaining a consistent viewpoint. Try to use the same 'personality' throughout the paragraph. If you write as 'I' at the start of the paragraph, don't suddenly change into 'we' later on. Similarly, if you start a description in the present tense, don't jump back into the past tense for no good reason.

Variety

Consistency does not, however, mean that you have to be dull. Find ways of avoiding numbing repetition.

There are a number of things you can do to avoid repetition of a key word:

> ➤ Use pronouns such as *he, she, it* and *they* instead of a noun.
> ➤ Use synonyms for the word.
> ➤ Use a phrase that provides a definition or explanation of the word as an occasional alternative to using the word itself.

In the paragraph below, the writer has used all of these techniques to avoid excessive repetition of the word *beginner*:

> **Beginners** *can easily become intimidated when* **they** *visit a foreign country.* **They** *tend to panic when they are confronted by unexpected replies, and some* **novices** *forget even the few words that they have learned. A few* **people who are unfamiliar with the language** *do, however, manage to communicate effectively by keeping calm and using a mixture of gestures and basic vocabulary.*

Just as repetition of words can be dull, so the use of just one form of sentence can also have a numbing effect on the reader:

> *The nature of employment is changing. People can no longer expect to remain in the same job for life. Work does not only happen between 9 and 5. Modern technology has contributed to this. E-mail and the Internet make working from home a more attractive and viable proposition. In many cases, however, people no longer aspire to the stable routine followed by earlier generations. They prefer to have a more varied working life.*

This paragraph can be enlivened by varying the structure of sentences, varying between simple sentences, compound sentences and complex sentences:

> *The nature of employment is changing. No longer can someone expect to remain in the same job for life, nor can many people guarantee that work will be something that only happens between 9 and 5. No doubt modern technology – especially e-mail and the Internet – has contributed to this, making working from home a more attractive and viable proposition. In many cases, however, it seems that people simply no longer aspire to the stable routine followed by earlier generations, but prefer to have a more varied working life.*

➡ The different types of sentence structure are discussed in more detail on pages 230–2.

Structure

In the two previous chapters of this book, we have looked first at how individual sentences are constructed and then at how sentences are combined together into paragraphs. The natural conclusion of this process is to look at how paragraphs can be arranged within a document to create a structure that puts forward your message in a way that is easy to read and understand.

The precise structure of a document will vary depending on its nature. In Part Three of this book we look at a wide range of documents and examine the requirements of each. However, there are some points about structure that apply to almost anything that you will write.

A beginning, a middle and an end

The Greek philosopher Aristotle, writing around 330BC, declared that 'a whole is something which has a beginning, a middle and an end' Aristotle was writing about the structure used by playwrights composing Greek tragedies, but his maxim holds good for any written document. Most writing requires three stages:

- an introduction
- the main body
- a conclusion

The introductory part of your writing should prepare your readers for what is to come. Put them into the picture by answering these questions:

- What is the subject I am going to write about?
- What particular problem, issues or questions about this am I going to address?
- Why are these issues important?
- What information am I going to introduce to address these issues?
- How am I going to arrange this information to get my point across most clearly?

After you have put your readers in the picture, you can set out your information, ideas and arguments in full. In this part of the document you need to concentrate on:

> ➤ organizing information into a logical order
> ➤ helping your readers to follow the course of your explanation

In the final part of the document, you should remind your readers of the main points you have covered and state any conclusions that can be drawn or any points that must be acted on. It is important that the conclusion follows naturally from the main body, which should contain all of the supporting evidence for it. A satisfactory conclusion may also look back to the points set out in the introduction and answer the questions:

> ➤ What particular problem, issues or questions about this was I going to address?
> ➤ What information have I introduced to address these issues?
> ➤ What possible conclusions can be drawn from the evidence?
> ➤ What is my personal reaction?
> ➤ What needs to be done to address the problem?

The idea of giving a structure to writing applies both to the document as a whole, and also to any self-contained sections that might exist within the document.

Organizing your material

Information should be presented in such a way that your readers can easily understand it. You might compare the task of structuring a written document to that of leading the reader on a journey. A good writer will make life easy for the reader by:

> ➤ having a clear idea of the intended goal
> ➤ moving forward in a series of logical steps
> ➤ avoiding unnecessary detours
> ➤ arriving at the destination successfully

The structure that you use will be determined by the nature of the material. Some common methods of organizing your material are:

> 'for and against' structure
> linear structure
> thematic structure

'For and against' structure

A 'for and against' structure is useful if you want to present two sides of an argument. Start off in your introduction by explaining that you will look at the points for and against a particular proposition. Then, in the main body, provide a series of paragraphs each listing a point for the proposition and a second series of paragraphs each listing a point against the proposition. The conclusion should indicate which points are the most significant, and will probably give an indication of whether you are inclined to support or oppose the proposition.

If you follow this approach you can either give the points for an argument first, followed by the arguments against, or give them the other way round. Generally, it is effective to present the points you do not agree with first, so that you can use the points you do agree with in order to have the last word. The crucial point is that you should not jump about between points for and points against.

The 'for and against' structure will work for many essay topics – particularly those that ask you to assess, discuss or examine, or those that are stated in the form of a question.

The essay plan below gives an example of this method of organizing information:

'The Vikings were not a naturally violent people.' Discuss.

> Introduction
> Points for the proposition: trade, religion, domestic life
> Points against the proposition: warfare, internal conflict, rituals
> Conclusion

Linear structure

A linear structure is useful if you want to provide your readers with a description, explanation, argument or justification. Start off in your introduction by saying what it is that you are going to describe or explain. Then, in the main body, give a paragraph to each stage in the process, showing how each follows naturally from the last one. The conclusion should summarize the process and may highlight particularly significant points in it.

This structure can be used if you are describing a process, moving from cause to effect. It can also be used to relate a chronological sequence of events, starting at the beginning and moving to the most recent.

The outline of a biography below gives an example of this method of organizing information:

Biography of Ben Hogan

- Introduction
- Family background
- Early career as a caddie
- Career as a professional at various country clubs
- Fight to the top
- Victory in three majors in 1948
- Bad car accident in 1949
- Triumphant return in 1953
- Later career
- Retirement
- Conclusion

Thematic structure

A thematic structure is useful if you are analysing or appraising a subject and there are a number of different factors to take into account. Start off in your introduction by listing the different factors involved. Then, in the main body, examine the subject in terms of each of the different factors. Deal with them one by one, devoting one or more paragraphs to each. The conclusion should draw together connections between the different factors and provide an overall assessment.

This structure can be used for writing about a wide number of subjects. It is particularly useful as a tool for talking about complex subjects, as it breaks them down into a series of manageable chunks of information. You can use it when writing about people, whether you are writing a report on an employee's performance or writing an essay about a literary character or a historical figure.

The outline of a discussion document below shows how you might use a thematic structure to analyse the effect of a proposal:

Discussion of proposal for new housing estate

➤ Introduction: description of the proposed development
➤ Political factors
➤ Social factors
➤ Economic factors
➤ Environmental factors
➤ Conclusion and recommendation

If you were analysing the qualities of a historical character, you might consider other themes:

Biographical sketch of George IV

➤ Introduction
➤ Physical appearance
➤ Family life
➤ Personality
➤ Intellectual qualities
➤ Public achievements
➤ Private interests
➤ Conclusion

Key points on establishing structure

Whatever structure you choose for presenting your ideas, keep the following points in mind:

➤ Let the structure you choose be dictated by what it is that you have to say and by the effect you wish to create.

➤ Keep the structure simple and transparent so that your readers know what is going on and are able to follow your train of thought all the way.

➤ Stick to the structure you have chosen throughout the document. Don't start off following one structural approach and then abandon it part-way through the document.

➤ The structure should be able to accommodate all of the necessary information.

➤ If a piece of information does not fit into the structure you have chosen, it is probably because it is not really necessary to include it. (If you are writing a report or an academic dissertation, you can use footnotes or appendices as tools for incorporating information that your readers may find interesting, but which is not essential to the thread of the argument.)

➤ Move forward steadily from paragraph to paragraph, giving each point as much attention as its role in the structure deserves. If one paragraph turns out to be especially short, check whether the point you make in it is actually worth making on its own, or whether it cannot be moved elsewhere or even deleted. If a paragraph turns out to be especially long, ask yourself if the point made in it is so important that it needs to be split up over several paragraphs.

➤ Try to complete the discussion of a point in one place rather than leaving a point and coming back to it later. If the structure demands that you do leave a point and return to it later, let your readers know where the discussion will be completed (*We shall return to the question of fish stocks when we discuss the environmental factors.*).

Guiding the reader

A clear overall structure should of itself help the reader to follow your train of thought and see how your message is developed. However, it does no harm to give the reader additional guidance.

In a longer document you can use a number of devices to help your readers understand the structure:

> Explain the way that the document is structured as part of your introduction.

> Break the document up into sections or chapters. You may want to give numbers to the different sections.

> You may even want to break some of these sections into subsections.

> Use headings and subheadings to introduce new subjects so that your readers can see immediately when there is a change of topic and what the new subject is

> Provide a table of contents at the start of the document. This can show your readers at a glance how the information is arranged.

A shorter document may not require the use of chapters and headings. However, you should still take steps to ensure that your readers know how things are progressing:

> Tell your readers when you are moving to a new topic.

> Make sure that your readers have enough background information to follow your argument. You may find that you need to define some terms briefly or clear up common misconceptions about the topic before you can develop your main theme.

> If you are going to discuss a number of issues, list them all and then examine each one in turn. This keeps your own mind focused as you write, and also allows your readers to navigate through the text easily, like a driver on a well-signposted road.

> Use tables, lists and diagrams to present information. A well-designed table or diagram can be easier to understand than a lengthy verbal description.

> Use linking devices throughout your writing to show your

readers how what you are saying relates to what has gone
before. (The following section explains these devices in more
detail.)

Linking devices

Linking devices take your readers from one sentence or paragraph to
the next in a smooth and coherent manner, helping them to follow the
line of your argument. They may consist of words, phrases or whole
sentences. Sentence adverbs (see pages 70–1) are commonly used as
linking devices.

You can use a linking device to move the argument forward:

> ***In addition***, *the Venturi effect between the two vehicles assists
> the swing.*

> ***Consequently***, *I am going to outline some of the philosophical
> beliefs about the nature of the mind.*

> ***For example***, *if the soldier cells are weakened, the chest can
> become infected.*

You can also use a linking device to counter or qualify the argument:

> ***Nonetheless***, *whatever success was achieved did not
> fundamentally alter the situation.*

> ***In contrast,*** *results in North America were hugely
> disappointing.*

> ***On the other hand***, *there is no doubt that the project has
> made a real difference to some people's lives.*

You can also use a linking device to sum up an argument:

> ***All things considered***, *the expedition must be considered a
> failure.*

> ***In other words***, *there was little genuine progress.*

> ***On the whole***, *he had a low opinion of human nature.*

More specifically, linking devices can be categorized as follows:

> ➢ those indicating that you are **adding** something: *also,
> furthermore, in addition, moreover, what is more*

➤ those indicating that you are introducing a **comparison**: *by the same token, likewise, similarly*

➤ those indicating that you are introducing a **contrast**: *but, conversely, however, in contrast, instead, nevertheless, nonetheless, on the contrary, on the other hand, rather, yet*

➤ those indicating a **consequence**: *accordingly, as a result, consequently, hence, therefore, thus*

➤ those indicating that you are introducing an **illustration**: *for example, for instance*

➤ those indicating that you are **restating** something: *in brief, in essence, in other words, in short, namely, that is*

➤ those indicating **chronological sequence**: *earlier, first of all, in the meantime, meanwhile, next, simultaneously, then, to begin with, while*

➤ those indicating that you are introducing a **summary** or **final assessment**: *all in all, by and large, in conclusion, on the whole, on balance, to sum up, to summarize*

Besides helping to guide the reader from sentence to sentence and from paragraph to paragraph, linking devices can also be used as 'signposts' to your readers, alerting them to how your train of thought is progressing. They can indicate when you are about to make a change in the general direction of your argument:

> ***Turning our attention from the social factors to the political factors***, *we must consider the electoral consequences of this decision.*

They can also remind your readers about things that have been covered in earlier parts of the document:

> ***As we have seen***, *there was little enthusiasm for the reforms among the urban population.*

> **!!!** Linking devices are hugely important for good writing. However, you should not use one every time you start a sentence, as this would become monotonous. Your readers can assume that you are continuing with the same thread of meaning until you decide to tell them otherwise.

Anticipating the reader's questions

A useful method to help you to create a coherent flow in your writing is to imagine that you are having a dialogue with the reader. After you complete each sentence, imagine what question a reader would be likely to ask. The answer to this question may provide you with your next sentence.

For example, a dialogue about the origin of the word 'Fascism' might run like this:

READER: *Where does the word 'Fascist' come from?*

WRITER: *It was the name of an Italian political party.*

READER: *Who were the Fascists?*

WRITER : *They were formed by Benito Mussolini in 1919.*

READER: *But why were they called Fascists?*

WRITER : *Because their emblem was the 'fasces', a bundle of rods bound around an axe, which in ancient Roman times was carried before a magistrate as a symbol of his power.*

READER: *What has a bundle of rods got to do with power?*

WRITER : *The sticks symbolized the magistrate's power to punish by beating, and the axe his right to carry out executions.*

In order to present a written explanation, the writer can remove the imaginary reader's questions, leaving the information that is required:

The term 'Fascist' comes from an Italian political party formed by Benito Mussolini. The Italian Fascists took as their emblem the 'fasces', a bundle of rods bound around an axe, which in ancient Roman times was carried before a magistrate as a symbol of his power. The sticks symbolized the magistrate's power to punish by beating, and the axe his right to carry out executions.

Writing Style

When we discussed organizing material into a coherent structure, we compared writing to guiding the reader on a journey. Of course, a really good guide will not only take you to the destination, but will also make the journey itself a pleasant experience. The role of the good writer is analogous to this: a well-written document should be not only clear but also interesting. Over the following three chapters, we shall look at how to ensure that reading your document is a relaxed, enjoyable and memorable experience.

Establishing your own writing style

Writing involves conforming to certain rules of spelling, grammar and punctuation. But although there are certain rules and conventions that writers need to observe, there is not necessarily a single correct way of expressing any given idea. Every writer has a personal style, which is a result of choices about which words to use and how to arrange them into sentences. Any piece of writing will therefore reflect the writer's personality and natural use of language.

This chapter will focus on how you can develop your writing style. There are certain aspects of style that are generally regarded as good practice because they make your writing easier to follow. Being aware of these may help you to eliminate some clumsy elements from your style and incorporate more elegant features into it.

Use the following principles to develop your writing style:

> - Keep it natural.
> - Write in the appropriate form of English.
> - Search for the right word for the occasion.
> - Eliminate unnecessary words.
> - Strive to express yourself clearly.
> - Be consistent.
> - Be aware of contentious points.

We shall look at each of these points in more detail below.

Keep it natural

Nobody likes having to work unnecessarily hard when they read. You may have come across writers who seem to use long words for no better reason than to show off or to make life difficult for the reader (or as they might put it: they obfuscate their intentions with sesquipedalian verbiage).

In order to help your readers, don't use words when you are not completely sure what they mean, and don't use difficult words merely for the sake of it.

> **!!!** As a rule, do not use more than one unusual or difficult word in a sentence. That way, if your readers are unfamiliar with a word, they may well be able to follow your meaning from the other words.

Write in the appropriate form of English

The different forms of English are described on pages 9–15. Make sure that you use a form of English that is appropriate to the document. Most documents will be written in Standard English, and this may sometimes call for a less informal style than you would use naturally.

Your writing style needs to be flexible enough to cope with the different sorts of document you have to write. This often means being aware of the elements of informal language and being able to eliminate them when you are creating a formal document. For example:

➤ Replace *lots* and *lots of* with *many* or *much*.

➤ Replace *sort of* and *kind of* with *rather* or *somewhat*.

➤ Use *as* instead of *like* as a conjunction in phrases such as *as I said …*

➤ Avoid colloquial contractions such as *haven't* and *won't* – use *have not* and *will not* instead.

Search for the right word for the occasion

Sometimes you will have the opportunity to use a range of words, all of which have a broadly similar meaning. Although the words you can choose may be similar, they are not necessarily completely interchangeable. A good writer will search for the word that is exactly right for the situation.

Some words have a particular nuance, derived either from their history or their usage, which marks them apart from words with a similar meaning. If you write about a launching a *crusade* against crime, you are suggesting that you are motivated by an almost religious impulse – like the crusaders of the Middle Ages. The word *crusade* creates a slightly different impression on the reader than other words that might be used, such as *initiative* or *campaign*.

The choice of word in any situation may be influenced by a number of factors:

➤ Does the word fit in well with the other words in the sentence?

➤ Does the word contribute to the effect you wish to have on your readers?

➤ Who are you writing for, and what is their relationship to you? Are they in authority, or is it an informal relationship?

➤ What do your readers already know about the subject?

➤ Will your readers understand and appreciate simple or more complicated vocabulary?

Eliminate unnecessary words

Watch out for words that do not contribute anything to the meaning of a sentence. You may be able to simplify your writing by removing unnecessary words and phrases, or by using one word instead of several.

Many clichéd phrases can be written in simpler terms:

PHRASE	SIMPLE FORM
and also	and
as to whether	whether
the reason is because	the reason is
because of the fact that	because
by virtue of the fact that	because
due to the fact that	because
in the event that	if
at this moment in time	now
in this day and age	now
on a daily basis	daily
with a view to	to
is located	is

Similarly, certain expressions often add nothing to the meaning of a sentence. It is usually desirable to eliminate the following phrases if the sentence can stand up without them:

> when all is said and done
>
> when it comes down to it
>
> in actual fact
>
> as a matter of fact
>
> in point of fact
>
> at the end of the day
>
> not to put too fine a point on it
>
> to all intents and purposes
>
> in a very real sense
>
> basically
>
> actually

Words such as *really, very, quite* and *extremely* are also often redundant. The American writer Mark Twain had the following advice for authors:

*'Substitute "damn" every time you're inclined to write "very";
your editor will delete it and your writing will be just as it
should be.'*

Another common fault is to say the same thing twice in the same
sentence. The highlighted words in the following sentences could and
should be eliminated, because the idea they express is already present:

*Let's continue **on** to the next village.*

*Finally, I would like say **in conclusion** that this an excellent film.*

In the first example, the word *continue* means that *on* is redundant; in
the second, the word *finally* means that *in conclusion* is redundant.

!!!   Don't use *again* after a word that begins with the
prefix *re-*. The idea of repetition is already present in the
prefix, and so *again* is redundant.

Strive to express yourself clearly

Your readers should not have to work too hard to interpret your
writing. Keep the following points in mind:

- Don't let your desire to show off your vocabulary get in the
  way of getting your meaning across. Your readers will not
  thank you for producing flowery prose sprinkled with
  unfamiliar words (*He averred that he was not able to
  apprehend the import of the epistle.*) when you could have
  used simple words instead (*He said that he was not able to
  understand the meaning of the letter.*).

- However, your readers *will* thank you for using a precise word
  rather than a meaningless general word. Follow the advice on
  avoiding overused words on pages 262–4.

- Many English words have several different meanings, and so
  careless writing can easily lead to misunderstanding. Look at
  the tips for avoiding ambiguity on page 187.

- Avoid complicated sentence structures. If a sentence runs to
  more than 30 words it can probably be split up into two
  shorter sentences.

➤ Longer sentences are easier to read if you use conjunctions such as *neither ... nor ...* or *not only ... but also ...* to impose a clear structure and indicate the train of thought.

➤ Life is much easier for your readers if you follow the basic rules of spelling and grammar explained on pages 23–92.

Be consistent

Remember that consistency is one of the 'five Cs' of good writing. If your writing is consistent, then your readers will know where they stand, and it will be easier for them to follow your message.

Consistency can take a number of forms:

➤ Be consistent in **reference**. Take care to present information in a consistent way throughout your document. Where there is a choice of ways of presenting something, decide on a policy and stick to it. (See pages 112–25 for suggestions about presenting information.) This gives your readers the feeling that you are in command of the situation.

➤ Be consistent in **argument**. Maintain the same approach to your subject throughout the document. Don't waver between opposing points of view or change your mind part-way through.

➤ Be consistent in **tone**. The way you write will often reveal the way you think about your subject. For example, you may write in an ironic way, a detached way or an enthusiastic way. Whatever tone you adopt, use it throughout the document.

➤ Be consistent in **register**. Use the same style of English throughout. Don't move between formal and informal language unless you are doing this to create a special effect.

There should be a single personality behind the writing, and being consistent allows your readers to become familiar with that personality.

Be aware of contentious points

Your aim should be to establish and keep up a good relationship with your readers. You want them to trust you and listen to your message. Often you want them to be persuaded by your argument or act in accordance with your request or recommendation.

The last thing that you want to do is to ruin this relationship by writing in a way that irritates or offends your readers. You therefore need to be aware of contentious subjects and develop a writing style that can deal with them.

Things that might irritate or offend your readers include:

- ➤ disputed points of grammar (see the tips on pages 84–92)
- ➤ incorrect spelling (see the tips on pages 44–6)
- ➤ incorrect use of easily confused words (see pages 142–70)
- ➤ controversial words (see pages 171–8)
- ➤ clichés (see pages 192–3)
- ➤ words that might be considered as taboo or offensive
- ➤ insensitive language (see pages 194–200)

Your aim should be to write in a style that puts your readers at ease, and does not distract them from the content of the document.

Keeping the Reader Interested

Getting your message across clearly is your first duty as a writer. Your second duty is to make what you say interesting to your readers. As you become more confident in your writing ability, you can start to think about using words more creatively and expressively.

Of course, there are many times when you do not need to worry too much about this. You may be working under the pressure of a tight deadline, or you may be producing a purely factual document. In such cases the creative use of language is not a priority. However, on other occasions – if you are preparing a talk, trying to influence people's opinions or trying to sell something – it may be important to write in a lively and entertaining style.

In this chapter we shall look at a number of techniques for making your writing more lively:

> variety of vocabulary

> variety of sentence structure

> patterns of sound

> figures of speech

> idioms

> examples

> analogies

> humour

Variety of vocabulary

Avoid using the same word repeatedly if there are useful alternatives available. If you find that you are using the same word over and over again, a thesaurus may suggest other words that you could use.

Some English words tend to be used excessively because they are very familiar and because they can be applied in many different circumstances. However, using easy, familiar words can lead to dull and repetitive writing. There are often alternative words that provide your readers with more precise information and give your writing more colour.

For example, the word *good* expresses general approval, but does not give the reader any idea of your grounds for this approval:

*a **good** question*

*a **good** solution*

Your reader may thank you if you use a word that expresses your point more precisely:

*a **pertinent** question* (good because it is relevant)

*a **penetrating** question* (good because it gets to the heart of the matter)

*a **workable** solution* (good because of practical value)

*an **ingenious** solution* (good because of the cleverness involved)

Similarly, the word *big* expresses greater than usual size, but does not give much indication of how much greater than usual the size is, or what impression this size creates:

*a **big** house*

*a **big** animal*

You can give your reader a clearer idea by using a more precise word:

*a **palatial** house* (big and grand)

*a **rambling** house* (big, but without clear organization)

*a **gigantic** animal* (unnaturally big)

*a **bloated** animal* (unhealthily big)

These are by no means the only words that are commonly overused. The list below includes some of the most overworked words in English. Before you use any of these words, stop to consider whether there is a more accurate or expressive alternative:

good	*nice*	*get*
bad	*happy*	*say*
big	*sad*	*very*
small	*go*	*thing*

easy	*fast*	*walk*
hard	*slow*	*run*

Variety of sentence structure

The different types of structure that can be used to construct a sentence are explained on pages 224–32. Good writers will constantly try out different combinations of clauses, reduce the sentence from two clauses to one, break up a sentence into two shorter ones and so on, until they are happy that the sentence is right. Some structures sound neater than others, so be aware of the possibilities.

Your aim should be to avoid repeated use of the same patterns:

> ➤ Don't always begin sentences in the same way (for example, with a main clause starting with the subject and verb).

> ➤ Don't repeat the same pronoun at the start of more than two successive sentences (*He entered ... He looked ... He ran ...*).

> ➤ Avoid excessive use of the conjunction *and* to join clauses. It is a simple tool for constructing a sentence which can quickly become tedious.

➡ See the advice on pages 272–3 on how to make use of different types of sentence structure to emphasize your point.

Patterns of sound

Paying attention to the patterns of sound created by words can make your writing more striking and effective.

The **soft consonants** *b, f, l, m, s* and *w* tend to express tranquillity. A description of a peaceful scene can be enhanced by using words that contain these sounds:

> *The murmur of lawnmowers emanated from a leafy village.*

In contrast, the **hard consonants** *c, k, p* and *t* tend to express vigour or harshness. A description of anger or violence can be enhanced by using words that contain these sounds:

There was a cacophonous crack as the car backfired.

Some particular sound techniques that you can use to make your writing more lively are:

- ➤ onomatopoeia
- ➤ alliteration
- ➤ assonance

Onomatopoeia involves the use of words that mimic the sound of the thing they describe. Thus, if you say that a ball *whizzed* past your ear, you are not only describing the speed of the ball, but you are providing your own sound effect as well. Other onomatopoeic words include *fizz*, *boo*, *hiss* and *squelch*.

Alliteration is the repetition of a consonant at the beginning of two or more words:

a fit of fiery fury

Assonance is the repetition of vowel sounds in words that are close together:

Twinkle, twinkle, little star.

Figures of speech

A figure of speech is a device that uses words in unexpected combinations to create a striking effect. Some of the more commonly encountered figures of speech are:

- ➤ similes
- ➤ metaphors
- ➤ allusion
- ➤ personification

A **simile** involves making a comparison between two unlike things, introduced by words such as *like* or *as*:

*She eyed the food **like a hungry lion**.*

*He was trembling **like a leaf**.*

For a simile to be truly effective it should be both **original** and **appropriate**. Many similes are so familiar that they have become clichés; the reader is not surprised by them and is not forced to think about the comparison that is being made:

as mad as a hatter

as long as your arm

as clean as a whistle

A **metaphor** involves using a word or phrase to describe something that it does not literally apply to. This unusual use of the word has the effect of making a comparison, although – unlike a simile – a metaphor does not use words such as *like* or *as*:

*Annie **sailed** into the room.*

In this example, the writer does not mean the reader to think that Annie literally travelled into the room in a ship, but that her progress was smooth and impressive, like a ship's.

If you use two metaphors in the same sentence, the result can be a **mixed metaphor** – a combination that creates an illogical or ludicrous image. This is often regarded as a sign of bad writing:

There are concrete steps in the pipeline.

An **allusion** involves using a form of words that makes the reader think of a particular person, object or event:

Never in the field of interior design have I seen anything like it.

These are probably the best sandwiches in the world.

In the first example, the words *never in the field* are an allusion to a famous wartime speech made by Winston Churchill (*Never in the field of human conflict ...*); in the second example, the phrase *probably the best* might put the reader in mind of a certain brand of lager.

Personification involves attributing human qualities to inanimate objects or abstract ideas:

The computer won't be happy if you don't log out properly.

Fear stalks the corridors of the building.

In the first example, the computer is pictured as being capable of human emotions such as happiness; in the second example, fear is pictured as a person moving threateningly about a building.

> ➡️ Some more unusual figures of speech are explained and illustrated on pages 378–80.

Idioms

An idiom is an expression with a meaning that cannot be understood from the usual meanings of the words that form it. Using an idiom can add colour to your writing:

> *She said that the directors were **fiddling while Rome burned**.*
>
> *Serge is one of those people who have **a finger in every pie**.*

However, because idioms are usually informal phrases, they can be out of place in more formal situations. Moreover, two idioms in the same sentence can create an illogical or ludicrous image, just like a mixed metaphor:

> *I've got a **few irons in the fire**, but I'm **keeping them close to my chest** for the time being.*

Examples

One way of making an explanation more lively is by adding examples to illustrate the point:

> *Even the most sought-after locations can became mundane to the people who live in them. For example, when visitors descend upon Cape Cod in the summer, many of the local residents go to Maine, New Hampshire or Vermont to avoid the crowds.*

Examples can also be an effective way of clarifying an explanation:

> *The date is recorded in a YYYYMMDD format and it represents the date when the document was created or finalized. 20 December 2004, for example, would be recorded as '20041220'.*

Analogies

An analogy is a comparison between one thing another. Analogies can be useful to writers as they allow unfamiliar things to be compared with familiar things:

Your lymphatic system can be compared to a motorway. When it is congested, nothing moves.

However, you should beware of pushing analogies too far. The analogy between the lymphatic system and a motorway is a useful general statement, but if you were to go on to look for elements in the lymphatic system that correspond to service stations, lane markers and the like, you might well end up making far-fetched statements that undermine the usefulness of the original analogy.

Humour

Humour can be used as a device for engaging your readers' attention. People who make public speeches often begin with a joke in order to win over the audience, and humour can have a similar role in writing, serving to 'sugar the pill' and make your message more palatable.

Some sources of humour that can be effective are:

> lively anecdotes – especially as introductions to an explanation

> apt quotations from well-known humorists

> gentle asides, in which you insert a personal remark or commentary into an account

Although the idea of using humour to enliven your writing can seem an attractive one, there are potential dangers:

> Don't make jokes at your readers' expense. If someone has to be the butt of the joke, it is better that it should be you.

> Topical allusions can quickly become dated. They may have lost their relevance by the time the document is read.

> Jokes can undermine a serious message.

> Humour is a very personal thing. What appeals to you may not appeal to your readers.

Getting the Point Home

When we speak to one another, only part of the message is communicated by the words themselves. We supplement our words by making hand gestures or by adopting certain facial expressions or body postures. We also pass on information by the *way* we speak, sometimes slowing down or pausing, sometimes talking more loudly, sometimes altering the tone of voice. All of these devices help to make our meaning clear to the person listening. They indicate which parts of what we say are particularly important and suggest what our attitude is and how the other person is expected to react.

These devices are not available to us when we write. That does not mean, however, that we cannot still give emphasis to important ideas. It just means that we have to use different strategies to get our point home. These strategies include:

- selecting vocabulary that reinforces your message
- using emphasizing words in sentences
- inserting 'signposting' language to guide your readers
- varying the way in which sentences are structured
- using punctuation to help get your meaning across
- choosing appropriate fonts, typefaces and page layouts

In this chapter we shall look at each of these points in turn.

Loaded vocabulary

Some words are more powerful than others, and come loaded with a particular association or tone that suggests either approval or disapproval. For example, the word *horse* is a fairly neutral word, but you can also refer to this animal as a *steed* (which suggests a magnificent specimen) or a *nag* (which suggests something that has seen better days).

Sometimes – for example, if you are writing the minutes of meeting – it important to use words that are neutral and do not carry overtones either of approval or disapproval:

*He is a reporter for the local **newspaper**.*

*The government **discontinued** the scheme.*

At other times – for example, if you are trying to influence another person's impression of a situation – it may be appropriate to use a more loaded word:

*He is a reporter for the local **rag**.*

*The government **ditched** the scheme.*

> ➡ If you are searching for the word with the right associations to express your feelings, you may find it useful to consult a thesaurus. See pages 131–2.

The choice of adjectives and adverbs plays a particularly large part in indicating approval or disapproval. A passage without descriptive adjectives and adverbs is likely to be neutral in tone:

The management has floated the idea of introducing performance-related pay. This idea appeals to some employees. However, others have expressed a desire to remain outside the scheme.

However, the addition of adjectives and adverbs can make it clear how you feel about someone or something. They can give an approving tone to a passage:

*The management has floated the **imaginative** idea of introducing performance-related pay. This **innovative** idea appeals to some **enlightened** employees. However, others have **inexplicably** expressed a **stubborn** desire to remain outside the scheme.*

A different choice of adjectives and adverbs might create a disapproving tone:

*The management has floated the **absurd** idea of introducing performance-related pay. This **bone-headed** idea **actually** appeals to some **misguided** employees. However, others have expressed a **perfectly reasonable** desire to remain outside the scheme.*

Emphasizing words

You can emphasize an important word in a sentence by adding certain adjectives, adverbs and pronouns.

Emphasizing adjectives, such as *absolute, complete, entire, sheer, total* and *utter* can be added to a sentence to stress a particular word:

> *The batch had to be scrapped.* (neutral)
>
> *The **entire** batch had to be scrapped.* (more emphatic)

Another way of adding emphasis is by using adverbs such as *absolutely, categorically, completely, entirely, thoroughly* and *utterly*:

> *He denied that there had been any wrongdoing.* (neutral)
>
> *He **categorically** denied that there had been any wrongdoing.* (more emphatic)

Emphatic pronouns, such as *myself, yourself, itself*, etc, can also be used to add emphasis:

> *The government approved the closure.* (neutral)
>
> *The government **itself** approved the closure.* (more emphatic)

Signposting language

On page 253, we discussed how linking words and phrases could be used as 'signposts' to keep your readers aware of how far you have progressed through an argument and where the argument is headed next.

You can also put these 'signposts' into the text when you want your readers to pay particular attention or to think about something in a particular way. They provide you with an opportunity to interrupt the flow of the language and add a personal comment or opinion. This can often be done in the introductory part of a sentence:

> ***This leads me to the irrefutable conclusion that*** *costs must be cut.*

You can also insert signposting language in the form of a parenthesis, using dashes or brackets to mark it off from the rest of the text:

> *The project has been – **and I cannot stress this point enough** – an unmitigated disaster.*

Emphatic sentence structures

The words in a sentence tend to fall naturally in the pattern *subject – verb – object*. However, you can often engage your readers' attention or focus on a particular word or idea by changing the natural word order. There are various ways of doing this.

You can emphasize a key word by making it the first word of the sentence. For example, a natural sentence structure might be:

She would not eat fish.

But if you want to emphasize the word *fish*, you can rework the sentence so that the key word comes first:

***Fish** was one thing that she would not eat.*

You can also emphasize a particular point by **repetition**. For example, a natural sentence structure might be:

I looked in the kitchen, the study and the dining room.

But if you want to emphasize the act of looking, you can rework the sentence so that the idea is repeated:

***I looked** in the kitchen, **I looked** in the study and **I looked** in the dining room.*

You can also use the form of a **question** – even though your readers are not in a position to supply a verbal reply to you – to make them take notice. For example, a natural sentence structure might be:

This did not discourage people from buying it.

But if you want to present this information in a more dramatic fashion, you can turn the statement into a question (and supply the answer yourself if necessary):

Did this discourage people from buying it? Not at all!

Another effective way of making a point is by **denying the opposite** of the sentence. For example, a natural sentence structure might be:

He was very unfit.

But if you want to present this information in a more interesting fashion, you can turn the sentence around, changing it from positive to negative:

He was certainly no athlete.

Many common idioms make use of this technique:

She is no spring chicken.

These guys are not exactly rocket scientists.

> **!!!** All these devices will lose their effectiveness if they are used too much, but if you use them sparingly, they can be very effective in helping you to get your point across.

Emphatic punctuation

The basic uses of punctuation have been described on pages 93–111. However, you can sometimes use punctuation in slightly more creative ways – especially in informal writing. The exclamation mark, quotation marks, capital letters and hyphens can all be used to highlight and emphasize words or sentences.

In formal writing, the **exclamation mark** is used sparingly to show that you feel strongly about something:

Nobody even bothered to look at it!

In informal writing you can use exclamation marks more freely, and you can even use more than one exclamation mark to indicate extreme emotion:

Finally!!!

Sometimes in informal writing you can combine an exclamation mark with a question mark:

Is this the best you can do?!

Sometimes an exclamation mark may be enclosed in brackets when the writer wants to draw the reader's attention to a particular word or detail:

He enjoys listening to heavy metal music (!) and has a worryingly large record collection.

You can also use **quotation marks** to show emphasis. You can put these around a word or phrase to show that it is being used in special way, when in speech you would pronounce it using a different tone of voice. This might happen when you are being humorous or facetious:

> *We had a few 'wee drams' at Victor's house.*

Or it might be that you want to show that you disagree with or question the use of a particular word or phrase:

> *What he calls a 'regional variation' is in fact a completely different language.*

> *The band have split as a result of 'musical differences'.*

Another way of drawing attention to a particular word is by using **capital letters**.

Writing a word or words in capital letters is usually the equivalent of announcing something in a loud voice, or of shouting at people to attract their attention:

> *This comes in a choice of three colours with FREE accessories!*

(This use of capital letters can be effective in advertising flyers or for promotional material, book covers and public signs.)

A further way of drawing attention to a word is to use **hyphens** to separate the individual letters. This is especially done to represent emphatic modes of speech:

> *Please speak v-e-r-y s-l-o-w-l-y.*

> *Of course I'm feeling c-c-c-c-c-cold!*

> **!!!** Even more so than with emphatic sentence structures, these devices will lose their effectiveness if they are used too much. However, they can be effective if used sparingly.

Typography

When writing is performed using pen and paper, there are only a few forms of presentation you can use for emphasis – you can use underlining and capital letters, but that is about all. However, when you use a computer, there are many other devices available to you. When you create a word-processed document, you can help to get your point across by considering:

➤ size of type
➤ typefaces
➤ fonts
➤ page layout

Size of type

The larger the size of type you use, the more you draw attention to the information contained in it. Very large type is used on posters and newspaper headlines, whereas legal and financial agreements are notorious for using small print to hide information from the reader.

You should think not only about what size of type you want to use for the main part of your document, but also about whether it is appropriate to use different sizes of type for different parts of the document. For example, you may decide to use a larger size of type for headings, or a smaller size of type for footnotes.

Typefaces

Word processors allow you to create text not only in the normal or 'roman' form, but also using **bold**, <u>underlined</u> and *italic* typefaces. You can use these options to highlight important words in the text.

Italic type is usually the preferred way of showing emphasis in normal text. It is also traditionally used to indicate certain special types of information (see pages 123–5).

Bold type is generally used for headings and letterheads. It can also be used to highlight individual words and phrases within a body of text, especially within a stretch of text that is already in italics:

275

> *October was originally the **eighth** month.*

Underlined text is used less frequently in word-processed documents. However, it can be used in the same way as bold type to emphasize a word or phrase within a stretch of italic text:

> *October was originally the <u>eighth</u> month.*

If you are using a typewriter rather than a word processor, you do not have the option of bold or italic typefaces, so underlined text is used for emphasis and to indicate special types of information.

Fonts

Word processors and desktop-publishing packages include a wide array of different fonts. Changing the font you use can give a document a very different look and create a very different impression on your readers. Here are a few examples of different fonts:

Book Antiqua

Arial

Georgia

Courier

Impact

Verdana

Fonts can be divided into **serif fonts** and **sans serif fonts**. In the list above, Book Antiqua, Georgia and Courier are serif fonts: they use small projections called 'serifs' at the ends of letters. Fonts that use serifs are usually easier to read, and it is preferable to use this sort of font for longer documents.

Font that do not use serifs, such as Century Gothic, Impact and Verdana, are known as sans serif fonts. Sans serif fonts are often considered cleaner and more modern-looking. These can create a striking impression, but they are usually best avoided for longer documents.

The font you decide to use will probably depend on the impression you wish to create:

Using a serif font, such as Courier, will help you to create a serious tone for reports.

Using a sans serif font, such as Comic Sans, will give your writing an informal tone for personal letters and e-mails.

Using a highly decorative font, such as Monotype Corsiva, may enhance a flyer or an invitation.

Page layout

Word processing also allows you to customize the layout of your page to create the effect you want. You should think about how you can use the following features to create a look that is both attractive and also in keeping with the message you are trying to communicate:

- ➤ What size and typeface do you want to use for headings? Headings need to be large enough to stand out from the surrounding text. You may choose to use different styles for different levels of heading to show that some are more important than others.
- ➤ What width of margins do you want? Using wider margins creates a narrower column of text and means that fewer words can fit onto each line.
- ➤ Do you want the text to be 'justified' (so that the margins are straight)? Having straight margins tends to give a more formal, authoritative look to a document, whereas a 'ragged' right-hand margin can make it appear more informal and accessible.
- ➤ Do you want the text to be single-spaced or double-spaced? Double-spaced text gives more room for readers to write comments on, and so may be required for some documents, such as essays or reports.
- ➤ Do you want to use different colours?
- ➤ Do you want to use graphical features such as borders, tables and bullet points to highlight certain types of information?

Part Three

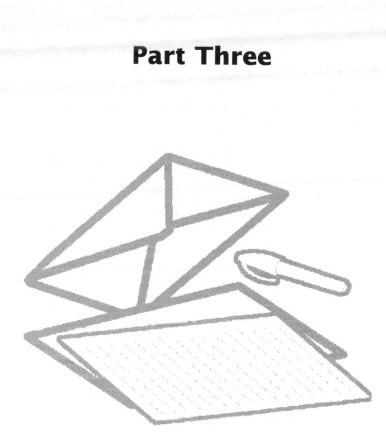

Writing in
the Real World

In the final part of the book, we look at applying the knowledge and skills you have acquired when you are **writing in the real world**.

We look at applying writing skills to various forms of personal communication, such as **e-mail and letters**, and at the standard ways of setting these out.

We then look at the various kinds of documents you might be called upon to write, whether you are **writing in the business world**, creating **academic writing** as part of an educational course or **writing for the Internet**. We look at the standard components of each type of document and at the conventional ways of setting them out, providing you with models to follow when you create your own documents.

Writing can also be an important tool for promoting a message, and so we look at **writing to attract attention** when you create documents such as newsletters or CVs.

Finally, we look at two very different and rather specialized forms of writing: **technical writing** and **creative writing**.

Whatever you write, you will be drawing on the 'tool kit' of information about language outlined in Part One of this book, and applying the general principles of good writing discussed in Part Two, but you will be need to work within the set of rules and conventions for the particular type of document.

Letters, E-mails and Texts

Public documents and personal communication

A piece of writing may be directed at a specific reader, or at readers in general. Novels, newspaper articles and advertisements are examples of public documents aimed at readers in general rather than a specific person. Letters, e-mails and text messages, on the other hand, are forms of personal communication. They are written with a specific person in mind, and so their contents are likely to be influenced by the writer's knowledge of the reader.

Later chapters in this part of the book will consider the various types of documents that you may write for readers in general. But firstly we shall look at personal communication.

Forms of personal communication

Anyone writing a book of this kind fifteen or twenty years ago would be concerned with only one type of personal communication: the letter. However, a lot has changed. As wireless communication technology has developed, people can now communicate 'in real time' from more or less anywhere in the world by sending e-mails and text messages.

In view of the ease and speed of new forms of communication, it is not surprising that people now spend less time writing letters and more time on the telephone or at the computer. The idea of writing anything more than a shopping list or a postcard by hand has come to seem less and less attractive.

Why write letters?

Although it is no longer the fastest or necessarily the most convenient way of communicating, there are still many occasions when writing a letter is preferable to using the telephone or sending an e-mail or text message. There are various reasons why this might be:

> Sometimes information needs to be exchanged so that everyone who is involved in something understands exactly what is being discussed or agreed upon.

> There are still some people – albeit fewer and fewer every year – who do not have access to e-mail and text messages, and a letter may be the only way of sending a written message to them.

> Sometimes the time and effort spent writing a letter is an expression of the personal relationship you have with someone.

The first of these reasons generally relates to formal letters and business letters, and the second and third relate to personal letters. These two kinds of letter tend to be written in different styles.

Two ways of setting out a letter

There are two common ways of setting out a letter:

> **Blocked** or **fully blocked layout** is a style that is recommended for formal letters and business letters.

> **Indented layout** is a style that can be used for more informal letters.

Blocked layout (for formal letters)

If you are writing to your local councillor or MP, to a potential employer or to the customer service department of a company when you want to ask for information or make a complaint, you should use **blocked layout**. An example of this layout is shown on page 283.

In a fully blocked letter:

> All paragraphs and headings are set against the left-hand margin, except for the top part of the letter, which is set on the right-hand side of the page, although it is still aligned to the left.

> The top part of the letter contains the address of the sender, usually together with the date.

> Below this is included the address of the recipient.

> Each new line and each new paragraph is set against the margin of the page, rather than being moved in slightly or 'indented'.

25 Julian Way
Broomloan
GLASGOW
G99 0ZZ

31st December 2004

The Manager
Glasgow and Scottish Bank plc
300 Great Scott Street
GLASGOW
G09 1YY

Dear Sir

Account No. 01234567 J D Haddington

This is to confirm my telephone call to the branch this morning asking that you stop payment of a cheque issued by me in favour of Breakneck Builders Ltd. It is cheque number 145678, written for the sum of £895.50 and dated 21st December 2004.

Breakneck Builders have informed me that they have not received the cheque, and I have therefore concluded that it has been lost in the post.

I would be grateful if you would confirm that the original cheque has been stopped, so that I may issue a new one.

Yours faithfully

James D Haddington

James D Haddington

➤ At least one line of clear space is inserted between each paragraph, and between every other separate element of the letter.

➤ In keeping with modern English usage, a more 'minimal' style of punctuation is adopted, so there are no commas in the address, in the date or in the opening and closing lines of the letter.

➤ Full stops are not generally used for abbreviations.

Indented layout (for informal letters)

For more informal letters, including those that are handwritten, the format most widely used is known as **indented** or **semi-blocked**. An example of this layout is shown on page 285.

In an indented letter:

➤ The sender's address is placed to the right, as in a fully blocked letter, but you do not generally include the recipient's address.

➤ The opening and closing lines of the letter are set against the left hand margin, but all other first lines are usually indented.

➤ Because the indenting shows where paragraphs begin and end, there are not usually clear lines between paragraphs. However, you can also include clear lines if you wish.

➤ Commas can be included in the date and after the opening and close if you wish.

➤ Full stops can be used for abbreviations if you wish.

Standard parts of a letter

A formal letter contains six standard parts:

➤ address
➤ other contact details
➤ date
➤ greeting
➤ main part of the letter
➤ ending

25 Laburnum Road,
ABERDEEN
AB6 6FW

Saturday, 17th April

Dear Anne,

I was delighted to get your long letter yesterday. I hadn't expected to hear from you so soon after your removal, as I'd been thinking you'd be much too busy arranging your new home and settling the children into their new school.

I'm so glad that all your lovely furniture survived the move intact, and that nothing is missing. I hope you have nice neighbours and that Tom and Chloe make friends quickly. Of course they will miss their old school friends for a while but they have so many hobbies and interests I'm sure they will soon belong to as many clubs as they did here, and that all their spare time will be occupied with interesting activities.

We all miss you, and I especially miss our daily chats. We must arrange to visit each other later in the year, perhaps in the school holidays. I'm sure you will want to come back to Scotland for the New Year, and of course you must stay with us.

I'm sorry to hear that your mother isn't very well. I'm sending her a 'get well' card, which I hope will cheer her up.

I'll phone you sometime next week.

Love,
Deirdre

The address

When you write the address:

> Include the separate elements of the address on separate lines.

➤ It is permissible to abbreviate words such as *Road* and *Street* to *Rd* and *St* even in formal letters.

➤ Add the post code in capitals on a separate line at the end.

➤ No commas are needed to mark the separate parts of the address in formal letters.

Other contact details

After the address you may wish to include your telephone number and other contact details:

➤ Make it clear to the reader what the number refers to by writing *Tel* or *Phone* in front of it.

➤ You might also include a mobile phone number on a separate line. Indicate that this is not a land phone by writing *Mobile* in front of it.

➤ Indicate an extension number by the letters *Ext*.

➤ Place your regional code in brackets, or put a dash between the regional code and your personal number.

➤ You may also wish to give your e-mail address (*E-mail:*), fax number (*Fax:*) and website address (*Web:*).

The date

For formal letters, write the month in words and the year in full, without using a suffix (*-th*) for the number of the day, and without using commas:

13 October 2004

For informal letters, you might prefer to include the day and miss out the year, and you can include a comma if you wish:

Monday, 27th January

Monday 27 January

The greeting

The beginning of a letter, where you 'speak' directly to the recipient of the letter, is formally called the **salutation**. There are various forms of words that are used:

➤ If you can, address the person by name (*Dear Dr Steadman*).

➤ If you do not know the name of the person or are not confident about the correct style of address, use *Dear Sir*, *Dear Madam* or *Dear Sir/Madam*.

➤ Remember that people can be sensitive about having their name given incorrectly. You want to avoid getting off to a bad start, so take care to get the name and style of address correct. Watch out for unorthodox spellings and for people who are styled *Dr*, *Lord*, *Lady*, etc rather than *Mr* or *Ms*.

➤ There are certain formal ways of addressing members of the aristocracy, the judiciary, the armed forces, religious groups and other people in authority. It is worth checking the correct form of address if you want to make a good impression.

➤ In more informal letters, you might prefer a salutation such as *My dear Joe* or *Dearest Mary*.

➤ In American English, full stops are more commonly used after abbreviations such *Mr* and *Ms*.

The main part of the letter

The aim of a letter is to communicate effectively. As with any piece of writing, think about what you are trying to achieve and what is the best way to achieve your aims:

➤ Make sure that your letter has a clear and coherent structure so that the reader has no problem in understanding any information and knows what action, if any, is required or expected.

➤ Think about the tone you wish to create. Do you want to appear impersonal and businesslike, or is a more familiar tone called for? Think about the advice on writing style on pages 255–61.

➤ Being formal is not the same as being long-winded or pompous. There is no need to write long complex sentences for the sake of it. Aim for a direct, easy-to-read style that uses the five Cs (Correct, Consistent, Clear, Complete, Concise).

➤ Create an uncluttered, more open feel to your writing by using punctuation only to avoid ambiguity or to allow the reader to pause in a long sentence.

The ending

The ending of a letter, where you 'sign off' is known as the **complimentary close**. The wording of the salutation at the beginning of the letter determines the wording of the complimentary close:

> *Dear Sir, Dear Madam* or *Dear Sir/Madam* is followed by *Yours faithfully.*

> If you mention the person by name (*Dear Janice* or *Dear Dr Steadman*), you use *Yours sincerely* for formal letters.

> In formal letters, no commas are needed after the complimentary close.

> In more informal letters, you might prefer a complimentary close such as *Regards, Best wishes, Yours* or *Kind regards.*

> In American English, the complimentary closes used are different from those used in British English. After *Dear Sir/Madam*, use *Sincerely yours, Truly yours* or *Respectfully yours*; after greeting the person by name, use *Yours sincerely, Sincerely yours, Yours truly* or *Truly yours.*

Creating a good impression

Formal letters should be written on A4 paper, usually a single sheet of good quality white paper: 90 grams per square metre is nice and heavy, but 80 grams per square metre feels a bit thin. For formal letters, only write on one side of the paper.

For informal letters, you can use a smaller size of paper if you wish, and you have more scope for expressing your personality through using coloured paper or writing on notelets.

Create a good impression by keeping the paper clean and using a matching envelope. It also helps if you can achieve a good balance between the size of your paper and the amount you write, and you can do this by spreading out whatever you write, however little, so that it always fills the page:

> Divide information logically into clearly identifiable paragraphs, even if these are only one sentence long.

> If your letter is very brief, try using two clear lines rather than one between paragraphs, and balance the space at the top with the space at the bottom.

➤ If your letter is long and takes more than a single sheet of paper, make sure that it is spaced well, so that the first sheet does not look cramped leaving only a few lines spilling over onto the second sheet.

Different types of formal letter

Formal letters tend to fall into a fairly small number of categories. We are going to look at some typical examples of each to show how they are laid out and give you an idea of what you might include in a letter of:

➤ application

➤ complaint

➤ apology

➤ request

➤ sympathy or condolence

> ➡ See also the advice on pages 320–8 concerning writing business letters.

Letters of application

A letter in which you apply for a job should be written with care. First impressions count, and your letter is the only thing that a potential employer has on which to base his or her impression of you.

The person who reads your letter will probably have read hundreds of other letters over the months or years, so it is worth taking a bit of time to try and get things right. As with any other formal letter, put your information across clearly and concisely, using correct, consistent language and making sure you include all the necessary information. At the same time, try to include some memorable or interesting detail in order to attract the reader's attention and provide something to talk about at a later stage.

Unless a job advertisement specifically asks for the application to be handwritten, send a printed letter with a signature at the bottom.

The letters on pages 291–3 show three examples of letters of application:

> a letter applying for a specific job, without a CV (*CV* is short for *curriculum vitae*, although it might also called a *résumé* in American English)

> a letter applying for a specific job, with a CV

> an unsolicited or 'spec' letter with a CV (It is unlikely that you would want to send a 'spec' letter without a CV.)

Letters of application without a CV

If you are sending a letter without a CV, you need to make sure that your letter is complete and includes all the relevant details, including:

> your home address

> your telephone number (or numbers)

> your e-mail address, if appropriate

> a clear and prominent indication of which job you are applying for

> where you heard about the job or saw it advertised

> your age (if relevant)

> your education and training

> your present job, or details of any voluntary or other work you are currently involved in, including job seeking

> any other experience, qualifications or interests that might be relevant or make you an attractive applicant

> the names and addresses of two or three referees, or a mention of any letters of recommendation that you are enclosing.

Covering letters accompanying a CV

Job advertisements often ask applicants to send a CV and a covering letter as the first stage of an application. It is also common for people to write speculative or 'spec' letters asking about whether or not work is available and offering their details to be kept on record if work does become available. Either way, because your CV will include all your personal details and your work history, you do not need to repeat all this information in the letter that you send.

Begin your covering letter with a short paragraph saying where you saw the job advertised, and mentioning that you are enclosing your CV. If

Flat 1
64 Plockenden Road
Islington
LONDON
N1 0ZZ
Tel: 01234 567 8910

Alexander Maxwell
Personnel Manager
Kingsway Shopping Centre
Walford
LONDON
N2 0ZZ

12th October 2004

Dear Mr Maxwell

Shopping Centre Supervisor

I am writing in response to your advertisement in this week's 'Retail News' for a shopping centre supervisor.

I am twenty years old, and have just completed a year's training in business studies at Thames College. I left school last summer with 5 GCSEs and two A Levels (English and Maths). During holidays and at weekends I have worked in a clothes shop as a sales assistant, and also in a newsagent's, where I was often left in charge. I am keen to follow a career in the retail industry, and think this post will give me the responsibility I am looking for.

Should you consider me suitable for the post, I can provide the names of three referees.

I look forward to hearing from you, and should you wish to, please do not hesitate to contact me at home at the above number.

Yours sincerely

Jonathan Lee

Jonathan Lee

200 Bairdmore Blvd
WINNIPEG
Manitoba
R3T 5HZ
September 16 2004

Ms A Dalrymple
Chief Analyst
Longthorn Investments
490 Akron Road
VANCOUVER
British Columbia
S4J 2NP

Dear Ms Dalrymple

Financial Analyst

I should like to apply for the above post which was advertised in today's Financial Post, and I enclose my current résumé for your attention.

I am an experienced financial analyst, consultant and presenter, having worked extensively in this sector both in Toronto and New York. I am currently looking for a position that will allow me to develop my skills and experience in a small, dynamic commercial team such as Longthorn Investments. I believe that my financial and academic background would be of benefit to your strategic financial planning and the building of partnerships with investment houses throughout North America and the Far East.

Thank you for considering this application. I look forward to discussing matters further with you at a future interview.

Sincerely yours

Robert Jones

Robert Jones
Financial Investment Analyst

45 Forest Way
CARDIFF
CA3 0NN

Tel: 1234 567 8910

L Hamilton
Personnel Officer
Globetech (UK) Ltd
75 Enderley Street
SWANSEA
SA1 0ZZ

15th July 2004

Dear Mr Hamilton

I wish to enquire about any vacancy you may have in your
Sales Department. Your customer services manager, Dewi
Griffiths, who belongs to a sports club of which I am also a
member, suggested I write to you. He tells me that your firm
is expanding, and will therefore be recruiting new people in
the very near future.

As you will see from the enclosed CV, I have a good
educational background and twelve years' experience in
sales, both as a sales representative and sales executive.

My present employers, Clearview International, are closing
their Cardiff factory at the end of August and I am to be
made redundant at that time. I am anxious not to remain
without work for long, and am willing to consider any
suitable post that becomes available.

If you consider my application favourably, I should be
pleased to attend an interview at any time.

Yours sincerely

William Preston

William Preston

you are writing a 'spec' letter, say what prompted you to write. Perhaps you have some connection with the company or with someone who works for it that will enhance your application.

In the next paragraph, draw attention to any parts of your CV that might be particularly relevant, and show how these make you a suitable candidate for employment. You may need to go into more detail than on the CV, and tailor your remarks to the specific requirements of the employer.

Finish with a short paragraph saying when you are available for interview.

Although the covering letter should be brief, its aim is to generate interest in the reader and ultimately an interview. Here are some useful points to remember:

- If you are replying to an advertisement, unless it asks for a handwritten letter, it is best to print it and then sign it by hand.

- Your application will look more professional if you use the same paper size, font and font size as you have used for your CV.

- Remember to include your home address, your telephone number and the date.

- Make sure you get the name and title of the person you are writing to correct. If you do not know who to contact, make an effort to find out, as a name is always better than *Dear Sir/Madam*.

➡️ Advice on how to present your CV is given on pages 363–5.

Letters of complaint

Avoid writing a letter to complain about something while you are too angry or upset to express yourself reasonably and clearly. If you use a letter as a way of letting off steam, then letting off steam could well be all that you achieve. If you want to receive something more tangible – such as compensation or an apology – it is worth taking a more measured approach. Here are some suggestions that might prove helpful:

- Make sure that you have all the relevant facts so you can quote prices, names, times, addresses and dates. This shows the reader that you are in control of the situation, and also helps your complaint to be dealt with more efficiently. If necessary, be prepared to quote any relevant pieces of consumer law.

➤ Make sure to include your contact details.

➤ Give your letter a heading. This should include any product details such as the order number, product number or model, together with the reference number of your receipt or invoice if you have it.

➤ Give details of the problem, stating that you are dissatisfied, and saying why. Then state clearly what you would like to be done about it, if necessary giving a date by which you would like matters to be resolved. Finally, refer to any further action you intend to take if your letter does not receive a satisfactory reply.

➤ Keep copies of all the letters you send and make a note of all the telephone calls you make, including times, dates, how long they lasted and who you spoke to. If you are making a claim of any kind, you may need documentary evidence if the claim is contested.

The following phrases are useful when making complaints:

I wish to draw your attention to ...

I wish to complain about ...

I wish to express my dissatisfaction regarding ...

We have identified the following defects ...

The service we were offered was unsatisfactory in the following ways ...

Under the terms of your guarantee ...

We were led to believe that ...

I look forward to hearing from you.

I look forward to receiving your written reply within the next seven days.

I look forward to your suggestions as to how the situation can be put right ...

I would be interested in any comments you might wish to make ...

If we are still not satisfied ...

---

7 Morningside Drive
EDINBURGH
EH9 4AY

The Customer Services Manager
Whitegoods plc
Lowburn Industrial Park
EDINBURGH
EH39 1GG

4th August 2004

Dear Sir or Madam

Kleanquik Automatic Washing Machine. Model number 9337.

I purchased the above model of washing machine from your Wallace Street store on 15th July 2004. It was delivered and installed by your service engineer on 19th July 2004.

On 30th July 2004, only eleven days after the machine was installed, it developed a serious fault, causing water to flood out of the front of the machine. I immediately telephoned the store and informed them of this. They advised me that an engineer would call on Tuesday 3rd August at 11 a.m. I waited at home for the whole of 3rd August, but no engineer called. I have telephoned the store repeatedly and each time was informed that someone would call me back. No one did.

I must therefore insist that you inform me in writing of your proposals to remedy this situation by providing me in the first instance with a firm date and time when your engineer will call. While I am prepared to give you a further opportunity to honour your guarantee and the terms of the service agreement that exists between us, I reserve my right to claim compensation for the inconvenience already caused to me and to reject the goods as unsatisfactory under the terms of the Sale of Goods Act 1979.

Yours faithfully

Jane Pearson

Jane Pearson (Mrs)

Letters making requests or arrangements

Making requests, making arrangements and confirming arrangements need not take long, but it is important to get the details right. Some points to bear in mind are:

> ➤ Make sure you refer to the reason for writing as early as possible in order to alert the reader, either using a heading or in your opening sentence.

> ➤ Mention if you are responding to an advertisement or recommendation.

> ➤ Be as specific as you can about what you are asking for or agreeing to so that there can be no misunderstanding.

> ➤ Include details of any special or unusual requirements you might have, so that arrangements can be made well in advance.

Novatel plc
56 Hill Place, London SE4 8WT
Tel: 020 7485 7896 Fax: 020 7475 8383
e-mail: admin@novatel.co.uk

Ms Emiko Nakamura, Training Manager   12 May 2004
Novatel Japan
1-22-7 Shimada Mansions
Setagaya-ku, Tokyo 155
Japan

Dear Ms Nakamura

Novatel 'Year 2004' conferrence

As discussed, I am enclosing the schedule for the 'Year 2004' conference which will be held here in London from 22-26 July this year. Could you please send me the names of the participants from your offices who will be attending, so that we can confirm hotel and local transport arrangements.

I look forward to hearing from you soon.

Yours sincerely

Ailsa Macauley
Ailsa Macauley
Organizer

---

7 Adelaide Street
BOSTON
Mrs F McLeod   MA 06743
Harkers Lodge   June 20 2004
HIGH RIVER
Alberta
A4G 7MX

Dear Mrs McLeod

This is to confirm the telephone booking I made on the
evening of June 18 2004.

My wife and I require a double room on the first floor
from September 16 to 19 inclusive; the room to have en
suite bathroom with shower. The all-inclusive price for
bed and breakfast for three nights, with dinner on the
evening of September 17, will be $375.00 as agreed.

I enclose my check for $85.00 as deposit.

Sincerely yours

Alan Nixon

Alan Nixon
enc

Letters of sympathy and condolence

Formal letters always have an element of distance, and when someone
is taken ill or dies it is always difficult to know what to say. However, it
is better to say something rather than nothing, and to feel embarrassed
saying it rather than feeling awkward for not saying it. A simple and
spontaneous acknowledgement of what has happened will almost
always be appreciated by those who are closely involved, whereas
avoiding the issue can make things worse for them and for you. Here
are a few suggestions that might be helpful:

➤ Messages of condolence are usually handwritten rather than
   typewritten.

> There is no need to include the address of the recipient.

> Even formal letters should mention the person by name

> Try to use simple, straightforward, everyday language rather than anything more formal, flowery or poetic.

> Be sensitive to the reader's faith and spiritual beliefs in the language you use.

---

405 Baird Drive
HOUSTON
Texas 0521

September 23 2004

Dear Mr Grosvenor

It was with deep sadness that I read of the sudden death of your business partner, Paul Cooper.
He will be greatly missed by the many clients who benefited from his professional advice over the years, and will be long remembered for the outstanding job he did on their behalf.
My staff join me in sending our sincere condolences and deepest sympathy to you and members of his family.

Yours sincerely

Arthur Jenkins

Jenkins and Paterson

Informal letters

When you write to friends and relatives, you can, of course, write anything you like, and will write in a more relaxed, conversational style than the one you use in formal situations. However, it is still a good idea to organize your writing into paragraphs, as a solid page of writing is more difficult for your reader to follow. The address and date do not need to be written out in full, but they can still record the time and place that a personal letter was written.

Unlike other letters, you can allow yourself to use a much more informal brand of language, including slang and colloquial words, and contracted forms.

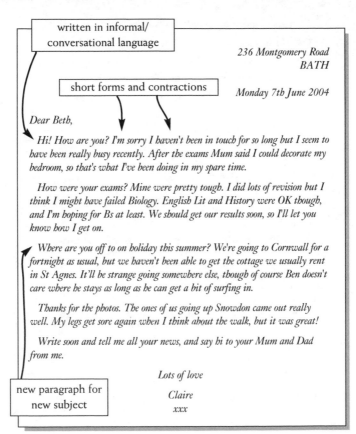

written in informal/
conversational language

short forms and contractions

new paragraph for
new subject

236 Montgomery Road
BATH

Monday 7th June 2004

Dear Beth,

 Hi! How are you? I'm sorry I haven't been in touch for so long but I seem to have been really busy recently. After the exams Mum said I could decorate my bedroom, so that's what I've been doing in my spare time.

 How were your exams? Mine were pretty tough. I did lots of revision but I think I might have failed Biology. English Lit and History were OK though, and I'm hoping for Bs at least. We should get our results soon, so I'll let you know how I get on.

 Where are you off to on holiday this summer? We're going to Cornwall for a fortnight as usual, but we haven't been able to get the cottage we usually rent in St Agnes. It'll be strange going somewhere else, though of course Ben doesn't care where he stays as long as he can get a bit of surfing in.

 Thanks for the photos. The ones of us going up Snowdon came out really well. My legs get sore again when I think about the walk, but it was great!

 Write soon and tell me all your news, and say hi to your Mum and Dad from me.

Lots of love

Claire

xxx

E-mail

It is now common to use **electronic mail** (usually called **e-mail** or **email**) instead of letters as a means of personal communication, although for some more formal types of communication, a letter is still more appropriate.

Whether you use e-mail or traditional letters (now often referred to as 'snail mail'), your aims are the same. You still need to think about presenting information clearly, so that the recipient gets the message and knows what is required. You also need to use language sensitively and strike an appropriate tone, so that you do not cause any unintentional offence.

However, because e-mail is rapid and informal, and is always created using a computer keyboard, it has come to differ from the traditional letter in a few respects. Some aspects of e-mail communication deserve special discussion:

> ➤ addresses
> ➤ headings
> ➤ writing style
> ➤ use of abbreviations and symbols

Addresses

An e-mail address is nearly always in lower-case lettering, with no spaces and its separate elements separated by full stops, referred to as dots. Sometimes the use of spaces is avoided by using underscores:

raj@fishtank.co.uk

marketing_dept@christmas.org

E-mail addresses are generally **case-sensitive**, which means that upper-case letters and lower-case letters are regarded as different characters, so you need to check this carefully before sending a message. In practice, nearly all e-mail addresses use lower-case letters throughout. Those e-mail addresses that do include upper-case letters in proper names have come to seem a bit 'fussy' and old-fashioned.

Headings

In order to send an e-mail, you need to state **the address of the recipient** and **your own address** (this is usually generated automatically). These addresses are written in the heading at the top of an e-mail.

The headings for e-mails are based on the heading of a traditional memo (see page 317). In addition to the addresses of the recipient and sender, you can also include other information in the heading:

> ➤ It is customary to include a **subject heading**, indicating what your message is about. If you are replying to a previous e-mail, your mail tool will create the subject heading using *Re:* and the name of the previous e-mail.

➤ You can type in the addresses of other people to whom you wish to **copy** the e-mail. An address written in the line called *Cc: (carbon copy)* will be displayed at the top of the e-mail as a recipient of the message; an address written in the line called *Bcc: (blind carbon copy)* will be sent a copy of the message without being displayed at the top as a recipient.

➤ The heading is also the place where you can add **attachments**, other files that wish to include as part of the message. You might include formal documents as attachments, with the e-mail itself acting as a cover note.

Writing style for e-mail messages

Because it can be sent quickly and casually, e-mail correspondence tends to be fairly informal in style. An e-mail is more like a note than a formal letter, which takes time to be composed, written, posted and delivered.

Some people use lower-case letters almost exclusively when writing e-mail. The logic for this lies in the quick and casual nature of e-mail, mentioned above, which militates against the unnecessary extra effort required to hold down the shift key to create capitals. The principle of reducing unnecessary effort can also lead in other directions:

➤ E-mail tends to use a lot of abbreviations and acronyms, some of which are listed below.

➤ Writers of e-mail are often less fussy about correcting of spelling mistakes when keying at high speed.

➤ Writing words in capital letters is the equivalent of shouting, and is generally frowned upon unless you are using it to express anger.

➤ There is less use of apostrophes and more subtle punctuation. Colons and semicolons are often replaced by dashes.

➤ Because all the information that is necessary to send, receive and reply to e-mails is included in the headings, salutations and complimentary closes are not required. However, many people like to start messages with a greeting of some sort, even if it is only *hi* or the first name of the person the message is being sent to.

> **!!!** Before you get too relaxed about spelling and use of lower-case letters, it is worth remembering that, although e-mail is more informal than letter writing, you should still be sensitive to what is and is not appropriate, especially with people you do not know or if you are e-mailing as a representative of an organization. In addition, you still need to be clear about what you are saying: inconsistent or incorrect language can be open to misinterpretation.

Using abbreviations in e-mail

It is customary to use many abbreviations in informal e-mail. These often take the form of a common expression being represented only by the initial letters of the words. Many of these are now use routinely, although it is a good idea to make sure the people you send messages to are familiar with these before you start to include them in your messages.

Here are some of the more common abbreviations encountered in e-mail:

ABBREVIATION	MEANING
AFAIK	as far as I know
ASAP	as soon as possible
ATB	all the best
BFN	bye for now
BTDT	been there done that
BTW	by the way
GAL	get a life
HTH	hope this helps
IMHO	in my humble opinion
IMO	in my opinion
IOW	in other words
LOL	laughing out loud (when someone has written something funny)
MYOB	mind your own business
OMG	Oh my God!
TVM	thanks very much

Another convention used by e-mailers is the use of **emoticons** (also called **smileys**). These are combinations of characters – mainly punctuation marks – which are used to show facial expressions and emotions:

EMOTICON	MEANING
:-)	*happy*
:-(	*sad*
;-)	*winking*
:-o	*shocked*

Using emoticons can help to express your mood to the person you are e-mailing. However, some people might not appreciate the use of such devices, and you are advised against using emoticons unless you know a person well.

Texting

An even more modern form of communication is the text message. Text messaging has certain similarities to e-mail in its speed and directness, but it also has some differences, due to the fact that text messages are sent by mobile phone rather than by computer:

➤ Unlike e-mail, capital letters are used as standard.

➤ The number of characters that can be included in a single message is limited (usually to 140 or 160).

➤ It is normal not to use punctuation.

Because of these limitations, text messages have developed their own style:

➤ Conventional grammar and spelling are largely irrelevant.

➤ Words are shortened in order to reduce the number of characters, with a single letter or number often used to replace a whole word or syllable.

➤ Certain conventional abbreviations have now become orthodox in text messages. For example, typing *TX* instead of *THX* when you mean *thanks* would immediately show you up as a novice, and might not be properly understood.

The language of texting

The most common way to abbreviate words when texting is to omit vowels, as in the following cases:

ABBREVIATION	MEANING
CD	*could*
FWD	*forward*
LV	*love*
MSG	*message*
PLS	*please*
PPL	*people*
SPK	*speak*
THX	*thanks*
TXT	*text*
WD	*would*
WKND	*weekend*
XLNT	*excellent*
YR	*your*

Letters are often used to stand for whole words, or syllables that sound like the letter, as in the following cases:

ABBREVIATION	MEANING
B	*be*
CU	*see you*
LO	*hello*
NE	*any*
RUOK?	*are you okay?*
XTRA	*extra*
Y	*why*

Numbers are often used to stand for syllables that sound like them, as in the following cases:

ABBREVIATION	MEANING
NO1	*no one*
SUM1	*someone*

1CE	*once*
WAN2	*want to*
2DAY	*today*
2NITE	*tonight*
B4	*before*
4EVER	*forever*
GR8	*great*
L8R	*later*
W8	*wait*

Colloquial shortenings and phonetic spellings are also used:

ABBREVIATION	MEANING
COZ	*because*
CUM	*come*
DA	*the*
LUV	*love*
RITE	*right*
SOZ	*sorry*
THRU	*through*
W/O	*without*
WOT	*what*

Some words of warning

E-mail and texting have given rise to new varieties of language, and these are valid ways of communicating. However, remember that two characteristics that mark out effective language users are:

> - the ability to adapt language use to a wide range of situations
> - the ability to tell what is and is not appropriate for any given situation

Although the extremely informal type of language described above might be appropriate for e-mails and texts, this does not mean that it is appropriate for letters, memos or anything else.

Writing in Business

Being professional

Every time you write anything to anyone, you are not just sending information, but you are also sending messages about yourself, your personality, your values, the way you relate to people and how well you write. If this is important in your personal dealings, it is also important in business, where you represent an organization or institution whose reputation may depend on the image you present.

This means that using English confidently and effectively not only makes communication easier, but also makes you and your organization look confident and effective. In other words, it makes you look professional.

Types of business document

In this chapter we shall look at the different kinds of business documents that you might be required to read or write. These may include:

> reports

> memos

> agendas

> minutes

> letters

Reports

A report is a document that presents information based on some kind of research or investigation. Whether it is a single page long or several hundred pages, a good report needs to be well researched, carefully planned, clearly laid out and written in a fluent and persuasive style, in accordance with the principles set out in Part Two of this book.

The process that ends with a finished report is likely to involve a number of stages, during which the report is planned, written and improved:

> the request for a report, or the decision to write one

> research, and collecting information

➤ selecting relevant and appropriate information

➤ organizing information into an order or structure

➤ the first draft

➤ redrafting and reorganizing

➤ writing a summary, if one is going to be included

➤ the final draft

The structure of a formal report

A formal report has a fairly standard structure, and below we shall look at its parts one by one, then show an example of a short formal report. However, you should bear in mind that you may be expected to follow your own organization's 'house style' in preference to the structure shown here. In addition, it might not be necessary to include all of the parts in exactly the order shown here every time you write a report, especially in the case of shorter or less formal reports.

The structure of a typical formal report might consist of:

➤ title page

➤ contents

➤ summary

➤ glossary

➤ terms of reference

➤ procedure

➤ findings

➤ conclusions

➤ recommendations

➤ appendices

➤ bibliography

Title page

The **title page** should include the title of the report, and usually also shows the names of its authors. It is also common to include the date on which the report was completed or submitted.

If you have not been given a title, choose a suitable title yourself. The people who read the report will usually appreciate a title that gives a clear indication of what it is about rather than a title that is cryptic or humorous. If you do want to use a clever or striking phrase for the title, it is a good idea to supplement this with a subtitle that clarifies the topic of the report:

Driving the Future: Transport Investment and Urban Planning

Contents

On the **contents** page the reader should be able to see a complete list of all the headings and subheadings that appear in the report, displayed in order and clearly numbered. This gives a view of the report's overall structure and makes individual sections easy to find, as not everyone will want to read the report in full.

Summary

It is usual to include a **summary** only as part of a long report. Its purpose is to describe briefly what the report set out to achieve and focus the reader's attention on the main conclusions and recommendations. Because it sums up the whole report, it is usually one of the last parts to be written. It can offer an overall view of the report and also help a reader to decide whether or not to read the whole report, which means it might be the only part that many people ever read. To do the report justice and help the reader, the summary needs to be accurate, clear and concise.

Sometimes a report will require an **executive summary**. This is a slightly longer document (usually one or two pages long), designed to provide a person who does not have time to read the full report with enough information to make a decision about its subject. An executive summary should cover the same ground as a standard summary, but be capable of being understood as an independent document without referring to the full report.

Glossary

A **glossary** is an alphabetical list that explains any abbreviations or technical terms that the reader might not be familiar with. You only need to include a glossary if the report is likely to be read by people who will be unfamiliar with such language. If you think that your report may require a glossary, make a note of the terms that need to be explained as you write the report. This will save you from having to go back through the report later to find them all.

Terms of reference

A formal report will often begin with a statement of the report's **terms of reference**. This is a brief statement setting out:

> - the issue that is being addressed (the purpose of the report)
> - how wide-ranging the report is (its scope and its limitations)
> - the instructions that were given to the writer (why the report was written, and who asked for it to be written, when they asked and when it was completed or presented)

Procedure

The **procedure** section can be used to explain what methods were used to gather information, where it was obtained, how much research was carried out and how long the process took. Sources of information that you list or describe in this way might include:

> - interviews
> - meetings
> - reference material (books, newspapers, magazines, journals, websites)
> - observation
> - visits
> - questionnaires and surveys
> - scientific measurements or experiments

In a short report, there will be no need for a summary, and the terms of reference and the procedure might even be described together in a single section – sometimes even a single paragraph – in the form of an introduction. The important thing is to make sure that the relevant information is clearly given somewhere at the beginning, however briefly.

Findings

The **findings** constitute the main part of the report. In this section, you set out under headings and subheadings all the information that has been gathered, together with any analysis of this information. The findings do not generally include the opinions of the writer.

It is usual to set out the findings in numbered paragraphs that identify clearly the sections and subsections into which the information has been divided:

1.	Spending on road-building schemes
1.1.	Public funding
1.2.	Private funding
2.	Road-building schemes in European cities
2.1.	France
2.1.1.	Paris
2.1.2.	Lyon
2.1.3.	Marseille
2.2.	Germany
2.2.1.	Berlin
2.2.2.	Hamburg

The example above is probably the most common format, and is the most straightforward to organize. In this, the headings for the various sections and subsections (and sub-subsections!) are identified by a system of numbering. It is possible to use other numbering systems. For example, you could use a combination of numbers, letters and lower-case roman numerals for the different levels of heading:

1) Spending on road-building schemes
   a) Public funding
   b) Private funding
2) Road-building schemes in European cities
   a) France
      i) Paris
      ii) Lyon
      iii) Marseille
   b) Germany
      i) Berlin
      ii) Hamburg

However you set out your findings, the most important thing is that the different levels of information are 'embedded' one inside the other, and that each section is numbered clearly and consistently. It is usual to begin the numbering from the very beginning of the report, so that the heading of the first section – whether it is a summary or an introduction – will begin with '1'.

The findings should flow smoothly. If from time to time you want to step back and make a brief comment on the information in the findings, you are advised to use footnotes or appendices so that the flow is not interrupted.

Footnotes are short comments that can be added either at the foot of a page or at the end of a section of text. Each footnote should be referred to in the main text by a symbol or number so that the reader is aware of its existence.

Conclusions

The **conclusions** of a report should state the significant results that have emerged from the findings. There should be no new material included here, and the conclusions should seem to follow logically from the information you have presented and the points you have previously raised.

Note that the conclusions of a report are rather different from the conclusion of an essay (see page 338–9). In a report you only provide essential information, so there is no need for the conclusions section to provide a summary of what has gone before or to make a personal judgement, as you might at the end of an essay. Indeed, if no significant points have emerged from the report, there is no need to include conclusions at all.

Recommendations

The **recommendations** of a report state what action should be taken. You may wish to list specific actions, or you may recommend that no action be taken or say that more investigation is necessary before a decision can be made. Your recommendations should follow logically from your conclusions, which should in turn be based on your findings.

Again, there should be no new material included here. However, this would be the place to deal with any objections or criticisms that might be raised. The best way to do this is to state what the objections are and then to answer them.

In a short report, the conclusions and the recommendations may be combined into a single section with a title such as *Concluding Remarks* or *Conclusions and Recommendations*.

Appendices

The **appendices** (or **appendix** if there is only one) contain material that supports the case being made but is too long, complex or distracting to be included in the body of the text. (Remember that the findings should be easy to follow, with a clear and logical structure, which should not be broken up by lengthy digressions.)

Appendices might include tables, graphs, diagrams, plans, photographs, maps or long extracts from other documents. It is common to have different types of information included as separate appendices, clearly labelled as *appendix A, appendix B* and so on. You should indicate the presence of any appendices to the reader by putting a reference to each one in the relevant part of the findings:

> *The figures for the southern region (table 5, appendix A) show that promotional events can have a significant effect on sales.*

References to appendices in the main text allow the readers who are interested in the detailed information to go to the appendices, but other readers to continue reading the findings without being distracted.

Bibliography

The **bibliography** or **references** section of a report should contain an alphabetical list of all the sources of information you have used. Different types of source are usually listed separately – for example, books and personal interviews would form two separate lists in the references.

> The standard format for setting out bibliographical information is shown on pages 342–3.

Language for report writing

The principles of good writing – the 'five Cs' – should stand you in
good stead for writing reports, as in most other types of document.
Although reports and other official documents require formal language,
you should not try to use excessively pompous language as a way of
making what you are writing seem more important than it really is. Let
the contents speak for themselves.

However, there are some points that apply specifically to report writing:

> ➤ Make sure that the first time you use any acronym or technical
> term that might be unfamiliar to your readers, you define it for
> them. If necessary, also include a glossary.

> ➤ Presenting the findings and the recommendations clearly is more
> important than imposing your own personality on the report. It is
> usually considered appropriate to avoid the first person and to
> use the passive voice, for example by writing *Mark Dawes was
> asked to ...* rather than *I asked Mark Dawes to ...*

> ➤ Use reported speech to summarize people's words rather than
> quoting people directly: *respondents to the survey said that ...*

Layout of reports

Because reports can be long documents with many different parts, it is
important that the information is presented in a clear and attractive way:

> ➤ Use bullet points or numbered lists rather than cramming a lot
> of items into densely worded sentences or paragraphs.

> ➤ Label any tables or diagrams clearly and simply (*table 6,
> section 3, paragraph 3.2.3* or *diagram 5*) without capital
> letters or full stops.

> ➤ Use only one font throughout, and try to vary the size of type
> as little as possible. Use either bold or underlined text for
> headings, but not both.

> ➤ To ensure consistency, it is a good idea to keep a 'style list' of
> issues that affect your layout, for example how your headings
> and subheadings are organized and presented, how you list
> items and how you cross-refer to other parts of the report.

> ➤ The overall look of the report should be simple and clear, with
> plenty of white space. Even if this makes it longer, it will be

easier to read (and easier to write!) and will create a better impression.

An example of a short formal report is shown below:

To: Julie Oliver, Managing Director
From: Alexander White, Training Manager
Date: 16 September 2004
Subject: Provison of in-house training courses

1. Introduction

The purpose of this report is to examine the feasibility of holding all training courses in house. External training providers were consulted, estimates of training costs were received and comparative costs examined. Questionnaires were completed by 80 employees from four departments and 10 of the respondents were interviewed by members of the training department.

2. Advantages

2.1 Following consultation with four of the company's regularly used external training providers, it was calculated that in-house training would reduce the present cost by 26% in the first year (see Appendix A).

2.2 It was felt by 65% of the staff that training courses could be better designed to suit the specific needs of the organization, and therefore bring benefit to the company as a whole.

2.3 45% of those who responded to the questionnaire felt that they were more likely to participate in training courses if they were held on site.

3. Disadvantages

3.1 Some respondents, particularly in the sales department, expressed concern that valuable business contacts arising from external training courses would be lost if all training was held in house.

3.2 Some training needs are very specific, and may only be required by one or two staff members. It was felt that these could not always be met by in-house training courses, as the necessary expertise could not always be brought in from outside.

3.3 Participation in external training courses is seen by 30% of respondents as a perk of the job, and it was felt that this motivational factor would be diminished with the provision of all training in house.

4. Conclusions

As a result of the analysis of the advantages and disadvantages of providing all training in-house, the following conclusions can be drawn:

- Considerable savings will be made in the immediate future if in-house training courses are introduced.

- The staff response is favourable overall, particularly at higher levels of management, although in some departments the loss of external training courses is seen to be a real disadvantage, with the loss of business contacts.

- While many employees feel that in-house training is a positive move and is likely to increase participation, 30% regarded it as a loss of a perk.

5. Recommendations

- In-house training courses should be introduced where a significant number of participants are required to attend.

- Where there are fewer than five participants, external courses should be an option.

- Staff should be consulted regularly as to the level of satisfaction with in-house training courses, and feedback regarding motivational factors should be addressed.

Memos

A **memo** (short for **memorandum**) is a short message sent between employees or colleagues within an organization, either in a particular building or between different places. Some business organizations have their own standard printed memos. In modern practice, the paper memo has largely been replaced by e-mail (see pages 300–4).

Like e-mail, a memo can be formal or informal depending on the relationship between the sender and the receiver, but however a memo is written, it is important that information is clearly expressed. It is also useful to remember that a memo is an official business communication, however informal, and on whatever subject, and that a copy might therefore need to be kept 'for the record'.

A memo generally has a number of items of information printed at the top, for example:

> ➤ name of the recipient
> ➤ name of the sender, often including a telephone number or extension
> ➤ department of the sender
> ➤ reference number (if the organization records memos using serial numbers or a similar cataloguing system)
> ➤ date
> ➤ names of anyone else who is to get a copy of this memo (the letters *cc*, standing for *carbon copy* are used to indicate this)
> ➤ subject (the word *re*, which is Latin for 'on the subject of' is used to indicate this

Although a memo is a kind of letter, it does not have a salutation (*Dear Anne*), nor a complimentary close (*Yours sincerely*). As with business letters, if an enclosure is sent with a memo, *enc* or *encs* should be added at the end, usually aligned with the text against the left-hand margin.

Agendas

An **agenda** is a list of the subjects that are going to be discussed at a meeting, set out in the order in which they are to be dealt with. Copies are usually sent out in advance to all those who might attend the meeting so that they can prepare themselves, for example by getting hold of any information they might need to bring along to the meeting.

An agenda should identify itself by stating clearly the nature of the meeting or naming the group, committee or organization that is holding the meeting. It should also include details of the date, time and venue of the meeting.

Although a single agenda will not necessarily include all of the following items, the usual order is:

- ➤ appointment of a chairman or chairwoman (if one has not been appointed)
- ➤ apologies for absence (sent by those who are unable to attend)
- ➤ reading and approval of the minutes of the previous meeting
- ➤ matters arising (anything from these minutes that people want to comment on)
- ➤ correspondence received (usually by officials such as the secretary or treasurer)
- ➤ reports from officials
- ➤ reports from other committees or working parties
- ➤ items of business (subjects that have been included on the agenda so that they can be discussed at the meeting)
- ➤ AOB, or any other business (subjects that are not on the agenda, but that someone attending the meeting would like to discuss)
- ➤ the date, time and venue for the next meeting

If a subject is going to be raised and discussed at the meeting, the full wording of a motion (or subject that is being proposed for discussion) should be included as an item of business.

Agenda

Training Development Programme

Date : 17 July 2004

Place: Room 202

1. Apologies
2. Minutes of last meeting
3. Matters arising
4. Report on Sept-Feb training programme
5. Proposed changes
6. Final arrangements for April-Oct programme
7. AOB
8. Date of next meeting

Minutes

Minutes are the formal written record of a meeting. They summarize what happened, and who said what, including any disagreements and complaints. Minutes are usually written in the past tense, using simple, impersonal language, with reported speech used rather than direct speech (see page 113) and, unless it is important who did or said something, the passive voice used instead of the active voice (see page 228).

Minutes need to be concise. They should present only the essential parts and dispense with any unnecessary details. It is best to write them in short sentences and short paragraphs. They also need to be neutral, clear and complete, so that anyone who did not attend the meeting can follow the discussions that took place and understand how and why decisions were made.

Minutes follow a standard format, which usually includes:

> ➤ a heading that states the type of meeting or its purpose, the name of the organization or group holding the meeting, and the date, time and venue

> ➤ a record of who was present and a note of any apologies for absence

> ➤ a record of corrections to the previous minutes if any are made, together with a statement that the previous minutes were read and approved

> ➤ a summary of what happened at the meeting, including correspondence that was received, summaries of reports that were presented, opinions that were expressed and decisions that were made

> ➤ if required, 'action points' can be added to record who made decisions about steps that have been agreed, who is responsible for carrying these out and when they need to be completed

> ➤ the date, time and venue of the next meeting

Each individual point made in the minutes needs to be numbered so that it can be easily referred to at the next meeting. If a numbered section includes several points, these should each be numbered in the style *2.0, 2.1, 2.2*, etc.

For obvious reasons, minutes should be based on notes made during the meeting and written as soon as possible after the end of the meeting. Copies should be sent to those who were present, and to those who should have attended but were unable to. The minutes can then be read through by everyone and, hopefully, approved without any bother at the next meeting!

Minutes of meeting held on 7 July 2004

Present: Joanna McGarrigle, Marie Eagelton, Bob Newman, Ana Maria Tejos, Steve Vandersteen, Diane Moore, Richard Mills, Denis O'Leary

1. Apologies

Apologies were received from Jill Thornton and Will Pidgeon.

2. Minutes

The minutes of the meeting held on 16 June were approved and were accepted as a true record.

3. Matters arising

BN reported that the business graduates have been notified about the dates of the project presentations.

DM thanked the Human Resources Department for their reports, all of which have been received.

Still awaiting confirmation of the Wright Rooms for September seminars.

4. Reports

The reports were distributed. SV suggested that each should be summarized. The chair stated that in view of the absence of JT and WP, this should not be done at this meeting. Following discussion it was decided that this could be done informally outside the meeting if anyone needed information that was not included in the reports.

5. ...

Business letters

We have already discussed letter writing in general in the previous chapter of this book. However, letter writing is an important part of business, and there are a number of conventions that relate to formal business letters that do not apply to other kinds of letter.

Obviously, if you are writing to someone such as a colleague or a client whom you know well, you might be quite informal. As a rule, however, business letters are polite, fairly formal, and as short as possible. They are word-processed rather than hand-written, and are laid out in the style known as **fully blocked** (see pages 282–4). As well as being concise, you should also be complete, giving details of any relevant times, dates, prices, addresses, serial numbers, product specifications and the like.

As we mentioned at the beginning of this chapter, people will use your writing to make judgements about how professional you are. Because of this, you need to make sure that your written communication sends out a positive message about the organization you represent. A business letter should look professional, and be easy on the eye as well as easy to read.

However short it might be, your letter should be laid out so that it fills the sheet of paper you are using. This means that the main body of your letter should begin about halfway down the page, with plenty of space for your address, signature and the like above and below this. Many word processors have a 'full page view' option that shows you what your document looks like rather than what it says, and this is a useful way of checking and adjusting your layout.

The layout of business letters

The letter on page 322 is a standard business letter – although not every business letter will require all of the elements shown. Each of its component parts is numbered and explained below:

1. Business letters are usually written on headed notepaper, which has the organization's name, address and other contact details printed at the top. This is often printed in a special font and is known as the **letterhead**.

2. There might be a **reference**, probably including the initials of the person who signed the letter, and maybe the person who wrote it, along with other details about its location in a file somewhere. Sometimes the letter might give the company's own letter reference (*Our ref:*) and also that of the letter that is being replied to (*Your ref:*). If this information is not included here, it might be added after the signature.

3. Leave two line spaces before the date. Write the date without any punctuation, with the month expressed as a word, and the

Swallow Books

1.   Address of company office, etc

2.   Ref: GD/cj

3.   1 June 2004

4.   Brown Brothers plc
          3 John Street
          LONDON
          N18 0RH

5.   Attention: Mr M. Smith

6.   Dear Sirs

7.   **Guide to British Birds**

8.1   Thank you for your letter of 26 May asking for two
          advance copies of the *Guide to British Birds*.

8.2   As requested, I am sending you two copies of the book
          under separate cover so that you can circulate them among
          your staff in order that you may gauge their reaction to the
          book and judge its suitability for your requirements. I feel
          confident that you and your staff will find the *Guide* the
          most comprehensive and helpful work of its kind. The
          method of classification and the detailed indexes, in
          particular, make it very easy to consult.

8.3   If you have any questions or comments about the book,
          please do not hesitate to get in touch with us again.

9.   Yours faithfully

10.   George Davidson
          Editor

11.   cc JW, MGU

12.   Encs

day of the month as a cardinal number (12) rather than an ordinal number (12th).

4. The name and address of the person the letter is being sent to is included, separated by two line spaces. (The reference or references, the date and the address sometimes appear in a different order, but make sure that they are all included if they need to be there. Most organizations have a preferred way of laying out this information, and although it may vary from business to business, it should be consistent within a particular organization.)

5. If the letter is for the attention of a particular person who is not mentioned in the address, something such as *Attention, For the attention of*, or simply *FAO* is included here.

6. This is the **salutation** (see page 286). If you are replying to a letter that was signed *pp*, you should reply to the person who wrote the letter, not the person who signed it. Follow the salutation with a line space.

7. You might like to include a **subject heading** to make sure that your letter reaches the right person quickly, or to focus the reader's attention on what the letter is about. The simplest way of drawing attention to the subject heading is to use bold type for it, although you could underline instead, but do not do both. Leave another line space after this. (If this were not a business letter, or if you were trying to be less formal, you would probably say something like *I am writing to you about* ... in the letter itself instead of including a subject heading.)

8. This is the main part of the letter. Like most documents, a business letter consists of three parts: an introduction, a main body and a conclusion:

    8.1. The **introduction** is a single paragraph, perhaps even a single sentence. It states the subject or purpose of your letter, and acknowledges any previous letter that was sent by the person you are writing to by quoting its date.

    8.2. The **main body** has one or more paragraphs. This deals with the subject of your letter in as much detail as is necessary. If you are doing something such as giving a list, describing a sequence of events or providing other detailed information, use bullet points, numbered headings or subject headings to make the information clear to read and easy to understand.

8.3. The **conclusion** is a single paragraph, usually containing some expression of goodwill. For business letters, it is better to put something fairly formal, for example *I look forward to meeting you* rather than *Looking forward to meeting you.*

9. This is the **complimentary close** (see page 288). Leave plenty of space for the signature after this.

10. A printed version of the name of the **signatory** (the person who is signing the letter) is included at the bottom, together with his or her **designation** (job or position). If the letter is signed on behalf of the sender by someone else – for example, a secretary or personal assistant – this person will sign his or her own name rather than using the name of the official sender. The name printed on the letter will still be that of the official sender, with *pp* before it. The abbreviation *pp* is short for *per procurationem*, which is Latin for 'on behalf of'.

11. This line shows whether or not copies of the letter have been sent to other people. The abbreviation *cc* stands for 'carbon copy', which dates back to the time before photocopiers when carbon paper was used to create duplicates of a document. (If this were not a business letter, or if you were trying to be less formal, you would probably say something like *I am sending a copy of this letter to ...* in the letter itself.)

12. The last line indicates if there are any **enclosures** being sent with the letter. (If this were not a business letter, or if you were trying to be less formal, you would probably say something like *I am enclosing ...* in the letter itself.)

Types of business letter

Business letters tend to be written for very specific purposes. Providing goods or services involves a lot of routine correspondence, so business letters are generally brief and to the point, rather than being particularly chatty or friendly. Common reasons for writing a business letter include:

➤ placing an order

➤ acknowledging an order

Watts Office Supplies
88 Prince Edward Road
BRISTOL
BS4 0ZZ

Customer Service Manager
Middlemarch Diaries
6 Consort Way
TUNBRIDGE WELLS
Kent
TN1 6BG

5th October 2004

Dear Sir

2005 Diary Order

I refer to your letter of 30th September enclosing your
catalogue of diaries for 2005. I would like to place an order
for some of the products advertised.

I enclose a completed order form. I assume that the amount
payable will be subject to the usual trade discount. Please
advise if this is not the case. Please also advise of the
preferred method of payment.

I look forward to receiving your confirmation of my order,
and would be obliged if you would advise me in advance of
the planned delivery date, so that I can reorganize my stock
accordingly.

Since I want to display next year's diaries from early
November, I would be grateful if you would give this matter
your urgent attention.

Yours faithfully

Charlie Watts

C Watts
Chief Buyer

cc B Jones

Watts Office Supplies
88 Prince Edward Road
BRISTOL
BS4 0ZZ

D George
KELPACK Ltd
44-48 Westbrae Street
BIRMINGHAM
B11 0JJ

23rd October 2004

Dear Mr George

Payment of Invoice no BD767

Thank you for the prompt delivery of our order no.
C00145.

Please find enclosed a cheque for £327.50 in payment of
your invoice no. BD767 of 30 September 2004.

Yours sincerely

David Wallace

D Wallace
Buying Assistant

> asking for a reference before supplying goods

> replying to an invoice

> responding to a complaint

> promoting goods or services

As you will see from the examples above, the layout of business letters
might vary in some ways, but should follow the general format
described on pages 321–4.

Dealing with complaints

One of the most difficult types of business letter to write is one in response to a complaint from a client or customer. Letters dealing with complaints are not simple exchanges of information, but require tact and delicacy:

➤ No matter how rude or incoherent the complaint, it should be dealt with in a calm and courteous reply.

➤ Deal with complaints promptly, as any delay seems rude and can make the situation worse.

➤ Deal with each complaint on a personal basis rather than simply issuing a standard response.

➤ If the letter lists a number of complaints or raises a number of points, make sure that you deal with all of them, in a bulleted list if necessary.

➤ Apologize for any errors or delays.

➤ Admit it if you are in the wrong, and offer some gesture of goodwill if possible.

➤ If appropriate, thank the complainer for drawing the matter to your attention and giving you the opportunity to improve the service you offer.

➤ Complaints might be bad publicity for a business, but resolving a complaint successfully can mean good publicity.

The following phrases are useful in dealing with complaints:

I was concerned to learn that ...

I would like to apologize for any inconvenience this has caused.

I appreciate that this must be frustrating ...

... put things right at the earliest available opportunity

Thank you for your patience.

If you have any questions, please contact ...

I am pleased to be able to inform you that ...

Please find enclosed ... with our compliments.

JOHN CARPENTER & SONS
38 Cardiff Road
NEWPORT
NP1 9FF

Mrs A S Swinton
6 Eastrow Cottages
NEWPORT
NP3 4DD

6th August 2004

Dear Mrs Swinton

Thank you for your letter of 4th August in which you advised that one of the new locks which were fitted at your property recently by one of our joiners is not working satisfactorily.

I am very concerned that if there is any question of faulty workmanship or a defect with the lock itself that this should be put right at the earliest opportunity, and therefore suggest that I call round on Friday morning at 9am so that I can examine the lock personally and have any necessary repairs carried out immediately. You may be assured that, if the fault lies with us, any repair or replacement will be carried out at no additional cost to you.

Please telephone me directly if the suggested arrangement is not to your convenience.

Yours sincerely

Robert Carpenter

Robert Carpenter
Director

Some common business abbreviations

Because much business writing tends to refer to the same things and
be written for the same reasons, a large number of specialist
abbreviations and acronyms has grown up to save time and space.
These are widely understood in business, but remember that you may
need to explain yourself more fully when dealing with people who are
not familiar with business terminology.

ABBREVIATION	MEANING
a/c	account
ad val.	ad valorem (according to the value)
AGM	annual general meeting
APR	annual percentage rate
asap	as soon as possible
av.	average
b/d	banker's draft (banking)
bc.	blind copy (of a memo, letter)
bcc.	blind carbon copy
be, BE	bill of exchange
c.	circa (approximately)
C&F	cost and freight
cc	carbon copy (copies to)
CEO	Chief Executive Officer
CFO	Chief Financial Officer
chq	cheque
C/N	consignment note; cover note; credit note
c/o	care of; carried over; cash order
Co	company, county
COD	cash on delivery
DD	direct debit
del.	delivery; delivered
Dir	Director
D/N	debit note
E&OE	errors and omissions excepted
enc(s)	enclosure(s)
FAO, fao	for the attention of

ABBREVIATION	MEANING
Inc.	*incorporated*
inst	*of this month*
L/C	*letter of credit*
Ltd	*limited company*
mgr.	*manager*
NIS	*not in stock*
O/D	*overdraft*
ono	*or nearest offer*
OOS	*out of stock*
p.a.	*per annum (each year)*
p&p	*postage and packing*
PAYE	*pay as you earn*
PLC, plc	*public limited company*
p.o.	*postal order*
pp	*on behalf of (Latin per procurationem)*
Pres.	*president*
rcd	*received*
re	*with reference to*
rec.	*recommend*
Ref	*reference*
req(d)	*required*
retd	*retired*
sae	*stamped addressed envelope*
sase	*self-addressed stamped envelope*
SO	*standing order*
SOR	*sale or return*
viz	*namely*
VP	*Vice-president*

Some useful words for business writing

Many of the words you use in business writing will be technical terms, either relating to business generally (*consortium, conglomerate, debit, demerger*) or to your particular business sector. However, there are also many non-technical words that are widely used in business writing. The list below contains some of the most frequently used non-technical words in business English. A command of these words is important for writing business documents:

benchmark anything taken or used as a standard or point of reference: *The aim was to provide a benchmark for future research.*

compliance agreement; assent: *The plans are examined by the council for compliance with the Building Regulations.*

convergence meeting, coming together: *These points of convergence should not be allowed to disguise important differences in values and assumptions between the two positions.*

criterion a standard or principle on which to base a judgement: *Every book must satisfy the very strict criterion of selling at least 100,000 copies.*

enhance to improve or increase the value, quality or intensity of something (especially something already good): *There are a number of complex schemes to reduce borrowing costs or enhance income.*

implement to carry out, fulfil or perform: *a difficult idea to implement; implementing the latest regulations.*

incur to become liable for (debts etc): *You are likely to incur a variety of additional expenses by virtue of your move overseas.*

ongoing in progress, going on; continuing; current: *The meeting was part of an ongoing international programme.*

orientate to acquaint (oneself or someone) with one's position, or their position, relative to points known, or relative to the details of a situation: *Most new firms copy existing companies and orientate themselves towards existing markets.*

statutory required or prescribed by law or a rule: *A person who is subject to a statutory duty cannot discharge that duty by entrusting responsibility for its performance to someone else.*

Academic Writing

In this chapter we shall look at a type of writing that we can refer to as 'academic writing'. If you are a student, a professional writer or someone else who works in the field of science or education, you might well need to produce writing in this style.

Academic writing refers to the writing required in schools, colleges and universities to produce things such as:

- essays
- dissertations
- write-ups of experiments

Even if you are not involved in education, the qualities that mark out good academic writing are those that also make you an effective user of written English. These include:

- identifying and focusing on a particular issue or idea
- presenting an argument clearly and supporting it with relevant evidence
- remaining objective and neutral, whatever you are writing about
- being comfortable using a more formal variety of English

Essays

An essay is a piece of writing that sets out to analyse a particular situation or idea, or puts across a particular point of view, supported by evidence. Editorials in magazines or newspapers are often in the form of short essays, and feature articles might be in the form of longer essays.

A magazine feature or an essay often has to be written in a set number of words, and the ability to say everything you want to in the number of words allowed is one of the skills that marks a good essay writer.

Essay titles

An essay usually begins with a title. Titles come in one of two kinds:

> a title that allows you to choose a topic of your own, either completely freely, or from a limited range of options. In this case, make sure you choose something that interests you – this may sound obvious, but it is easier to write effectively about something when the subject motivates you to do the relevant work.

> a title that gives you specific instructions about what to deal with, and how to deal with it. In this case, make sure that you answer the question or deal with the issue effectively.

Answering the question

Essays take time and involve careful thought and planning. Begin by reading the title or question carefully in order to find out what it is that you are meant to be writing about – not just in terms of the subject matter, but also in terms of how to deal with it. It is important to do this before getting started on anything else, as it will give you a clear sense of direction from the outset.

Make sure you actually answer the question you are being asked, rather than another question that you happen to know more about or are more interested in. Answering the right question also involves being selective, so avoid just writing down everything you know about the topic in the hope that the relevant material will be in there somewhere.

Although essay-writing involves being careful and thorough, it need not be difficult. Essay titles are usually carefully written, and often contain a 'key verb' or 'key phrase' that suggests what is required and what your approach should be. In fact, essays can be separated into five categories, according to the key verb in the essay title:

> describing

> analysing

> comparing and contrasting

> arguing

> explaining

Describing

These essays are probably the most straightforward to deal with, as all you need to do is select and present relevant information in a logical order. Key verbs in the title will be:

> *state/describe/give an account of* – asking you to present a detailed, relevant description

> *outline/trace* – asking you to present the main features

> *summarize* – asking you to present briefly the main features

> *illustrate* – asking you to present the main features and give relevant examples

Analysing

These essays not only require relevant knowledge, but the ability to separate a topic into different parts and examine these parts individually. Key verbs in the title will be:

> *analyse/examine/investigate* – asking you to separate, define and look closely at the main features

> *assess/evaluate/say how far/say to what extent* – asking you to present your opinions or reactions, supported by evidence

> *define* – asking you to give a detailed explanation

> *explore* – asking you to look at the subject from different points of view

Comparing and contrasting

This requires a combination of fact and opinion, or opinion supported by evidence, and asks you to look at what you regard as the most important similarities and differences between two or more things. Usually, the differences are more striking or important than the similarities. If this is the case, deal with the similarities first in a single section then go on to examine the differences one by one.

Sometimes you can reach a conclusion about which option is preferable, on other occasions you might not. Either way, make it clear what you have decided.

Arguing

This kind of title often presents you with a controversial or extreme statement of some kind, for example *'All art is quite useless.' Discuss.* You can then either take a balanced view, weighing up the arguments for and against the statement, or else adopt a particular point of view that you argue forcefully.

Whichever of these approaches you decide on, it is important to show that you are aware of both sides of the issue and can deal with arguments against your own point of view.

Explaining

Like essays that ask you to describe or outline something, these essays require you to display your factual knowledge. Here however, in addition to showing your own understanding, you might also need to show what you know about the development of important or influential ideas or achievements in a particular field.

These titles tend to begin with an open question such as *What?, Why?* or *How?*

Developing your ideas

Titles sometimes seem rather intimidating when you first see them. It might be hard to know where to begin with a topic such as *'The First World War was a mistake.' Discuss.* If this seems difficult, try rethinking it as a question (*In what way could the First World War be seen as a mistake?*). The subject then becomes easier to grasp. Rephrasing something as a question can often be useful, because a direct question like this is easy to respond to. It can also generate further questions, for example, *Who might see the First World War as a mistake?* or *Who might be to blame for this mistake?*

If you have been given a topic such as *Is photography an art form?*, try asking yourself a series of questions, starting by examining the words that are used in the title:

> What exactly is an *art form*?
> What different kinds of *photography* are there?

➤ Can any or all of these be regarded as art forms?

➤ Why/why not?

Questions like these will lead to answers, which can give you ideas and might offer you an underlying structure for what you are going to say.

Organizing your ideas

Once you have a clear understanding of what the essay involves, you can go through the processes of research, planning, drafting and revising described on pages 205–14.

The planning stage requires special care. You may have a number of different ideas that do not fit together easily into a coherent structure. You may have to sift through your ideas and decide which ones are essential to the essay and which can be left out:

➤ Which of your ideas are linked? You can show their relationship by joining them with arrows or by numbering them in your notes.

➤ Which ideas seem most important? Emphasize them by underlining, circling or highlighting them.

➤ Are there any good arguments that can be made against your main points? Add these to the plan.

➤ Is each idea strictly relevant to the essay title? If it is not, remove it.

➤ Does any point seem trivial or uninteresting? If it does, delete it, and only keep what is important or interesting.

➤ Have you gathered enough material for your essay? If not, gather more material or develop your existing points further.

The final plan into which you organize your ideas should contain three distinct stages: an introduction, the main development of ideas and a conclusion.

➡ See pages 245–50 for a detailed discussion of what to put in each of these parts and how to decide on an appropriate overall structure for your writing.

Constructing arguments

Many essays involve presenting an argument. In the context of an essay, an 'argument' has nothing to do with angry exchanges of temper. An argument is a carefully constructed and well-developed expression of a point of view which attempts to persuade the reader that what you are saying is correct. An argument should be:

➤ **Objective**: you should assure the reader that you are not influenced by personal prejudices, and that you have not allowed your emotions to intrude.

➤ **Fair**: you should consider a range of possible points of view and treat each one seriously. If you do not agree with a point of view, make it clear what your reasons are for rejecting it. Accept any limitations that your argument may have.

➤ **Incisive**: you will be more likely to convince the reader that you are right by being clear, precise and direct. Don't waste space on detail that does not advance your argument.

➤ **Logical**: make sure your points are not put down at random but follow an order that makes sense. Bear in mind that what might seem an obvious connection to you and thus not worth mentioning (perhaps because you are especially knowledgeable about a subject) might not appear so to others. Make sure it is clear how you have arrived at your conclusion.

In developing an argument, take the reader through a series of stages:

➤ Introduce the subject: provide the reader with any background information that will be necessary for them to follow your train of thought.

➤ Introduce supporting evidence: this might be in the form of statistics, facts or quotations. The reader might not believe you if you simply state something is true, but if you can present evidence then you are more likely to be taken seriously.

➤ Analyse the evidence: look at what information the evidence provides and how it can be interpreted.

➤ Make an inference: show that the evidence leads you to a natural conclusion.

> Introduce any contrasting evidence: mention any statistics, examples, documents, etc that might be brought forward in objection to your conclusion.

> Refute the contrasting evidence: explain why you do not think that it effects the truth of your argument. Perhaps the evidence is unreliable, or perhaps there is a reason why it does not apply in this case.

Presenting evidence

Your arguments will be more persuasive if the evidence you bring forward is clearly presented:

> Statistics are often easier to digest if they are presented in the form of tables. However, make sure that tables are clearly explained so that the reader can see how the information in them relates to your argument.

> Similarly, make sure that any diagrams or pictures are labelled so that their connection to the argument is obvious.

> Facts and statistics are more impressive if you are able to trace them to a reputable source. For example, simply writing that a third of all marriages in Britain end in divorce is not as impressive as writing that a government survey published in 2001 showed that a third of all marriages in Britain end in divorce.

> An occasional quotation from a reputable source can be an effective way of supporting your argument. Make sure that quotations are reproduced accurately and are correctly attributed. If you are unable to check the quotation, it is better to summarize the content than risk misquoting your source. (The correct form for presenting quotations is shown on page 114.)

Drawing conclusions

The final part of the essay is one of the most important. A good conclusion will summarize the ideas that you have been developing and leave the reader with a clear impression of your opinions on the subject. Don't be tempted to rush it:

> Briefly remind the reader of your main points, but don't repeat specific examples.

➤ Let the reader know your own opinion. You could do this directly by coming down on one side or other of the argument, or you could do it indirectly by putting in a quotation or anecdote that highlights your point of view.

➤ Leave the reader something to think about: an essay that ends with a sentence such as *Thus we see that the statement in the title is not true* attempts to close down the argument and encourages the reader to switch off their mind. It is far better to give the reader something new to take away with them and think about, like a parting gift at the end of the journey. You might hint at a future development or a problem that is related to the topic. In other words, maintain the reader's interest right until the end.

> One of the best ways to improve your essay-writing skills is to read essays written by other people. Try reading well-known essayists such as E M Forster, George Orwell and, in the scientific arena, Stephen Jay Gould. You could also look at the articles written by regular columnists in magazines and newspapers. Observe how these people structure their writing to achieve the effect they want and note what devices they use to hold the reader's interest.

Writing essays under examination conditions

You might have to produce essays for an examination. The difference here is that you have a lot less time, so you need to know your material well enough to identify the relevant points quickly. A few tips are:

➤ Make sure you are familiar with the key facts. Memorize important figures and quotations beforehand so that you are confident about reproducing them quickly. Trying to dredge half-remembered information up from your memory wastes valuable time and can be stressful.

➤ Write an introduction, main body and conclusion as for a regular essay, but keep each part short. This will show that you know what the most important points are, and also that you can organize your information effectively.

➤ Before you start writing the essay itself, write an outline of the structure, listing the key points in note form. This helps you to gather and organize your information before you start, and is useful to refer to as you write, saving you from having to stop and think every few minutes. Once you start writing, you should have a lot to say and will not want to stop!

➤ Divide your time up between the questions you have to answer, and stick rigidly to this division of time. Try to make sure that you are finishing your conclusion as the time allocated for the essay finishes. If you have not made all your points in the time allocated, mention them briefly as part of your conclusion and then move on.

➤ Keep an eye on the time as you work. Make sure that you don't spend too much time on any one part of the question or too much time making notes before you start writing.

Dissertations and theses

A **dissertation** is basically a long essay, often 5000 words or more, and is an important piece of written work on many education courses, for example as part of a degree.

A **thesis** is longer than a dissertation, and might even be produced over a number of years as part of a high-level postgraduate qualification such as a doctorate.

The longer the dissertation or thesis is, the greater the need for clear organization so that all the parts contribute to the whole, and so that the writer (or the reader!) does not get lost in the text, or lose a sense of what the piece of writing is about.

Longer pieces of writing are usually divided into separate sections or chapters. These might be treated as individual essays, each of which deals with a particular aspect of the overall work. Despite this, each introduction should connect with what has gone before, and each conclusion should look forward to what is to follow so that there is a sense of continuity.

Layout for a dissertation or thesis

Because a dissertation or thesis is usually arranged into sections rather than consisting of one continuous piece of writing, it will often share many of the features of a report and need to be organized in a similar way.

 See pages 307–15 for a description of how to organize and set out a report.

Most institutions that require students to produce dissertations or theses have their own guidelines about format, length and style, and might provide a supervisor or mentor as well. Make sure that the way you set out your work is in keeping with your institution's published guidelines.

Usually, however, a dissertation or thesis will contain:

- a title page, with an explanation of the title
- a full list of contents
- a summary (often called an 'abstract') providing an outline of the piece
- clear headings and subheadings to make it easy to navigate through the text
- footnotes for any comments that would be distracting if they were included in the text itself
- appendices for material that is too long to include in the form of footnotes, and for graphs, charts and tables
- a bibliography

In some cases, a thesis will also have an index listing all of the terms and ideas discussed in it. This makes it easy for all references to a term or idea to be found and compared. (After all, if information cannot be easily found, it might as well not be there.)

Most of the features that go up to make a dissertation or thesis are discussed on pages 308–13 with reference to writing reports. However, the bibliography needs to be discussed in more detail here.

Bibliography

A dissertation should contain a **bibliography** that gives an alphabetical list of all the sources of information you have used.

It is important to make sure that you acknowledge all the sources that you have used to obtain information and ideas. The charge of plagiarism or intellectual theft is a very serious one and can lead to a piece of work being rejected or taken a lot less seriously.

The most common system for a bibliography or list of references is known as the **Harvard system** or the **author–date system**. Although there are slight variations, this system gives some information in the text itself:

> ➤ the author's surname
> ➤ the year of publication of the text or texts
> ➤ the pages being quoted or referred to

For example:

She refers only briefly to this theory (Pollock 1985, p. 267), although her successor goes into more detail (Davis 1976, pp. 333–5; 1987, pp. 766, 798).

Fuller details are then included in the bibliography:

> ➤ the author, arranged by surname in alphabetical order
> ➤ the year of publication
> ➤ the title of the book (in italics or underlined, to make it stand out), or the title of the article followed by the book or magazine it was published in (with the article in italics or underlined, and the publication in roman)
> ➤ an edition number, if this is appropriate
> ➤ the name and location of the publisher

For example:

Davis, George 1976. <u>Emerging Mind</u> Psychology Review 45, pp. 53–68

Davis, George 1987. <u>The Myth of Mind</u> 3rd edition. New York: Box Press

Pollock, Anne M. 1985. <u>Women in Mind</u> London: Tolpuddle Books

The advantage of this system is that it does not take up much space in the text, yet it allows different books to be quickly and easily identified.

If you have used material from the Internet, it may be that you are not able to attribute it to a particular author. In this case you can use the word *Internet* and a number in the main text, as follows:

> *This has been called 'the single greatest advance in our understanding of the mind' (Internet 1), although writers are more sceptical (Internet 2).*

You can then explain these references in the bibliography by having a separate *Internet* section, in which you list the websites in the order you have referred to them:

> *1. http://www.psych_review.org/papers/pck3.html*
>
> *2. http://www.tolpuddle.com/publications/psych/pck/wim.http*

Academic style

The style for academic writing should follow the same principles as any other writing, as summed up in the 'five Cs' (Correct, Consistent, Clear, Complete, Concise). Academic writing is one of the more formal types of writing, and so it calls for a few special considerations:

> ➤ Do not use contractions (*they've, it's, he'll*), or informal vocabulary (*great, quite good, get started, a bit of research*).

> ➤ Use a fairly impersonal style (for example, *this was done* rather than *I did this*), although it may be appropriate to address the reader directly in this way for the introduction. Generally, you need to 'keep your distance' rather than seeming to be too personally involved.

> ➤ Avoid expressing strong opinions directly: academic writing should generally aim to offer evidence for objective consideration, rather than seeking to persuade directly (for example, *many writers have suggested that ...* rather than *maybe ...*).

> ➤ Being formal does not mean that you have to be pompous or difficult to understand. Don't use very long sentences if they can be avoided, and where possible use simple language, even – in fact, especially – when discussing complex ideas.

➡ See pages 255–61 for a more detailed discussion of writing style.

Some useful abbreviations for academic writing

There are a number of abbreviations that are commonly used in academic writing. Many of these are derived from Latin. Although they might seem rather obscure to begin with, these abbreviations are very convenient when referring to books and articles.

et al. is short for the Latin *et alia* or *and others*. It is used when referring to a group of people such as authors or editors:

> *(Jones et al., 1956 p. 12)*

et seq. is short for the Latin *et sequens* or *and what follows*. It is used when referring to an unspecified number of pages that follow an individual page that you have mentioned. An alternative is *ff.*:

> *in the rest of the third chapter (pp. 65 et seq.)*
>
> *in the rest of the third chapter (pp. 65 ff.)*

ib. or *ibid.* is short for the Latin *ibidem* or *the same*. It is used when referring to a work that you have just quoted:

> *This is mentioned briefly in the introduction (Jones et al, 1956 p. 12), and in more detail later on (ibid., pp. 87–92).*

op. cit. is short for the Latin *opere citato* or *in the work already quoted*, and is used when referring to a work that has been quoted earlier:

> *a process that was also alluded to by Davies (op. cit., pp. 23–8)*

Scientific writing

Although scientific writing is like other academic writing in that you should be clear, concise and should also 'keep your distance' by remaining as neutral as possible, there are a few particular points that are worth remembering:

> ➤ If you refer to a published work in the main body of an essay, give a paraphrase of the relevant information rather than an exact quotation. The precise words do not matter (as they might do in an essay about literature); what matters is that you show your understanding of the material by presenting it in your own words.

➤ Always use SI units of measurement, and make sure you give the units using the standard abbreviations. A list of the main SI units is shown on pages 346–7.

➤ Names of SI units are not written with a capital letter, even when they are derived from a proper name, for example *newton*, *ampere* and *kelvin*. Note that even though the French surname *Ampère* has an accent, you do not need it for the metric unit that is derived from it.

➤ You do not need full stops after abbreviations for units of measurement, and they should not be pluralized.

➤ Avoid starting sentences with a number. Either write out the number in words or restructure the sentence so that the number does not come at the start.

Using numbers in scientific writing

Scientific and technical writing uses some conventions about numbers that are different from those of non-technical writing.

In writing large numbers, the convention is to use spaces rather than commas:

23 678

167 983

2 569 746

Note that no space is required if the number contains only four figures:

9765

You can abbreviate amounts of more than a million using whole or decimal numbers together with *m*:

a population of 6.2m

However, if this abbreviation will clash with other abbreviations, such as *km* meaning *kilometres*, it is better to give the number in full:

6 200 000 km from the sun

Very large or very small numbers can be expressed as decimal numbers multiplied by powers of ten:

$8000 = 8 \times 10^3$

$0.007 = 7 \times 10^3$

$6\ 000\ 000 = 6 \times 10^6$

$7\ 750\ 000 = 7.75 \times 10^6$

The word *billion* (sometimes abbreviated to *bn*) is nowadays understood to mean one thousand million (one and nine zeroes, which is 1,000,000,000 or 10^9). Formerly, in British English a billion was one million million (one and twelve zeroes, which is 1,000,000,000,000 or 10^{12}). Similarly, *trillion* is now understood to be one million million (the former British billion), rather than one million million million (one and eighteen zeroes, or 10^{18}). If you need to use these terms, it is a good idea to indicate the number in figures to avoid confusion about which definition of the word you are following.

SI units

The SI (*Système International*) units are the internationally recognized units for scientific measurement. Always express measurement using these units in scientific writing.

There are seven base units, from which the others are derived:

QUANTITY	UNIT	SYMBOL
length	metre	m
mass	kilogram	kg
time	second	s
electric current	ampere	A
temperature	kelvin	K
luminous intensity	candela	cd
amount of substance	mole	mol

Some of the most common derived SI units are shown in the table below:

QUANTITY	UNIT	SYMBOL
force	newton	N
pressure	pascal	Pa
energy	joule	J
power	watt	W
frequency	hertz	Hz
conductance	siemens	S
electrical charge	coulomb	C
potential difference	volt	V
capacitance	farad	F
resistance	ohm	W
radioactivity	becquerel	Bq

Biological classification

If you are writing about an organism, make sure you use the standard conventions that apply for biological classification:

> ➤ Classification names should be given in italics.

> ➤ Classification names have two parts, the **genus name** or **generic name**, which begins with a capital letter, and the **species name** or **specific name**, which begins with a lower-case letter (*Homo sapiens*, *Rattus norvegicus*).

> ➤ Classification names behave like proper nouns, so they are not preceded by *the* or *a*: isolated populations of *Arnoglossus laterna*.

> ➤ Always write out the classification name in full the first time that you use it. You can then abbreviate the genus name if you use it again (*A. laterna*).

> ➤ If the organism also has a widely used common name, give both the common name and the classification name the first time you mention the organism, and then use the common name on subsequent occasions: *We observed colonies of the brown rat (Rattus norvegicus) in several locations.*

The use of Latin and Greek in science

Scientific language relies heavily on words derived from Latin and

347

Greek. Take care to distinguish between the singular and plural forms of nouns that come from Latin and Greek words. Here is a list of some common scientific words that have Latin or Greek plurals:

SINGULAR	PLURAL
analysis	analyses
bacterium	bacteria
criterion	criteria
datum	data
diagnosis	diagnoses
focus	foci
fungus	fungi
genus	genera
hypothesis	hypotheses
index	indices
larva	larvae
locus	loci
matrix	matrices
medium	media
nucleus	nuclei
ovum	ova
phylum	phyla
pupa	pupae
spectrum	spectra

Writing up experiments

When you write about an experiment, what you are doing is writing a specialized type of report, which has a standard format:

- ➤ title
- ➤ abstract
- ➤ introduction
- ➤ materials and methods
- ➤ results
- ➤ discussion
- ➤ references

Each section should have a clear heading and be dealt with according to a standard procedure.

Title

The title should be clear, informative and as specific as possible, so that the reader can see at a glance what the report is about. Make sure you include:

> the name of the substance, organism or whatever is being studied

> the particular aspect being studied

> the purpose of the experiment

Abstract

As the abstract is a summary of the report itself, you should not write it until the end. The abstract should be short (no more than one paragraph) and should not go into detail. The reader must be able to understand it without having to refer to anything else. Make sure you include:

> a description of the topic

> a summary of the methods you used

> a summary of the results

> a summary of the main conclusion

Introduction

In the introduction you should mention:

> how the experiment is relevant to your broad topic of study

> what the aim of the experiment is. If the aim is to test a hypothesis, then make sure you also state what the hypothesis is, the thinking behind the hypothesis and the predictions that you are testing.

> any relevant background information on the topic. Mention and discuss briefly any relevant experiments that have been carried out by others.

Materials and methods

In this section you should describe what you actually did in the experiment, without referring to the results. Write clearly and in detail – it should be possible for someone else to repeat the experiment after reading your description. Be sure to include information on:

> the materials you used

> how you used the materials

> sizes, measurements and concentrations

> any special equipment you used

> any statistical methods you used to analyse the data

> the location and date, if it is a field study

Make sure that you:

> give only necessary information (for example, do not refer to the size or condition of equipment unless it is needed to understand the experiment)

> avoid mentioning irrelevant matters such as how to clean up after the experiment

> avoid details that are specific to your personal circumstances

> show the reasons why you carried out a particular action

> write in the past tense – a report is meant to describe what you have actually done

> write in a neutral, objective style

> describe your actions in the passive voice (see page 228)

Results

In this section you should give the results of the experiment, but without referring to how they affect the aim of the experiment:

> Describe the main trends of your results. Refer to the appropriate illustrations, graphs and tables in the order in which they appear.

> If you carried out a statistical analysis, you must mention whether the trends that you observed were statistically significant.

Graphic information

Follow these guidelines if you are including graphics, such as diagrams, charts, graphs and tables, in your write-up:

➤ Give each graphic a number, followed by a title. Each type of graphic should be numbered separately, so if you had two illustrations or diagrams and one table, they would be *Figure 1, Figure 2* and *Table 1*.

➤ Make sure that each title is clear and informative so that the reader can make sense of the illustration or table without having to look anywhere else. Place the number and title at the bottom of an illustration, but at the top of a table. Remember to give a scale for each graph or chart if necessary.

➤ Do not repeat data in the text that you have already given in a table. Instead, refer in the text to the illustration or table by its number: *figure 1 shows that ...*

Discussion

In this section you need to explain the significance of the results with regard to the stated aim of the experiment. You should:

➤ explain to what extent the results achieved the aim of the experiment and to what extent they supported your hypothesis

➤ take into account any other ways in which it might be possible to interpret your results

➤ discuss any possible errors that might have affected your interpretation of the results

➤ explain to what extent the results have contributed towards an understanding of your topic of study

➤ make recommendations for further experiments that might help to resolve any remaining difficulties in achieving the aim of the experiment or in testing the hypothesis

References

An experimental write-up should conclude with an alphabetical list of all the sources of information you have used. Follow the guidelines for presenting bibliographical information set out on pages 342–3.

Writing for the Internet

Electronic text

In previous centuries, when we wrote everything by hand, written communication had certain characteristic features:

- It required a lot of thought and planning.
- It was time-consuming to produce.
- It was troublesome and time-consuming to correct or rewrite.
- It required a legible handwriting style.
- It was bulky.
- It was costly to print and distribute to others.
- It took time to transport from one place to another.

For better or for worse, computers have now changed the way we use language, and have also transformed our relationship with information of all kinds. Much electronic text has very different features:

- It requires almost no effort to produce.
- It is easy to change or correct.
- It is easy to read.
- It can be made available to millions of people at the touch of a button.
- It takes up hardly any space.
- It costs next to nothing.
- It can be sent to a person on the other side of world in an instant.

On pages 300–6 we looked at electronic forms of personal communication in the shape of e-mail and text messages. In this chapter we are going to look at the way that electronic text can be used for public communication on the World Wide Web.

Creating web pages

Until quite recently, creating pages for the World Wide Web required a knowledge of HTML (Hypertext Mark-up Language). Although HTML is not terribly complicated, it is quite time-consuming to learn, so the creation of web pages tended to be left to specialists.

However, it is now possible to use automated **web-authoring programs** to create web pages just as easily as word-processed documents. This means that, in theory, anyone can have a website.

Websites

Many individuals and organizations now have their own websites, and many of these websites contain hundreds of pages.

Companies and organizations that have large websites often use people known as **content creators** to produce material for the site. The content creators work with technical specialists who are responsible for the format of web pages and create the look and feel of the site and make the site easy to use.

Weblogs

Weblogs are documents that are put on the Internet by individual people. Like websites, these have become increasingly popular now that authoring software is freely available. Weblogs can be divided into two main categories, although these categories might overlap to some extent:

> ‘filter’-style sites that consist largely of links to other websites and weblogs, with personal comments and observations on issues such as current affairs, culture, sport and politics

> ‘diary’-style sites that are updated frequently and take the form of a continuous journal about a person’s everyday life

Weblogs offer you the chance to express your own opinions about anything and everything without restriction. In many ways, they are the opposite of the large-scale corporate websites.

Retrieving information from the Internet

In order to understand the requirements of writing for the Internet, it is necessary to think about how information is retrieved from web pages.

Traditional documents are generally read by **linear access** or **random access**. **Linear access** involves starting at the beginning of a document and proceeding in a continuous path to the end. This approach has obvious limitations if you want to locate information quickly, or if you want to compare different parts of a piece of writing. In these circumstances, you need to retrieve information by **random access**, flicking through the pages of a book, using an index or looking a word up in a dictionary.

On a computer, however, it is possible to take the idea of random access a step further. Not only is it possible to move from page to page within a particular document (using the 'forward' and 'back' buttons), but it is also possible to flick from page to page between documents, so that you are in effect using the electronic 'links' that are provided on web pages to flick through an entire library. This is what is meant by **hypertext** – your very own virtual reference book allowing access to a whole CD-ROM, or the entire Web. What is more, the Web is a multimedia environment, so this means that you can access pictures, diagrams, animation, video images and sound as well as straightforward text.

Because hypertext is so fluid, it places particular demands on those who write for the Web. Information needs to be planned in such a way that everything is properly connected to everything else, and the process of moving about or 'navigating' the Web needs to be made as easy as possible.

Features of English on the Internet

What has been said in previous chapters about the use of written English still applies when you write for the Internet. You still need to think about the 'five Cs' (Correct, Consistent, Clear, Complete, Concise), and you still need to have a coherent, logical structure and to use language that is appropriate for your readers and your material.

However, much Internet English is more informal than other kinds of written English (although this can vary depending on whether you are reading an official government website or a personal weblog).

Some people who visit a website will read the text in a linear fashion in order to obtain information. However, many visitors will be casually 'browsing' or 'surfing'. This means that text needs to attract and retain the casual reader's interest – it needs to be 'sticky', in terms of what it says and also in terms of how it looks.

The usual requirements for on-screen text are therefore:

> ➤ simple, direct language
> ➤ short sentences
> ➤ short paragraphs – often consisting of a single sentence (a maximum of about 30 words is recommended)
> ➤ a reasonably large size of type and a clear font to take account of various screen sizes and grades of screen
> ➤ not too much visual 'clutter' – although graphics are easy to insert and might make a page look interesting, too many graphics can make the screen look very 'busy', be off-putting and make text difficult to read, especially when text is superimposed over graphic material. This is the opposite of 'sticky' design and content.
> ➤ hyperlinks to provide access to other pages, other websites, help pages and FAQs (Frequently Asked Questions)

Writing to Attract Attention

Promotional material

This chapter looks at writing to promote or sell a product. In this sort of writing, language is used actively to persuade rather than to make indirect or tentative suggestions. Promotional material therefore needs to be:

➤ noticeable

➤ memorable

➤ clear

➤ positive

This is true whatever kind of promotional material you are referring to. In this chapter we start by looking at the general qualities that go to make effective promotional material, and then move on to examine some specific kinds of promotional material:

➤ advertisements and leaflets

➤ newsletters

➤ press releases

➤ CVs

Being noticeable

The first thing that promotional material needs is 'stickiness'; the ability to attract and retain people's attention. You are probably not the only person with something to promote, and other people will be competing for the customer's attention. Those with the loudest voice or who are the most amusing or interesting will be the ones who succeed in capturing the customer's attention – at least for a second.

This brief moment is the beginning of the process of promotion – even before it is read, written material needs to be noticed, otherwise it will be ignored.

Being noticed depends on:

➤ **Impact** – something large is easier to see then something small. Something bold is easier to see than something timid or subtle.

➤ **Design** – what graffiti and advertising catches your eye while you are driving? Generally, material that is easy to read quickly from a distance; things that are simple and direct rather than complicated or 'busy'. Strong, contrasting colours and simple designs are usually the most effective from this point of view.

➤ **Relevance** – even if something is difficult to read, if it appeals directly to you (your values, your fears, your sense of humour, your vanity) it is more likely that you will make the effort. Trying to appeal to as many people as possible is known as broadcasting or mass marketing, and trying to appeal to only a few is known as narrowcasting or niche marketing.

➤ **Style** – in order to attract attention, many advertisements are very direct, and either ask a question that people will want to answer in particular way (Do you want the best for your family?), or make a proposition that people will want to accept (Save while you spend!). Flyers and leaflets often use capital letters and question marks or exclamation marks – the written equivalent of shouting at people to gain their attention.

➤ **Strangeness** – sometimes, a gimmick or unusual feature can attract attention, and this is why you see people in animal costumes or other bizarre outfits handing out promotional leaflets. As you might expect, strangeness stops being strange when everybody tries to do it, at which point you need to be even stranger or try a completely different approach.

Being memorable

Besides having the power to attract attention in the first place, successful promotional material should also stick in the mind after it has been read. Many of the most memorable product names, advertising slogans and political soundbites are based around a few simple but effective techniques.

Some use simple **rhyme**:

You can do it if you B&Q it.

A Mars a day helps you work, rest and play.

Some use **repetition** of words:

> *Tough on crime, tough on the causes of crime.*
>
> *Have a break, have a Kit Kat.*

Some use **alliteration**:

> *Get it? Got it? Good!*
>
> *Bob the Builder*

Some use **wordplay**, such as the laundry service called *The Iron Lady* or the hairdresser called *Fringe Benefits*.

Some catch the eye by breaking the rules, deliberately spelling words in creative ways:

> *Kwik-Save*
>
> *Beanz Meanz Heinz*
>
> *Weetabix*

Being clear

Before you can decide on what you are going to say, you need to be clear in your mind about two things:

➤ What are you trying to achieve? It often helps to focus the mind by expressing this on paper; this is what a 'mission statement' tries to do.

➤ How are you going to achieve it? Produce a simple list of objectives, rather than a sophisticated flow chart.

Once you know what your message is, you want to get it across quickly and clearly:

➤ Use short, simple words and short, simple sentences.

➤ Use the right language for your audience, whether you are broadcasting or narrowcasting.

➤ Use a simple, clear layout.

➤ Check all your punctuation and spelling – any mistakes may be seized upon and used as negative publicity.

Being positive

In all forms of advertising and promotion, it is important to deliver a positive message wherever you can.

If you are advertising a product, use positive words such as *new, better, best, free, fresh, delicious, full, clean, special, real, big, easy, great, more* and *extra.*

If you are promoting yourself in a job application, you need to describe your skills, experience and personality in a way that emphasizes positive things about you, rather than sounding negative or simply remaining neutral. This is not the place to be objective.

Advertisements and leaflets

Advertising is a multimedia activity. This means that it operates in print, on the radio, on TV, in the cinema, on the Internet, and on clothing, badges, posters and hoardings. It also means that language is only one part of the advertising process. It works alongside other tools such as colour, graphic design, still and moving images, music, sound, celebrity endorsements and promotional events.

Nevertheless, copywriting – the job of coming up with simple, effective text and catchy slogans – is still a hugely important part of the advertising process. Even on the smallest budget, unadorned black words on white paper can still be effective, as long as they are the right words and are well presented.

Whether you are planning a national advertising campaign or a flyer for a local shop window, the same principles apply:

➤ Be noticeable, memorable, clear and positive.

➤ Be creative. Good ideas are more important than large budgets, and a strong image or effective slogan is worth a thousand words.

➤ Keep it simple. A line drawing can work at least as well as a slick photograph if used imaginatively. Simple, strong design is not expensive to produce.

➤ Be consistent. If appropriate, try and adopt a logo, together with a 'look' or 'brand image' for your graphic design so that the colours, fonts and layouts are always recognizable even before the material is read.

➤ Be direct. Ask simple questions and make simple propositions.

Newsletters

A newsletter is a combination of news and a letter – it offers current information in a friendly format. Newsletters are produced regularly, and they tend to have an informal style, offering information in relatively small chunks that are easy to read.

A newsletter is usually produced for a specific audience or interest group, whether this is the parents of children at a local school, the members of a professional scientific body or the customers of a national supermarket chain. Even if newsletters do not all start with *Dear Parent* or *Dear Customer*, they try to give the feeling that they are addressing the reader directly.

If you find yourself in charge of producing a newsletter, you might consider including the following types of information:

➤ an editorial piece in which you comment on or draw your readers' attention to things that have happened, things that are happening or things that are going to happen

➤ reports and reviews of things that have happened since the last newsletter, or of products that have been released

➤ diary and calendar announcements about forthcoming events

➤ features about ideas or issues that might be of interest to readers

➤ appeals for money or support

➤ advertisements and requests for information

A newsletter is likely to be well received by its readers if you:

➤ have a clear idea of your readership and deal with issues that will be relevant to them

➤ use humour and human-interest stories to create a strong initial impact

➤ present information in a lively and eye-catching way, making use of illustrations and graphics

➤ make sure that it always contains accurate and up-to-date information

Press releases

A press release is a short specially written announcement or statement that is distributed to the media. It provides information either about something you want to draw attention to, or something they want to know about. In addition, it gives you an opportunity to take control of what is happening by presenting things from your point of view.

A press release needs to seem important or dramatic if it is to create an impact, and might be accompanied by a promotional event such as a press conference or photo opportunity where pictures can be taken. Alternatively, images might be provided with the press release. It is not unknown for a press release and photo opportunity to be organized as part of an election or advertising campaign rather than being concerned with 'real' news.

A press release needs to capture the attention instantly. The most important or dramatic aspect of the press release should therefore come first, presented in the most dramatic terms, with an explanation being given in more ordinary language further down. A press release is usually written in short paragraphs, each of which might consist only of a single sentence.

Press releases are structured in this way because news reports are often organized with an 'attention-grabbing' item first, and an explanation later. The fact that the two are presented in the same way makes the job of reporting your event easier for the reporter. It also, you hope, makes it more likely that the reporter will present the report from your point of view and use your language.

SAFECO GOES GREEN!

24/06/04

Supermarket giant Safeco is going green, with backing from organic farmers across the country, and special offers on prepared organic meals.

The Green movement turned out in force today for the launch of Safeco's 'Greening the High Street' organic produce range. This continues Safeco's long-term commitment to protecting consumers, offering great value, and increasing choice.

Many organic farmers, including a representative from HUMUS, the organic food movement, turned out to sample the range, which includes basic ingredients and prepared meals, and is supported by special offers and in-store recipe suggestions.

HUMUS chief Barry Field said: 'This is a step in the right direction'. Safeco manager Hugh Park agreed, adding: 'This proves that Safeco is at the forefront of the campaign for healthy food and great value'.

Contact: Hugh Park, Safeco Public Relations, 09768 987 654

www.safeco.co.uk/organics

CVs

CV is an abbreviation for **curriculum vitae**. A CV is a summary of your personal details, work history, education, skills and training. It is often required instead of an application form if you apply for a job, and it is usually accompanied by a **covering letter** (see pages 290–294). Some examples of CVs are shown on pages 366 and 367.

It is common nowadays for employers to prefer a CV that consists of a single-page summary, with more detailed information provided on extra pages. This allows an employer to get a quick impression of a candidate without having to read through a long, complicated account of the person's life and career.

Although you might have a standard CV stored on your computer, it is always a good idea to tailor your CV to the specific job you are applying for. This allows you to emphasize particular aspects of the information, and to ignore others if they do not happen to be relevant. If you do not do this, your CV might look to the employer like the equivalent of an impersonal standard letter rather than one that has been written with him or her in mind. Remember that this is a promotional document – even if the promotion is done more subtly than in an advertisement.

Writing your CV

When preparing a CV, it is important to create a good impression, not just in terms of the content, but also through the way it looks. Present information in a clear and concise fashion, using bulleted points rather than solid paragraphs for listed information.

There is no single standard format, but the usual way of organizing a CV includes the kind of information that most employers are likely to be interested in:

➤ personal details
➤ work experience
➤ education and qualifications
➤ skills and achievements
➤ memberships

➤ interests

➤ referees

Personal details

Include here all that you think might be relevant:

➤ name

➤ full address

➤ telephone number or numbers

➤ e-mail address, website, fax

➤ date of birth

➤ nationality

You might like to actually include the words *name: ...*, *address: ...*, as part of the CV, but if the information is displayed clearly at the top this might not be necessary.

Work experience

Start with your current or most recent position and work backwards from this.

Focus on your responsibilities in each post, and give examples of your achievements, rather than just listing names and dates.

Education and qualifications

List the places where you were educated and the qualifications gained at each place, along with the dates:

➤ You do not need to go back too far unless the qualifications are relevant to your application. Few employers will be interested in your primary school career.

➤ If you are a recent graduate, mention any achievements at university that provide examples of responsibility, teamwork or other skills that could be important in a working environment.

Skills and achievements

List any skills you have that relate to leisure-time activities and voluntary work, together with examples of success or achievement:

➤ Many things you do outside work might provide evidence of the skills that employers are looking for and, even if they do not, will make you more interesting and well developed as a person.

➤ Mention recent achievements as well as things from the past to show that you are still interested in personal development.

➤ Make sure that you describe the person you are rather than the person you think other people want you to be – if you are dishonest or misleading, you will soon be found out.

Memberships

Mention memberships of professional bodies and organizations associated with non-work activities, along with positions of responsibility. You could equally incorporate this information into the previous section.

Interests

List two or three leisure-time interests that help to show you as a rounded, balanced person:

➤ Make sure that you include only what will be viewed positively by an employer – this is one reason why you need to tailor your CV to the particular job you are applying for.

➤ If you mention subjects here, make sure you know enough to be able to talk about them if you are interviewed!

Referees

Give the names and addresses of two people that you trust to be positive about you, or you can simply state that references are available.

If you have different referees for different job applications, you can also include this information in your covering letter.

Cameron Grant

Address: 14/3 Greenknowe Ave., Potts Point, NSW 2055,
Australia
Tel: 2883 455
e-mail: cgrant@alc.com
Nationality: Australian
Date of birth: 1 May 1969

Work History

1998 to date: International Business Manager, Haircare Ltd,
Sydney
Producer of hair care products

Responsibilities:
- *marketing in Europe and the Far East*
- *packaging development and design input*
- *setting up and developing distribution network*
- *negotiating contracts with major retailers*

1991-1995: Overseas Marketing Manager, Fourstar
International, Tokyo
Manufacturer of broadcasting equipment

- *formulated strategy, developed distribution network, dealt with agents and customers*
- *produced sales material*
- *represented company at trade fairs worldwide*

Education

1997 MBA, London Business School
1991 BA Economics and Japanese, Sydney
University, Sydney, Australia

Skills

fluent Japanese
holder of pilot's licence, four hundred hours of flying

Interests

keen interest in flying
hiking
member of Greenpeace

Beverley Roberts

Personal details

Address: 122 Honor Oak Road, Forest Hill, London
                SE23 4NM
Tel: 669 3439
e-mail: broberts@goserve.net
Nationality: British
Date of birth: 4 October 1981

Education

2004   MSc Computing for Business and Industry,
                Napier University, Edinburgh
2003   BA Business Administration (2.2), University
                of South Wales
1999   Hull Grammar School. 'A' levels in Italian
                (A), Computer Studies (A) and Economics (B)

Work Experience

Summer 2003 Website design, Hypercommunications Ltd,
             Cardiff
Summer 2001 Adventure camp group leader, Nottingham
             Responsible for sailing tuition

Skills

- full driving licence
- fluent Italian
- experience of sailing training with under-sixteens
- first aid certificate

Interests

- member of university sailing team until graduation
- contributor of articles to yachting magazines
- keen painter with a strong interest in modern art

Names of referees available on request.

Technical Writing

What is technical writing?

Of all the types of writing dealt with in this book, technical writing is perhaps the least understood and most often overlooked. It covers material such as:

- ➤ instructions
- ➤ directions
- ➤ operating manuals
- ➤ health and safety documentation
- ➤ recipes

What all these things have in common is that they are designed to pass useful information from someone who knows about something to someone who does not. This kind of writing is a strictly one-way, impersonal kind of communication with the widest possible audience in mind. If the communication becomes two way, this suggests that there has been a failure of some kind, and that the writer has failed to create a self-sufficient text.

How long is a piece of string?

Sometimes technical material is long and complex, and is written over a relatively long period by specialists (for example, when producing an operating manual). Sometimes it is written quickly by people needing to provide short, easy-to-follow instructions about how to do something or how to get somewhere. The commonest kind of technical writing is probably the recipe: many people have probably read, written or tried to follow one at some time or other, with varying degrees of success. On a more modest level, even the instructions on how to re-heat chilled meals count as technical writing.

Technical writing is deceptive – in fact, the easier it is to read, the more difficult it can be to write. Small panels of text appear on hundreds of everyday products, and if you have ever had to struggle with unhelpful instructions, you will appreciate the importance of performing this kind of writing well.

In this chapter we shall look at some problems that can arise with technical writing of various kinds, and then suggest some ways of making things better.

The unfortunate reader

From the point of view of the reader, technical material is usually read unwillingly, often at speed or impatiently, maybe under stress or as a last resort. Perhaps it is read quickly, and only re-read when problems arise. For example, after pressing all the available buttons over and over again or switching an unco-operative machine on and off several times.

Many readers are intimidated by the idea of technical writing. The very word *technical* is sometimes associated with things that are complicated and confusing, and therefore to be avoided unless there is no other option. Although this way of treating technical writing is understandable, it is not very sensible!

The unfortunate writer

From the point of view of the writer, technical material is written to make something potentially difficult or dangerous as straightforward or safe as possible for others. However, something that is 'easy when you know how' may be all but impossible when you do not know how. Although technical writing is meant to fill this gap, problems can arise with:

➤ knowledge

➤ language

➤ the world

Knowledge can get in the way

Writers who are very familiar with the thing or process being described have a tendency to write 'from the inside out' – as an 'insider' in a position of knowledge and experience – rather than writing 'from the outside in', adopting the point of view of the reader, the 'outsider'.

Often, the reader is in a position of ignorance, and therefore needs to know things that might be **simple**, but not **obvious**. Good technical writers put themselves in the position of an 'outsider' and give complete explanations that do not assume any prior knowledge of the subject.

Language can get in the way

Language can get in the way of successful communication for two reasons:

> ➤ Documents may be written by technical experts who lack the ability to write in simple, clear, concise English.

> ➤ Documents may be written (or translated from another language) by language experts whose lack of technical expertise leads them to make inaccurate or incorrect statements.

When it comes to technical writing, you need both technical expertise and writing expertise, and it is rare for these skills to be combined in the same person. This means that the saying 'two heads are better than one' often applies. A successful document may be the product of a technical expert who understands the process involved and a language expert who is able to explain the process in clear, concise language.

The world can get in the way

The world can get in the way of successful communication because it is constantly changing. Information that was accurate at the time it was written may cease to be accurate within a few months or even days. For example, an out-of-date telephone number or website address can mean that a document offering technical support becomes useless.

Technical writing may need to be checked and regularly updated to ensure that it remains accurate. It is also important to make sure that it conforms to legal requirements. For example, manufacturers might be worried about being sued for failing to provide adequate warnings about when it is and is not safe to use a particular product.

Getting it right

Not everyone designs and builds complex equipment that requires a lot of documentation. However, many people are required to produce technical writing on a smaller scale. This may take the form of a set of directions telling people how to get to your organization's headquarters, or perhaps instructions to your colleagues about how to operate a particular computer program.

If you have to produce this sort of document, it is important to be aware of the things that can get in the way of successful communication. Getting it right can be time-consuming, so be prepared to spend some time thinking, writing and rewriting if necessary.

The following guidelines will help you to succeed:

➤ Put yourself in the position of your readers. Treat them as intelligent but do not assume they have any previous knowledge of the subject. Use simple, clear language that is absolutely unambiguous, and if necessary provide a glossary of technical terms.

➤ If technical material is divided into sections in the same way as a report, not everyone might want to read it from start to finish. Because of this, make sure that different sections are clearly labelled and a full index is provided if you need one. To use an analogy, the best library in the world is useless if its books are hard to find.

➤ If you are describing a process, make sure that the order of events makes sense and that no stages – however trivial – have been left out. If any preparations are required, say so at the beginning. Many problems result from the writer failing to realize that things that are trivial or simple may not be obvious to someone who is unfamiliar with the process.

➤ If you are describing a process or a route that is complex, go through it yourself to test whether your instructions are valid, or get someone else to do this. If the instructions turn out to be deficient, make any necessary corrections.

➤ Remember that two heads might be better than one. If you are

an expert, involve non-experts and try material out on them. A
fresh pair of eyes can often help by seeing things you would
not notice yourself.

➤ Having said 'two heads are better than one', it can also be the
case that 'too many cooks spoil the broth'. A document that
contains several sections each produced by a different
specialist can lack coherence. Make sure that the complete
final draft is read by a single person to ensure that there is
continuity between the different parts.

➤ Make sure there is enough space for material to be laid out
clearly, with numbered lists or bullet points instead of dense
blocks of text. The techniques of laying out information for
maximum effect are discussed on pages 275–7.

➤ The best recipe books are not necessarily the ones with the
glossiest colour photographs – a simple line drawing might be
all you need as long as it is clear, and a well-placed illustration
or diagram can say more than a hundred words in the right
situation.

Creative Writing

What is creative writing?

Creative writing is a rather different form of writing from most of those discussed in this book. It is characterized by imagination and originality, rather than by ideas of correctness or standardization. Furthermore, it exists as a way of enjoying language for its own sake, rather than to communicate information.

Because creative writing is such a personal form of expression, there are no standard formats to follow. However, there are techniques and ideas that can help you to be more creative and original if you are interested in this sort of writing.

In this chapter we shall look very generally at some types of creative writing, give some suggestions about thinking creatively and offer some information that might make you aware of using words and language in new ways.

Types of creative writing

We can consider four general types of creative writing here.

➤ narrative fiction

➤ reportage

➤ poetry

➤ drama

Narrative fiction

Narrative fiction can range from full-length novels to short stories. In between, there are 'long short stories' or novellas.

Technically speaking, there is a difference between a **story** and a **narrative**. A story is a simple relating of events (for example, *A met B, then C happened, then D happened*). A narrative is a story in which the writer or storyteller controls the ways that the reader finds out about things, and the ways that the characters find out about things, both of which can create suspense and surprises.

Many narratives belong to a particular 'genre' or type, such as horror, crime, science fiction, fantasy, romantic, legal or historical fiction. Each genre has its own ways of doing things, and writers who work in a particular genre are expected to familiarize themselves with and – usually – follow these conventions.

Narrative fiction is often linear in form – like a line, it runs from start to finish, building towards a climax, with a resolution at the end. However, many modern novels experiment freely with ideas about time, space, plots, characters, the nature of reality and language itself to the extent that sometimes there is no actual story.

Reportage

Reportage takes the form of personal accounts of travel, war, places, personal experiences or historical events. Biographies and autobiographies might also be written as reportage.

Many of the aspects of narrative mentioned above also apply to reportage. What you are doing is telling a story, although the story in this case is meant to be true and seem real. What gives reportage its own identity is the inclusion of background details and extra information to set things in a context and make what you are describing sound convincing and authentic.

Poetry

Poetry is perhaps the most personal form of creative writing, and the most difficult to comment on. Poetry can explore ideas and images without relating them to people and events, can investigate comparisons between different things to stimulate the mind and the senses and can aspire to turning language into music.

Traditionally, poetry often involves **rhyme** and has a regular **metre** or beat to structure it. Verse that is written in a particular metre is divided into lines with a regular pattern, or into regular groups of lines called stanzas. However, much poetry is now written in **free verse**, and is expressed and organized by the writer in whatever way seems appropriate.

Drama

Drama is written to be performed by actors, so consists almost entirely of speech. Like narrative fiction and reportage, much drama involves storytelling, but because it involves actors and speech, the emphasis is also on character – what people are like, how they speak, how they behave and how they are changed (or not changed) by relationships and events.

Drama may be written to be performed 'live' in the theatre, but can also take the form of scripts for radio, television and film, all of which have very different characteristics. However, all of these media are based on speech, and dramatists need a good 'ear', a sensitivity to how language works when it is spoken rather than written down. This means that dramatic dialogue requires the writer to focus on aspects of language that are suppressed in other forms of writing.

Being creative

If you want to produce creative writing of any kind, you need to put yourself in the right state of mind, and you need to work at it, just as you do with most other things that you enjoy doing and want to do well.

Here are some suggestions:

➤ If in doubt, write – anything. What you write about is not important if you want to make a start, nor is how you write it. Keep a diary or journal about things that interest you, write down your dreams, your responses to the world around you, comments about the things you love or hate. Carry a notebook around to jot down ideas whenever and wherever you have them, then develop these ideas later. Creativity is a process, it involves producing things, and you will learn more about writing practically, by doing it, than you ever will by thinking about it or reading about it.

➤ Make mistakes. Creativity is not about being perfect; it is about experimenting, about trying things out, about making mistakes and learning lessons from them. Be playful as well as serious: try breaking the rules about 'proper' English that you have to follow everywhere else, and see where it gets you.

➤ Be persistent as well as playful. Take an idea or theme and explore it in detail. Give yourself the time and the space to work and rework things that you have written so that you get a sense of technique, of how easy or hard it is to achieve particular effects, of how to organize things, of what works for you and what does not.

➤ Believe in yourself. If you do not, who else will? Follow your intuition and trust your judgement. You have your own way of dressing, of talking, of decorating your home. If you develop a particular way of writing, this is also an aspect of your personality, so be who you are, and make the most of it.

Being poetic

In the past – although less so nowadays – poetry, drama and much narrative fiction were written using their own language, which involved special poetic vocabulary and was more elaborate than the language used in everyday life. This poetic language was thought to reflect the specially intense, heightened feelings of the writer.

Because of this poetic tradition, you will often come across rather elaborate, formal and often quite old-sounding words in poetry. Even if it does not feel natural to you to use such words, an awareness of poetic language can be interesting for its own sake and can open up new possibilities by:

➤ expanding your vocabulary and your appreciation of language for its own sake

➤ helping you to appreciate poets and writers of previous centuries, who had much the same feelings as us about many things but wrote about them differently

If you look up a common word in a thesaurus (see pages 131–2), you will find a number of alternative words, some of which might allow you to express yourself in a more striking and original way.

The table below gives some examples of the sort of poetic alternatives you might find in a thesaurus:

WORD	POETIC ALTERNATIVES
beautiful	alluring, beauteous, exquisite, fair, radiant, ravishing
big	elephantine, gargantuan, gigantic, immense, titanic, vast, voluminous
dark	drab, dusky, ebony, glowering, murky, shadowy, sombre
evening	crepuscule, dusk, even, forenight, gloaming, sundown, twilight, vesper
full	ample, brimful, chock a block, curvaceous, gorged, orotund, replete
hate	abhor, abominate, despise, detest, execrate, loathe
hurry	dash, fly, hasten, hightail it, scoot, scurry
love	adore, cherish, desire, dote on, idolize, prize, treasure, worship
old	ancient, antique, grey-haired, grizzled, hoary, prehistoric, venerable
red	coral, crimson, damask, rosy, scarlet, vermillion
sea	briny, deep, the drink, foam, ocean, oggin
sky	azure, blue, empyrean, ether, firmament, heavens, sphere, vault, welkin
speak	articulate, converse, declare, express, pronounce, utter
strong	burly, forceful, Herculean, muscular, puissant, strapping
stupid	dim, doltish, gormless, obtuse, sluggish, vapid, witless
sun	daystar, disc, light, orb
villain	blackguard, knave, libertine, miscreant, rapscallion, rogue, scoundrel

Some descriptive adjectives

Adjectives tend to be used more frequently and more prominently in poetic writing than in other forms of English. People engaged in creative writing will probably build up a stock of adjectives that can be used to create vivid descriptions. A few examples of strikingly descriptive adjectives are given below. Listen out for others that appeal to you and make a note of these so that you can use them in your own writing:

benighted lacking culture, intelligence or a sense of morality: *the poor benighted villagers of that region*

capacious having plenty of room for holding things: *slipped it into her capacious pocket*

evanescent quickly fading from sight: *wreathed in an evanescent white mist*

galvanic sudden, or startlingly energetic, as if the result of an electric shock: *His comments drew a galvanic response.*

marmoreal like marble, especially in being cold, smooth and white: *the marmoreal surface of the water*

oleaginous oily; obsequious: *a smirking, oleaginous fellow*

plashy full of puddles: *walking through the plashy meadows*

stentorian describing a voice that is loud and strong: *A woman was sounding off in stentorian tones.*

Stygian dark and gloomy, like the river Styx in ancient mythology: *She lowered her head and entered the Stygian darkness.*

verdant covered with lush green grass or vegetation: *a landscape of verdant valleys*

vitriolic extremely bitter or hateful: *a vitriolic tirade against hunting*

Some more figures of speech

Creative writing makes frequent use of figures of speech to experiment with the boundaries of language and attempt to find new and interesting ways of expression. Some common figures of speech, such as metaphor, simile and allusion have been described on pages 265–7.

In addition to these common figures of speech, there are various other devices that can be used to make writing more interesting.

Anaphora is the repetition of an initial word or phrase to connect otherwise unattached clauses:

> *We shall fight on the beaches, we shall fight on the landing grounds, we shall fight in the fields and in the streets, we shall fight in the hills; we shall never surrender.* (Winston Churchill)

Anastrophe is the reversal of normal word order:

> *Far have I travelled, and much have I seen.* (Paul McCartney)

> *Into the valley of death rode the six hundred.* (Alfred Tennyson)

Antithesis is the balancing, usually symmetrically, of contrasted clauses, phrases or words:

> *feared by the bad, loved by the good*

Apophasis is the device of expressing something by saying you will not do so:

> *I wouldn't dream of mentioning that you failed your driving test!*

Apostrophe involves speaking directly to an absent person, inanimate object or abstract idea that would normally be referred to in the third person:

> *O death, where is thy sting?* (Bible)

Hyperbole is the use of extreme exaggeration to make a particular point:

> *there are a thousand and one reasons*

> *not for all the tea in China*

Irony is the expression of a meaning opposite to the one apparently expressed:

> *I can't wait!*

> *Oh, very funny!*

Litotes is the use of extreme understatement to make a particular point, for example by denying the opposite:

> *She is not unattractive.*

> *It is a bit of a disappointment.*

Metonymy is the use of a term to refer to something that is closely associated with it:

>   *an oath of allegiance to the crown* (instead of *to the monarch*)

An **oxymoron** is a phrase composed of words that have contradictory meanings:

>   *a **bitter-sweet** love story*

A **paradox** is a statement that, although apparently self-contradictory, contains an element of truth:

>   *You've got to be cruel to be kind.*

>   *Expect the unexpected.*

>   *Less is more.*

Pleonasm is the use of words that are not strictly required, usually for emphasis:

>   *I saw it with my **very own** eyes.*

A **rhetorical question** is a question that is asked to emphasize a point, without expecting an answer:

>   *Is the Pope a Catholic?*

>   *Do I have to do everything myself?*

Syllepsis is the use of a word (usually a transitive verb or a preposition) that relates to two others, creating a different sense with each:

>   *She went home in a flood of tears and a taxi.*

Synecdoche is the use of a word denoting a part of something or someone to refer to the whole:

>   *a safe pair of hands*

>   *a new set of wheels*

Tmesis involves inserting a word into another word:

>   *Oh, abso-blinking-lutely!*

Zeugma is similar to **syllepsis**, except that one word relates to two nouns but can only normally be used with one of these:

>   *He hung up his coat and his bad mood in the hallway.*

Index